DOWNHILL FROM HERE

DOWNHILL
FROM HERE

RETIREMENT INSECURITY IN
THE AGE OF INEQUALITY

KATHERINE S. NEWMAN

METROPOLITAN BOOKS

Henry Holt and Company   New York

m

Metropolitan Books
Henry Holt and Company
Publishers since 1866
175 Fifth Avenue
New York, New York 10010
www.henryholt.com

Metropolitan Books® and m® are registered trademarks of
Macmillan Publishing Group, LLC.

Library of Congress Cataloging-in-Publication Data

Names: Newman, Katherine S., 1953– author.
Title: Downhill from here : retirement insecurity in the age of inequality / Katherine S.
    Newman.
Description: First edition. | New York : Henry Holt and Company, [2019] | Includes
    bibliographical references and index.
Identifiers: LCCN 2018028311 | ISBN 9781250119469 (hardcover)
Subjects: LCSH: Social security—United States. | Retirement income—United States. |
    Older people—United States—Economic conditions. | Equality—United States.
Classification: LCC HD7125 N455 2019 | DDC 306.3/80973—dc23
LC record available at https://lccn.loc.gov/2018028311

Our books may be purchased in bulk for promotional, educational, or business use. Please
contact your local bookseller or the Macmillan Corporate and Premium Sales Department at
(800) 221-7945, extension 5442, or by e-mail at MacmillanSpecialMarkets@macmillan.com.

First Edition 2019

Designed by Kelly S. Too

Printed in the United States of America

3   5   7   9   10   8   6   4   2

To the memory of my dearest friend,

M. Elaine Combs-Schilling, 1949–2016

CONTENTS

Introduction   1

1. Teamsters in Trouble   13

2. White-Collar Damage   47

3. Municipal Blues   77

4. Gray Labor   113

5. Two-Tiered Agreements and the Dilemmas of Gen X   147

6. Retiring on Next to Nothing   179

7. Keeping the Promise *by Rebecca Hayes Jacobs*   213

Conclusion   249

Notes   267

Acknowledgments   307

Index   313

DOWNHILL FROM HERE

INTRODUCTION

Millions of Americans are approaching the end of their working lives with a deep sense of financial insecurity. Nearly half of all private-sector employees in the United States—some fifty-eight million people—had no company-sponsored retirement plan in 2018.[1] And the plans that do exist increasingly expose workers to the vagaries of the stock market instead of guaranteeing a stable pension.[2] The retirement situation in the United States isn't just bad, it's moving in the wrong direction.

Baby boomers and the generations following behind them are at risk for an old age that is significantly less secure than the one they imagined. Recent federal legislation, for instance, has enabled massive cuts in pension benefits. Terry, a seventy-five-year-old retired trucker living in Troy, Michigan, got the unwelcome news that his Teamster pension was among those on the chopping block.[3] Told that he would receive "special consideration" because of his age, he found that his benefits were set to be cut by more than 45 percent. "I was shocked beyond words," he says. "My wife and I are wracking our brains trying to figure out how we can live with half a pension check. No medicine? Food stamps? Welfare? What will we do? Sell the house? And move where?"

Gary, a fellow retired trucker in Altoona, Iowa, is a decade younger and has been told that his benefits will be slashed by 60 percent. He seethes with anger as he tries to make sense of where he has ended up. "I worked thirty-seven years of twelve to sixteen hours a day to live a decent life in retirement. How can people in Congress be so cruel?" he asks. "I bet their pensions will never be cut. How many have gone to Washington and come home millionaires? Next year is an election year. Vote every one of the SOBs out!"

Blue-collar workers like Terry and Gary are hardly the only retirees caught in this maelstrom. High-skilled professionals working for profitable major corporations like Verizon and United Airlines have also found themselves profoundly affected. And the crisis has also spread beyond the private sector. Elsie, a sixty-year-old woman, has worked for the city of Detroit since she was thirty. As a result of her city's bankruptcy, she has been stripped of her health insurance, lost part of her pension, and has even been ordered to return to the city some of the payments to her retirement accounts approved by pension authorities years ago. Elsie has plenty of company in Detroit and elsewhere in the country: three small cities in California have already followed Detroit's lead by threatening the benefits promised to their retired public servants.[4]

Across the spectrum, workers have responded to the crisis by planning to work for many more years than they had expected, only to find that they cannot hold on to the jobs they had in their fifties. Aching backs make physical labor too difficult, and employers are often looking for ways to ease out older, more expensive workers. Those who do find employment past sixty-five are likely to be relegated to positions that are far below the status—and the salary—of the jobs they once held.

Economists and policy scientists are warning of an impending financial meltdown as companies and cities walk away from their obligations to retirees. The good fortune of longer lifespans is colliding with the inadequacy of the public policies that we assumed would undergird financial stability in retirement. Elder poverty, a problem we thought was resolved during Roosevelt's New Deal, is again rearing its head.

Pensions are regarded by most workers as among the most durable of promises. Americans assign government the responsibility of protecting this sacred bond against any firm tempted to raid retirement accounts for their own purposes. Increasingly, though, this once-unbreakable promise has become a discretionary benefit. Employers can abandon it when the stock market falters, when a firm goes through financial reorganization, or simply when shareholders demand higher profits. Insecurity is becoming the standard across many kinds of employment. And younger generations are finding that the concept of retirement itself is slowly fading away, replaced by a work life that does not end at the traditional age of sixty-five. As private pensions, Social Security, and Medicare become increasingly inadequate, working life simply has to go on.

Of course, this problem is not universal. In late 2015, the Institute for Policy Studies and the Center for Effective Government copublished a report entitled *A Tale of Two Retirements* that substantiates what many have long suspected: while companies default on pensions and benefits for most of their workers, up in the C-suite the weather is fine. Not only are CEOs socking away millions of dollars in executive retirement plans, but they are enjoying such benefits on a tax-deferred basis. In 2014, Fortune 500 chief executives put $197 million more into their retirement accounts than they would have been able to do if they were ordinary workers, saving $78 million on their tax bills in the process.[5] They won't start paying a dime of taxes on those funds until they retire, thus depriving the country—at least for now—of critical resources needed to run schools, hospitals, and other public institutions.

Retirement insecurity is an increasingly serious manifestation of the vast inequality that is eating away at the social fabric of America. The same forces that are eroding pension rights are also leading to historic levels of wage inequality, the uneven distribution of wealth, a hollowing out of the middle class, and polarization in the economic trajectories of racial groups. Roaring stock markets exacerbate inequality by driving increases of wealth at the top. Middle-class equity is tied up in the housing market, which has gyrated in ways that have placed increasing downward pressure on retirement savings for the majority.[6]

The problem of inequality has moved from an academic preoccupation to a growing theme in national and local politics. The 2013 election of Mayor Bill de Blasio in New York was the first real political victory attributable to citizens demanding its reversal. Inequality was the centerpiece of Bernie Sanders's 2016 presidential campaign, and eventually a leitmotif for Hillary Clinton as well. Tellingly, when members of Congress returned to their districts to test out messages for the 2016 election season, the one issue that resonated among their varied publics was "Do something about retirement."

We know a lot about the impact of such inequality on children, on youth, and on working-age adults. It has been the subject of many books (including several of my own). What we don't know is what those same forces mean to those who are at the end of their work lives. *Downhill from Here* dwells on the lived experience of retirement insecurity. It gives voice to the experience of retirees, those on the cusp of retirement, and those in their forties and early fifties for whom retirement is just coming into view.[7] The people featured here hail from many different occupations, geographies, and racial and religious communities, but almost all of them have something in common: in their various ways, they've been brought to the brink.

In the United States, economic security in old age was for a long time seen as a social question and a national obligation. From the birth of Social Security through the end of the twentieth century, the common assumption has been that we have a shared responsibility to secure a decent retirement for our citizens. That certainty is weakening rapidly now. Instead, we are starting to hear echoes of the mantra of self-reliance that characterized "welfare reform" in the 1990s. You alone are in charge of your retirement destiny, the new theory goes; if you wind up in poverty in old age, you have only your own inability to plan, save, and invest to blame.

THE "DEFINED BENEFIT" pension was the traditional retirement instrument of the second half of the twentieth century, familiar to the fortunate generations who began their working lives after World War II but before the age of inequality.[8] A defined benefit pension provides a steady, fixed income throughout retirement, and is the fiduciary responsibility of the employer. Companies offering them had to manage the investment of pension funds to guarantee that enough money would be there for the workers they covered.[9]

These generous pension plans were never universal. In 1980, for instance, only 30 percent of the unionized or high-skilled workers in the United States could count on this kind of retirement plan.[10] But because defined benefit pensions are often bequeathed to survivors, millions of their spouses were beneficiaries as well. Accordingly, the impact of these solid, reliable pensions spread well beyond the number of employees who "owned" them directly. Diminishing union membership, though, has reduced the bargaining power necessary to command or retain such pensions. In the last thirty years, unions have disappeared at a rapid clip and now cover only 10.7 percent of American workers, most of them in the public sector.[11]

As defined benefit pensions have fallen away, their opposite, "defined contribution" pensions—typified by 401(k) plans—have become the predominant form of retirement savings. These programs require employees to save and manage their own retirement funds, which doubtless is why they were originally intended only as supplements to "real" pensions.[12] Americans have never been very good at discretionary savings, and those of us who are not professional fund managers know very little about investing. What's more, the temptation to raid the stash we have in 401(k) plans when we hit a rough patch— as so many households did during the Great Recession of 2008— has drained many a saver's resources and left them unprotected in retirement.

The 2008 downturn also taught the country a devastating lesson about the risks involved in making up for missing pension resources by relying on home equity, as many in the middle class do. The crisis sent house prices plummeting. People who had been counting on using their housing equity—either through reverse mortgages or downsizing— to provide for their health care and monthly living expenses often woke up to find that the value of their homes had fallen, and that houses were no longer saleable because mortgage lending was tight and qualified buyers in short supply.

In the good old days of defined benefit pensions, economic upheavals in the housing market would not have been so consequential. Yes, older Americans would have felt the pain of declining assets. But they would have had reliable monthly pension payments and could depend on Social Security payments to fill in the gaps. Unfortunately, this kind of pension is now a distant memory for all but a very small number of private-sector retirees, while Social Security simply doesn't stretch as far as it used to. And the problem will only get worse: we are living much longer, on average, than the Social Security system can support at current benefit levels, unless we increase the taxes we devote to it.[13]

The costs of health care are also rising significantly faster than the cost-of-living adjustments built into Social Security. In 2016, the cost of Medicare coverage for doctor visits and outpatient services, known as Medicare Part B, jumped by 16 percent for about a third of the participants. And while the Affordable Care Act, popularly known as Obamacare, provides some security—which American households have come to value much more than they did when it first passed—it has been under attack by conservatives in Congress and the Trump White House.

Those lucky seniors who do have cash savings—an increasingly small proportion of the population—have seen interest rates hovering close to zero for nearly a decade. Hence they have not been able to increase the value of their cash through the instruments of interest-bearing savings accounts, certificates of deposit, or any other once-normal approaches. Even for those with resources, escaping the retirement crisis has been getting harder and harder.

For low-income workers, the luxury of a funded retirement is completely beyond reach. This particularly affects minorities: 62 percent of working-age African Americans and 69 percent of Latinos have no retirement savings at all.[14] The jobs they hold rarely provide good employer benefits, are often seasonal or part-time, and barely clear the bar for Social Security benefits. Their ability to save from their earnings is negligible, and family obligations to both older and younger generations stretch the income of the working-age generation in the middle in multiple directions. Many have also been the victims of unscrupulous lenders targeting minorities for subprime mortgages; African Americans and Latinos suffered the largest losses in the housing meltdown of the Great Recession.[15]

The fragile finances of many low-income minority workers mean that many of them will need to fall back on the support of their grown children when they are elderly. (Few poor families can afford assisted living or other amenities that make upper-middle-class retirement a more palatable, if less kin-based, experience.)[16] Millions of low-income women suffer this fate, but for men, the options are frequently even more constrained. Years of distant or frayed relations—and, in some cases, bouts of incarceration—often mean they have weaker ties to their children and must find others to count on in their senior years.[17] The least fortunate elderly workers find that their adult children are in economic distress as well. They may never be able to retire from their obligations to them.

These problems do not affect seniors alone. Indeed, members of younger generations, who never had true pensions and are almost entirely reliant on the 401(k) system, may find themselves in worse trouble in due course. They had insufficient resources to get into the stock market or to take advantage of the housing booms that previous generations could benefit from. And powerful headwinds generated by rising inequality—a stumbling entry into the labor market, slower prospects for advancement, and stark differences in savings—compound the volatility of 401(k) programs, threatening to undermine the economic security of these younger generations when they do reach retirement age.

IN MANY WAYS, Americans are enjoying a time of remarkable longevity and good health. That is a gift. But given the fiscal problems we confront as a society, and the political compromises and capitulations we have accepted, it is not an uncomplicated state of affairs.

As millions of Americans reach retirement age in the coming years, the implications of the vast economic and social shift toward do-it-yourself retirement will be profound. The underlying premise—that retirement is a personal responsibility to be managed by each worker individually, rather than a social responsibility of institutions such as employers and the government—resonates with contemporary values. But its wisdom is dubious, as becomes clear when recessions and stock market gyrations expose the deep vulnerability of workers and retirees. Shining a light on the diverse individuals, households, and communities affected by the abandonment of the social contract with working Americans, *Downhill from Here* makes clear that this isn't a problem for other people—it is a problem for all of us.

Chapter 1 focuses on the Teamsters whose retirement savings were bound up in the Central States Pension Fund, a multiemployer trust covering over four hundred thousand workers and retirees. Starting in 2015, retired truckers began receiving ominous letters threatening the cancellation of as much as 70 percent of their pensions. In years past, when deregulation in the trucking industry began to pull their companies down, many of these truckers forfeited significant portions of their salaries to help keep the firms they worked for afloat. But after being forced to leave their retirement assets in the hands of the federal government, they have learned the hard way that their sacrifices were no guarantee of security. Now they feel betrayed by everyone: their union, the Treasury Department, the politicians who enabled the attack on their pensions, and a society that seems to have little respect for blue-collar workers.

Chapter 2 explores the experience of skilled white-collar managers and technical experts caught in the retirement retrenchment. In 2005, Verizon Communications announced that fifty thousand of its managers would see their pensions frozen. Many other firms, including United Airlines, followed suit. "This is just a continuation of a trend amongst many companies that have moved away from defined-benefit plans as a principal source of retirement income," noted the head of the American Benefits Council. Half the defined-benefit plans in the United States vanished in a period of just ten years.[18]

Private-sector workers have borne the brunt of restructuring and the resulting retraction of earned benefits. Yet in chapter 3 we see that public-sector workers are learning the hard way that the civil service—critically important for upward mobility, especially for African Americans—is now also vulnerable to the same pressures. Cities experience different paths to fiscal disaster, but the implications of bankruptcy for public-sector workers are always the same: struggling municipalities invariably reduce their payments into employee pension funds. The pension liabilities sitting on their books depress cities' bond ratings, pushing city governments to walk away from their promises.

With real retirement becoming impossible for many, those who are able to continue working are joining the "gray labor force." Chapter 4 takes us inside the lives of employees over the age of sixty-five. Between 1977 and 2007, as the number of workers in the overall labor force rose by 59 percent, the number of employees over the age of retirement increased by 101 percent. (The number of workers seventy-five and older saw an even more dramatic uptick of 172 percent.)[19] Some of these older employees, to be sure, simply want to stay active and find retirement a bit boring. But for many, the income from these "encore jobs" is a lifeline without which they could not cover their bills. For them, these jobs often represent downward mobility, since the "real jobs" they had in their prime working years were more skilled and better paid. More and more people over sixty-five are doing entry-level jobs in chains like Walmart, CVS, Home Depot, Walgreens, Duane Reade, and assorted grocery stores.

The generations that have followed the baby boomers—gen Xers and millennials—may face an even bleaker future.[20] As chapter 5 reveals, these younger workers are often on the losing end of two-tiered wage and benefit agreements that many companies, searching for a politically palatable way to reduce pension obligations, have negotiated with their unions. Such agreements spare retirees (and workers on the cusp of retirement) the worst of the pain, but they make up for it by savaging the younger members of the workforce. To the extent that gen Xers and millennials have retirement plans at all, they come almost exclusively in the form of 401(k)s and similar schemes based entirely on optional contributions.[21] These cohorts have also been battered economically, as many lost jobs during the Great Recession. Millennials lacked the resources to buy houses or invest significantly in the stock market, and hence have missed out on booms like those that previous generations benefited from. And, of course, they worry about forecasts that the Social Security trust fund will be "exhausted just as Gen Xers start hitting retirement age in the mid-2030s."[22]

Those who have been hardest hit by rising inequality are the poor. The proportion of Americans over the age of sixty-five whose income is less than half of the federal poverty line is growing.[23] Chapter 6 looks carefully at the US city with the highest rate of elder poverty: Opelousas, Louisiana. Seventy-five percent African American and Creole, Opelousas is home to men and women who worked all their lives, but mostly in jobs that provided no employee benefits at all—retirement or otherwise. Few were entitled to sick leave or health care coverage while they were working, and virtually none can count on a pension to support them when they reach retirement age. Instead, retirees in Opelousas are almost entirely reliant on Social Security for their income—and for some, even that is out of reach. People whose working lives were exceptionally unstable, a patchwork of jobs that were part-time, seasonal, or prone to layoffs, receive very modest Social Security benefits. And workers at the bottom of the labor market often find that they cannot make it all the way to eligibility for retirement-linked Social Security: they develop chronic illnesses, face debilitating injuries, and are laid off at an earlier age than their middle-class counterparts. For them, aid such as the Supplemental Nutrition Assistance Program—food stamps—offer the only hope, but such programs are neither easily accessed nor particularly generous in a red state like Louisiana.

In chapter 7, we learn that the problems besetting Opelousas are not universal. For example, Ogden, Utah, has found better ways to take care of its retirees. A small city nestled at the base of the Wasatch Mountains, Ogden has earned the notable distinction of having the narrowest wealth gap among America's largest metropolitan statistical areas.[24] What made things work better in Ogden? Part of the answer comes from the economic opportunities available in Ogden courtesy of the federal government: it is home to a large Air Force base and a big Internal Revenue Service office. No one in Opelousas has had the opportunity to work for such steady employers, and the wages these federal workers enjoy underwrite Ogden's economic equality. Another factor is that the majority of city residents belong to the Mormon Church, a common commitment that means that older people are socially integrated, even in widowhood. Mormons also take care of one another financially through the tradition of the tithe, their own form of social insurance.

Of course, if the special nature of Ogden only affected the members of one church, it would be a less interesting place to analyze, because its solutions could not be easily generalized. But Ogden is now more diverse than it has ever been: 40 percent of the city is not Mormon. For the most part, these residents are Catholic migrants from Mexico, who share neither the religious background nor the educational advantages of the Mormon population. But as chapter 7 makes clear, these non-Mormon retirees also benefit from Ogden's steady employment and community-level social policy. Thanks to these, Ogden retirees are largely protected from the economic distress experienced by people in places like Opelousas.

The United States is an aging society. Birth rates have dropped, and the enormous baby boom cohort sits on top of the population pyramid. These demographics exacerbate the problem of financing retirement systems, since a relatively small number of workers are supporting a big generation of retirees. But the United States is not unique in this predicament: virtually all affluent, postindustrial countries are growing older. Not all of them are facing a retirement crisis, however. Some are managing the demographic pressures far better than the United States. The book's conclusion looks at what kinds of policies have made a difference in countries like the Netherlands and Australia. For there is no getting around this crisis: it is here today and it is likely to get worse tomorrow, especially for younger generations who are only now recognizing that they have no idea how they will navigate retirement.

Rita Lewis touches the photo of her husband, Butch, memorialized on the podium at the Teamsters' Washington, DC, protest against the threat to devastate their pensions.

1

TEAMSTERS IN TROUBLE

Rita Lewis never imagined she would find herself addressing a crowd from a podium on the National Mall in Washington, DC, or testifying before a committee of the US Senate.[1] She came from a modest midwestern family, a textbook example of twentieth-century blue-collar America. But in a twist of fate, the retirement crisis would make her the public face of a social movement, made up of thousands of Teamster retirees looking to take their crusade to the country's political leadership.

Rita's father, Floyd Lanter, drove a tractor trailer out of Cincinnati his whole working life. When Rita was in high school, she had ambitions for college, but she had to abandon them because money was too tight in the family. Next, attracted like many other teenage girls of her generation to the idea of seeing the world, she dreamed of becoming an airline stewardess. But in the 1960s, flight attendants had to be at least five feet two inches tall. She was an inch short. "That was that," Rita remembered, in her matter-of-fact way.

Instead of flying, at age seventeen she became a receptionist at a trucking company where her father had an "in" with the hiring manager.[2]

"The guys all took bets that I wouldn't last even three months," she chuckles. They underestimated this Teamster's daughter, who knew a good thing when it happened to her. At a time when the minimum wage was only $1.00 an hour, she was making $2.25. "I loved that job. I really, really did," she recalls. "I was very good at what I did. It felt like home."

Rita's high school sweetheart, Butch Lewis, volunteered to go to Vietnam in the summer of 1967. Within a few months, he was badly wounded, nearly losing his leg to the load of shrapnel embedded in his knee and thigh. He was airlifted to an American military base in Okinawa, then sent to Germany to recuperate. When Butch came back to the United States, he and Rita got married, and she left the workforce once their first child was born. Rita and Butch had long ago decided that it was best for their children if Mom was at home.

Over the course of the next forty years, Butch would endure thirty-two knee operations and three knee replacements. Years of physical therapy never quite calmed the pain from those injuries, and they would continue to plague him in the freezing winters and the humid summers. Still, the most pressing concern when he came home from the war was not his aching leg, but the need to find a job. Floyd Lanter came through once more, connecting Butch to a temporary position as an on-call truck driver. With that experience under his belt, Butch then easily transitioned to a much larger trucking firm, Holland Freight, where he worked from 1974 until the day he retired.

Rita grew to be a "proud . . . middle class, blue collar woman," the daughter of a union trucker and the wife of another. Rita's men were traditional fathers and husbands who took care of their own, asking for no help from anyone. Floyd and Butch were careful about their finances and modest in their lifestyles. Teamster wages were solid as blue-collar jobs went, but in the best of times that meant $60,000 annually—enough to take out a mortgage, run a couple of cars, and, in a good year, take the family to Disneyland. Even that depended on a working wife bringing in some money, which everyone thought of as "extra" but really wasn't.

Butch and Rita built a good life for themselves, drawing on the security he had with Holland Freight. The company was good to Butch and he, in turn, was loyal to them. He would volunteer to take on extra freight to help generate business. Long before the dawn of cell phones, Butch bought a pager—then a new technology—so that he could pick up extra loads the company booked on the spot. One year, Rita remembers, he brought in $1 million in extra revenue all by himself, which was unheard-of among the rank and file.

From the outside, the Lanter and Lewis families looked a lot like those of the teachers and cops that lived in the neighborhood: homeowners with limited savings, careful about their finances and modest in their lifestyles. Most importantly, they trusted in dependable pensions and union-paid health benefits to the end of their days. The stability and security they enjoyed was the reward for many years of hard and unforgiving work. Unlike teachers, who can depend on the respect of the community and the status that comes with white-collar work, Teamsters are "grunts," the invisible army we rarely acknowledge that moves the goods we use every day.

Floyd and Butch relished the brotherhood of fellow Teamsters and the protective cloak of the union. Those bonds mattered. Periodic layoffs, the unforgiving cold of the loading docks, the sweltering heat of trailers where they off-loaded their cargo—none of that had to be explained to their buddies in the union. Everyone endured these things for the salaries and retirement accounts that swelled with time on the rig. For someone like Floyd, with a seventh-grade education, that prospect made all the trouble worth it. He was a self-taught man who appreciated every dollar he made.

Between the end of World War II and the mid-1970s—Floyd's prime working years and the early part of Butch's time in Cincinnati Local 100—an expanding economy and a growing federal highway system put thousands of trucks on the road. Rising affluence generated insatiable demand. Consumers who had waited through years of shortages demanded furniture and food, refrigerators and air conditioners. Industries had to have spare parts, pipes to lay in the ground, cables to string for telephone wires, and logs to feed the construction industry. A rich America translated directly into steady work for the nation's Teamsters.

For men with no college education, trucking was a good line of work in many respects. As long as they could get enough hours, the income and retirement benefits were on par with the best of the nation's factory jobs. True, they suffered through layoffs and callbacks as orders surged and then receded. But that was the lot of most blue-collar workers in the 1960s and '70s.

Bill Ackerman, a tall, broad-shouldered man from the south side of Milwaukee, is a second-generation Teamster. As a kid, Bill grew up hearing about the strikes of the 1930s, as union truckers fought for wage increases and fair pensions.[3] His father started hauling freight in 1954 and stayed with the same firm for thirty-four years until his retirement. Bill followed in his dad's footsteps and reveled in the same romance of the road. "It's a freedom that people who work in offices can't feel and will never appreciate," he explained. "Your windshield is your office . . . You're meeting people everywhere from all different walks of life. And it's a great opportunity to see this country and get paid for it."

The stereotypes of truckers as workers with no brains hurt, though. "We're not given due respect," Bill complains. "Most people," he says, believe that "a monkey can do this job." A trucker is "looked down upon by management as a second-class citizen or lower, uneducated person." Bill remembers being called a "dock pig" by managers who seemed to feel that making truckers feel worthless was part of their jobs. "You were just wallowing in the mud out there moving freight," while "supervisors wouldn't want to get their nice shirts and ties dirty so they wouldn't even come out on the docks."

That disdain was heaped on people whose working conditions were backbreaking. Teamsters like Doug Flynn learned to take the punishment. "When you work the dock at two o'clock in the morning and it's January, February, and there's no bumpers on the doors, all the wind and the snow is coming in . . . Ice dripping from your nose gets frozen on your mustache," Doug recalls. He would work "sixty, seventy hours a week. Every week. And there were times at one company that I would work twenty-eight straight days." It was what they had to do to provide for their families.

Teamsters on the docks always looked forward to the day when they could get the specialized license for driving a big rig and take to the road. The union bargained on behalf of all of them, but compared to the loading bay, sitting inside the cabin of an eighteen-wheeler was a comfort. Still, it wasn't easy. "Oh my god, the trucks back then," Larry Williams, a second-generation Teamster from Cincinnati, remembers.

> I started in '67 and never drove my first truck with power steering until probably 1980 . . . And you'd go back up to the dock with a trailer and these things steer so hard you'd have to stand up and put two arms around [the steering wheel] to crank the thing so you can get it into the dock . . .
>
> You'd never get heat out of these early trucks. The only time you'd ever get any heat at all is when you'd run the expressway. You've got to run the truck and . . . raise the temperature up in the engine to get any heat. And the windshield wipers! They had air[-driven] windshield wipers and they'd go flip, flip, flip! Oh my god it was horrible.

Out on the road, Teamsters lived off NoDoz caffeine pills to stay awake, ate in cheap diners with lousy food, lifted heavy cargo on and off their big rigs, and twisted their torsos to steer unwieldy trucks. Back injuries and knee pain were part of the job description. Working-class boys would start as soon as they scored a driver's license, and many put in three decades on the job before they turned fifty. But it was not unusual for them to hang it up shortly thereafter. Physically, they were spent. Floyd Lanter was done by the age of sixty-two, and that was a long career for a Teamster.

Those long years took a toll on the drivers and on their wives. Especially before cell phones, Teamsters' families worried about the safety of their loved ones out on the road. Larissa Kammerer, whose husband, Tim, was a member of an Ohio local, remembers those nights alone all too well. "You can't imagine what it's like when someone you love goes out in a blizzard, and they're driving miles and miles away and you can't reach them."

Teamsters tended to keep their problems to themselves. But women like Larissa Kammerer and Rita Lewis knew very well how hard their fathers and husbands were working. "Driving a truck is a challenging task, mentally and physically," Rita explains.

> You have your bosses to contend with, sometimes your coworkers. You've got the traffic. You have to pass your DOT test. If your blood pressure's too high, or you have a health issue, you can be redlined, which means you can't work. You have to make sure that the freight gets there on time. You're out there in all kind of weather. Battling all kind of elements, all kind of pressure coming at them all the time. And being physically fit was imperative.

Rita thought Teamsters deserved more respect, more money, more of everything for enduring these working conditions. Instead, the pressures they faced on the job were compounded by fears of layoffs, wage cuts, and bankruptcies.

And if the job was hard on the white working class, trucking life was that much more difficult for African American and Latino Teamsters. Where white workers found fellowship and support within the union, black workers discovered they were second-class members of the brotherhood, unwanted competitors for whatever opportunities there were. In many a coffee shop and motel along the interstate, minority drivers were not welcome. This came as little surprise to African American truckers in the South, where the legacies of Jim Crow had barely faded. Hostility in the North was more surprising, but sadly still fairly common.

Kevin Staples is an African American who grew up thirty miles outside of Milwaukee. When Kevin was a teenager, his family began tumbling down the economic ladder. By his junior year in high school, his father had lost his small business, and his mother had been forced back into the labor market after many years as a housewife. She landed a job with a manufacturing company, where she worked for the next thirty years.

With that somewhat rocky past in mind, Kevin was looking for security when he graduated from high school and leaned on the advice of a buddy who passed along a tip: a nearby trucking company was looking for reliable workers. He put in an application, but curiously never heard from the firm. Other people, young white men he knew, got those calls instead. So Kevin tried the company again. When they told him that they weren't hiring, he pursued a discrimination suit and, to his surprise, won the case. But that would be "the beginning of me being blackballed in the industry. No freight company would touch me," he recalls.

"I was discriminated against in this industry by my own people who were supposed to represent me in the union," Kevin laments. "This very industry that was supposed to . . . help people find jobs and get fair treatment, was also the one that allowed employers to just slam the door in your face." He wouldn't break into the freight business until 1993, when he linked up with a business agent who sympathized with his situation.

Barry Barkley, another African American truck driver, had much the same experience. At meetings of the Local 100 retirees, Barry is often one of only a handful of black men in a crowd of several hundred. He graduated from an integrated public high school in Cincinnati, trained in a vocational program as an auto mechanic, and then put those skills to use in the Marine Corps in the early 1960s. With the service behind him, Barry found a part-time job at GE in Cincinnati and enrolled in a local university in hopes of improving his chances for better wages. But when he dropped out of college to seek full-time work, he hit a wall almost instantly. Application after application was declined or ignored.

"In 1971, a black man could not get a union job in the city of Cincinnati," Barry recalls, a scowl crossing his face. "I don't care what kind of experience he had . . . Civil rights laws were enacted in '64, '65, but the government did not [start to] enforce them 'til late '60s or early '70s. That's when you started seeing black guys get jobs." And when Barry did finally find his way into the trucking industry, he discovered how hard it was for a black man to navigate social conditions on the road. "We couldn't go into a lot of restaurants on the interstates," he says. Police pulled him over all the time, especially at truck stops. White truck drivers would refuse to work beside him on long hauls because they would have had to share sleeping quarters.

Whether black or white, truckers had hard jobs and got little respect.

Yes, there was fellowship among the Teamsters, especially the long-haul partners who spent days on end in one another's company. And true, the wages were good, especially for men whose education tended to stop with high school and perhaps some military experience. But the day-to-day experience of trucking was grueling, and it took its toll on workers' health. "Teamsters or truck drivers really don't have a very long lifespan," Larry Williams notes in a matter-of-fact way. "Most of them don't eat right, they smoke, they drink. And it's a very dangerous job. I don't know how many people I've seen killed through thirty years. So you don't know how many years you've got. My father"—a Teamster—"only made it to sixty-six."

With this grim prospect hanging out there, truckers like Peter Farber saw their pensions as a reward they had earned and the main reason for the sacrifices they had made over many years in unforgiving jobs. Peter's craggy face shows the toll his work has taken on his health. "Teamsters give the majority of their life to . . . their families and to their employers," he says. And a lot of them don't make it. "The manual labor jobs kill 'em before they get there. I know some that retired on Monday and by Friday the next week were dead. It ain't right. It ain't right."

What made it worth it, then? Rita likens it to a college student pursuing a degree. The Teamster's "skill is driving that truck, and their degree is that pension that was waiting for them at the end of their life," she says. "That's what they worked forty years for: that pension."

For Teamsters, as for many military men, the overriding goal was getting to retirement in one piece. And the pension dangled out there in the future as the reason to pull through another day on the loading dock and contend with another chronic ailment. Most wanted nothing more than to retire as early as they possibly could while protecting their income and their families.

The pension was the main reason for enduring the hardships of the job and giving up so much time with their loved ones, Tim Kammerer explains. On Ohio primary day, his "I voted" sticker plastered to the pocket of his leather motorcycle jacket, Tim thinks of what a good working-class American wants out of his job. "The main thing for me was that pension. I knew I couldn't save up myself," he says. "I always looked out there and I thought, well, when I get my thirty years . . ."

DEREGULATION AND ITS CONSEQUENCES

Beginning in the 1980s, the kind of security that pensions offered became less and less certain. Deregulation would be the beginning of its end.

During Jimmy Carter's presidency, and continuing with even more devotion under Ronald Reagan, deregulation became America's guiding economic policy. As an advisor to the Interstate Commerce Commission at the time puts it, Democrats and Republicans alike led a "crusade for significant deregulation of major industries—broadcasting, banking, telecommunications, oil and gas, air, rail, bus, and trucking. That movement was coupled with deregulation in less-industry-specific areas such as antitrust enforcement and environmental, safety, and health standards."[4]

The connection between this 1980s policy change and today's retirement debacle is now clear enough: the competition that deregulation engendered put pressure on firms to cut their costs, which ultimately included contributions to retirement accounts. Some firms simply stopped paying in altogether, even when they were legally required to do so. Others raided pension funds in order to improve their balance sheets. Many cut their unionized workers and picked up cheaper labor. All the way around, deregulation put downward pressure on America's blue-collar workers, and wobbling pensions were among its results.[5]

The Motor Carrier Act, passed by Congress in 1980 and signed into law by Jimmy Carter, removed requirements for entry into the trucking business, paving the way for the proliferation of nonunion truck driving, increased competition, and wage cuts.[6] The legislation greatly weakened the power of the Interstate Commerce Commission, which had been established in the 1880s to regulate the railroad industry and was placed in charge of regulating trucking in 1935. The agency was terminated altogether in 1995.[7] Meanwhile, a number of US Supreme Court cases overturned state regulations on truck lengths, permitting larger, heavier trucks to move across state lines.[8]

Government deregulation, the expansion of the interstate highway system, a wave of corporate mergers, and the promotion of intermodal transport all combined to increase the coordinated movement of goods.[9] Thanks to the interstate system, it became possible to move goods five hundred miles overnight by truck. Suppliers could ship their goods at any hour of the day.[10] The highway system became an immense rolling warehouse.[11]

Deregulation encouraged the entry of hundreds of new carriers, many of them nonunion.[12] The big losers in the deregulation sweepstakes were the unionized drivers. In 1997, a study found, the "median union member earned $44,000 annually, 26% more than non-union-members."[13] It did not take long before the wages of the organized workers took a tumble. Deregulation reduced their hourly earnings by approximately 28.6 percent.

Even very experienced Teamsters, who had carried union cards for decades, had to contend with increasing turmoil. Their jobs became more uncertain as the unionized firms they worked for faced increasing competition from the nonunion carriers. Larry Williams, one of Butch Lewis's fellow members in Cincinnati's Local 100, worked for thirteen different trucking companies from 1967 to 2002, all union. Only two of them are still in business today, and even those surviving companies have had to periodically lay people off when there weren't enough contracts to go around.

Divisions between union and nonunion truckers played out on the ground as trucking companies began to employ "wildcat" truckers, former farmers who were firmly independent and anti-union. "Unimpeded by union organizers or government regulators, these 'asphalt cowboys' began piloting ever larger tractor-trailers down federally funded highways," writes historian Shane Hamilton. "Trucking firms became the primary movers of the nation's farm products and foodstuffs, setting the stage for a 'free market' revolution in the postwar countryside." The deregulation of trucking, he argues, contributed to the low-wage, low-price "Walmart economy" of the 1980s onward.[14]

Reagan's all-out war on striking air traffic controllers in 1981 was a signal that unions were in trouble across all industries. Companies that were subject to collective bargaining found it hard to compete with nonunion shops that paid less and could lay off workers on a moment's notice. Steel mills, auto plants, and the rest of the nation's manufacturing firms packed up and deserted the Midwest and the East Coast, heading for the Southeast and the South—to the right-to-work states where wages were lower and "flexible" labor policies meant management had the upper hand. Nationwide, unemployment zoomed above 10 percent in the first two years of the Reagan administration. With millions on the unemployment lines, workers who still had jobs found that their power to press for wage increases or preserve their benefits was drastically reduced.

As high-wage blue-collar workers with expensive benefits, Teamsters were exactly the kind of employees at risk in this business climate. Companies like Holland Freight, where Butch Lewis worked, began to sweat. Management turned to workers and asked them to swallow wage cuts to help the company weather the storm. In return, truckers were promised more generous retirement packages. "If you sacrifice now," they were told, "you will see that reward later."

Butch and his coworkers gave back 15 percent of their annual pay to help Holland Freight stay afloat. That was no small amount of money for the Lewises. But Butch and Rita figured it was in their best interest for Butch to have a job to hold on to. Besides, those givebacks were putting cash in the bank for the day when Butch could hang up his keys and settle down in his easy chair.

For many years, the Lewises were confident that this tradeoff was worth it. They thought of Holland Freight as family. When someone close to you runs into trouble, you are supposed to pitch in and help. That's what the Lewises were doing. But they weren't fools. They didn't give up a portion of Butch's wages so that his employer could make more money. Their sacrifice was a matter of enlightened self-interest: they expected to see the reward on the back end, in retirement.

They had reason to believe that this quid pro quo model was realistic, because they had seen it in action before. And indeed, as business conditions deteriorated, the leadership at Holland Freight did what they could to protect their drivers. They kept them on the job rather than lay them off, as less loyal firms did. They steered Butch toward overtime so he could recoup wage losses. They tried to support loyal Teamster families by hiring drivers' sons (and daughters like Rita) when they could.

Yet a decade after Reagan's first inauguration, the consequences of deregulation were only getting worse. By the 1990s, givebacks from workers were no longer enough to keep companies from losing money. Waves of company failures began to crash into the rust-belt towns where the trucking industry employed thousands of men like Butch Lewis. Small firms went down first; they couldn't compete with the bigger players, who started taking over their businesses. Some companies tried to stay alive by discounting their prices, but for many the end was unavoidable. Multiple bankruptcies swept the trucking industry.[15]

THE CENTRAL STATES PENSION FUND

Collective bargaining agreements have established multiemployer pension plans in many industries in which employees frequently move among firms. They enable workers to switch jobs while keeping constant access to their pensions, to which assorted employers contribute.[16] But when many companies within an industry stop making their required contributions, or go bankrupt altogether, multiemployer plans run into trouble.

The problem was particularly acute in the trucking industry. Some four hundred thousand Teamsters in the Midwest and on the East Coast received their retirement benefits through the Central States Pension Fund, one of the largest multiemployer funds in the country.[17] The employers that participated in Central States banded together in the 1950s to pool their investment power and moderate their risks.[18] But even as more and more pensioners came to depend on Central States, fewer participating firms were left to support it.

Other industries are facing a similar predicament. Somewhere between one hundred fifty and two hundred plans, covering 1.5 million

American workers and retirees, could run out of money in the next twenty years. (The Central States Pension Fund and the United Mine Workers, another behemoth multiemployer pension player, account for about one-third of those affected.)[19] *Forbes* magazine has noted that multiemployer plans have assets of approximately $450 billion, but liabilities in excess of $600 billion.[20] The math is not favorable.

In the case of Central States, there is a further complication: as far back as the Kennedy administration, the International Brotherhood of Teamsters was accused of collusion with organized crime. Both JFK and his brother Bobby, the attorney general, were critical of the Teamsters, convinced they were extorting from the firms they organized. Pensions were particularly ripe for abuse and corruption. Accordingly, the federal government moved in to oversee the Teamsters both as a union (supervising its elections and overseeing its expenditures and organizing practices) and as a financial concern. Teamster brothers were furious over the open, sneering disrespect for their leader, the larger-than-life Jimmy Hoffa Sr.[21] In 1989, management of the Central States Pension Fund was taken away from the union and placed under the authority of the Treasury Department.[22]

The Treasury didn't actually manage the Central States pension fund itself. The department turned over those responsibilities to Wall Street titans Goldman Sachs and Northern Trust, two of the biggest money managers in the world. These companies would be in charge of making investment decisions and reporting back to the federal government. With managers like these, how could Central States go wrong? Butch and Rita Lewis were concerned, but also confident that their precious pension was at least in capable hands.

For decades, Central States was indeed rock solid. Even in the era of deregulation, it stood for financial security. While member firms started to wobble in the 1980s, the fund was still able to provide secure retirement benefits to retirees. This was a bit misleading, however: the money was there only because high returns in the stock market during that period swelled the pension coffers. The fund's promises to retirees depended on sustaining this trajectory. During the roaring stock markets of the Clinton presidency, that rosy future appeared entirely reasonable—until it didn't. Suddenly, Central States itself was on the verge of going broke.

The final backstop for troubled pension plans is the Pension Benefit Guaranty Corporation (PBGC), a federal agency created by the 1974 Employee Retirement Income Security Act (ERISA). Pension plans are required to pay premiums to the PBGC, which provides insurance in case a company goes bankrupt and its pension accounts are underfunded. The PBGC pays full pensions for most workers they cover, up to a cap of approximately $60,000 a year.[23] Workers in single-employer plans whose benefits exceed that cap, however, stand to lose money if the agency takes over their pensions.

In 2015, the PBGC paid for monthly retirement benefits, up to that guaranteed maximum, for nearly 826,000 retirees in 4,800 single-employer and multiemployer pension plans that could no longer pay promised benefits. Including those who have not yet retired, the PBGC is responsible for the current and future pensions of about 1.5 million people.

For most workers covered by troubled multiemployer plans, the maximum payout from the PBGC (especially if they take early retirement) is significantly less than what they would have received if their firms had stood by their obligations. Josh Gotbaum, who served as director of the PBGC from 2010 to 2014, explains that this discrepancy has historical roots: "When the multiemployer program was set up in 1980, folks didn't think PBGC insurance would be necessary, because the other employers would take up the slack if one employer went bankrupt. They hadn't considered the possibility of whole industries going into distress."

Gotbaum comes from a storied family of labor stalwarts; his father, Victor Gotbaum, was the legendary leader of District Council 37 of the American Federation of State, County and Municipal Employees, the largest union in New York City. Before being named the head of PBGC, Gotbaum worked with unions in distress situations as an investment banker and investor. His perch at the PBGC gave him a unique perspective on the nation's largest private pension systems, and his account of how the Central States Pension Fund got into trouble is instructive for the way it pinpoints the assumptions behind the fund's debacle. Somehow, the people in charge of its finances came to believe that what goes up in the stock market will not come down.

In the 1990s, Gotbaum notes, most pension plans in the country were fully funded; some were even overfunded. The economy was doing well, firms were contributing what they had contractually promised, and the stock market was exceptionally strong. Indeed, it easily outpaced the returns that actuaries had used to determine companies' required contributions to the pension funds and retirees' benefits from them. "The Central States pension fund was listening to its actuaries," Gotbaum recalls, "and saying, okay, for each dollar you put in under the Teamsters contract, we'll give you so many cents' retirement benefits when [they] retire after thirty years." Looking at these forecasts, Central States and other pension systems like it increased benefit levels. But the stock market reached a peak in 2000, and the tech bubble burst in 2001. Suddenly, investment returns fell far below the actuaries' estimates. Pension funds turned from being well funded to being woefully underfunded.

Gotbaum surmises that the actuaries at the Central States pension plan knew they were in trouble after the stock market decline of 2001. "But they thought it was a manageable level of trouble," he says. However, in 2008–9, the stock market truly cratered, and actuaries knew for sure they had a catastrophe on their hands. After they had predicted steady growth, assets plunged by 25 to 30 percent. The losses were the largest the economy had witnessed since the days of the Great Depression. And they took the Central States Pension Fund down.

There are many culprits to blame for the benefit retractions Rita and Butch Lewis were notified about in 2015. From Josh Gotbaum's perspective, the most important of them was the Great Recession itself. "Anybody who says that this [disaster] wasn't primarily caused by '08–'09 is entirely kidding themselves," he says. "This was largely a consequence of the meltdown."

The question became: Who is going to make up the shortfall? It wasn't the actuaries. It wasn't the Wall Street firms that had managed the pension funds, making large investments of Teamster funds in bonds tied to junk mortgages, among other assets. It wasn't the trucking companies that had disappeared into bankruptcy, leaving behind "orphan" pension plans that Central States still had to pay out. The only parties remaining were the owners and current employees of the remaining firms in the multiemployer plans—and the retirees themselves. It was Butch Lewis who would have to pay.

"CRITICAL AND DECLINING STATUS"

Before 2014, federal law safeguarded the rights of retirees in multiemployer pension plans via ERISA, which set minimum standards for most voluntarily established pension and health plans in the private sector.[24] The law requires employers offering retirement benefits to fully fund them and keep their hands out of the pension till. It sets fiduciary obligations for managers and enables all those covered to submit grievances and appeals. Workers can sue if the fund managers default on their responsibilities. Moreover, workers covered by ERISA are assured access to information about the health of their pensions.[25]

But in December 2014, new legislation undercut those guarantees. The law, known as the Multiemployer Pension Reform Act (MPRA), reflected the conclusions of a committee housed and funded by the American Federation of Labor's National Building Trades Council. This committee included both labor and business interests, and it was concerned about "living" companies having to shoulder the costs of pensions for "orphan" employees of firms that had gone bankrupt.[26] Its influential report, "Solutions Not Bailouts," offered the MPRA as a solution.

The bill was passed as part of the two-thousand-page omnibus federal budget, with most members of Congress unaware of its provisions. It enabled pension fund managers to ask for drastic cuts in benefits if a plan was deemed to be in "critical and declining status"—in lay language, going broke.[27] Financially troubled plans were defined as those unable to pay 100 percent of benefits within fifteen (or, in some cases, twenty) years. For such plans, trustees would decide how to make cuts, which could vary depending on the age of retirees and the extent of the shortfall.[28]

The Central States plan, which is only 53 percent funded, is one of the plans in hot water.[29] Thomas Nyhan, the executive director of Central States, calculated that the fund would be bankrupt by 2026 if it had to meet its full obligations to its retirees.[30] In that case, current workers paying into the plan right now would be left with nothing when they retire. To avoid that scenario, Nyhan applied to the Treasury Department in 2015 for permission to enact severe cuts on pensions going to existing retirees. While he waited for Treasury approval, 273,000 Central States beneficiaries were notified of impending reductions in their benefits.

The letters started appearing in Teamster mailboxes throughout the Midwest in November. Rita and Butch stared at theirs in disbelief and called the union, hoping to learn they had misunderstood. No, they were told, the letter was accurate: if Nyhan's application to the Treasury Department was approved, 50 percent of Butch's pension would disappear. Teamsters whose benefits were coming from orphan firms had it worse: they would be hit with 70 percent pension cuts.

Leon Barnett, retired from a southwest Ohio local, exploded when his letter arrived. Clearly he was expected to go back out to work, because no one could survive on the benefits that would be left. "I'll be sixty-nine years old in June," he said, shaking his head.

> Where do I go to get a job? Maybe as a greeter at Walmart? I don't think I could stand on my feet for eight hours at a time. I've got arthritis in my clutch foot, from, you know, driving a truck. Arthritis in my hands from changing gears and stuff. So . . . Who's going to hire me at sixty-nine years old?

Peter Farber agrees. When his letter arrived, all he could think was that no hiring manager would take him on. And even if a manager were kind enough or rash enough to give him a second look, it would barely make a difference. His physical stamina was so low he couldn't imagine being able to work anyway.

I've got back injuries that are so bad that I have to take pain pills all the time. I've got nerve damage in both arms, in both legs, I've got nerves pressing against bone. Growth in the back of my neck that gives me migraine headaches. I lost my vision while driving across [Interstate] 275. The whole right side of the vision is gone.

I passed out the other day on steps, wrenched my knees, turned my ankle . . . I can't go back to work. If I do, I'll end up dead . . . So what do I do? I've got to live on something.

Peter had no answer to this question. If his pension was gutted, he would be stuck. Thousands of retirees across the Midwest faced the same quandary.[31]

DISTRIBUTING THE BLAME

The arrival of the warning letters sent a wave of anger and recrimination through the Teamster retiree community. In union halls and taverns, living rooms and church basements, the conversation alternated between despair and fury. Teamsters, their wives, their leaders, and eventually the politicians they turned to for help searched for someone to blame for the looming disaster. They wanted to find a way to get the cuts reversed.

There were many targets for their outrage. Rita Lewis argued that a sinister effort to undermine the union movement, one that went back decades, was surfacing again. "There's been an attack on organized labor for forty years," she insisted. "Reagan started it when he wanted to do away with unions." No one in the Treasury Department was looking out for them, she argues, because they *wanted* the unions and their benefit packages to fail. Those in power are not going to shed any tears when the little people, the Rita and Butch Lewises of this world, get the short end of the stick.

Rita is still bitter about the government taking over the pension funds years ago, based on what she sees as phony corruption charges aimed at Jimmy Hoffa Sr. "They took our pension out of our hands," she says. "If we would've handled it on our own, we [might have] mismanaged it. I would've said that's our fault. But they took it from us." And once they had it, Rita wonders, how could they have let the funds be so poorly managed? Isn't this what experts in the Treasury Department were supposed to know how to do?

Rita and her compatriots don't buy the idea that the pension losses merely reflected gyrations in the market that no human being could be blamed for. They have a hard time believing that innocent, well-intended actions could have produced such a catastrophe. Instead, retirees reason, there had to be sinister motives at work on the part of the well-heeled and powerful. Perhaps it was even a conspiracy. "When these losses were coming in, why didn't [government officials] say something?" Rita asks. The answer seems clear enough to her: they had something to hide.

Teamster fury also focuses on the big Wall Street firms that were given the responsibility by the Treasury Department to manage pension investments. As losses mounted during the Great Recession, Teamsters watched with growing anxiety. How could people who were supposedly the best investors in the world lose all that money? In the absence of any credible explanation, class resentment, always latent, began to rear its head. In the truckers' opinion, those rich elites with their fancy educations, their bloated salaries, and their Fifth Avenue mansions could not be expected to care about the blue-collar workers whose money they held in trust. And why should they? As Rita points out, bankers made fistfuls of money even when the accounts they managed were losing millions. Paid by the transaction rather than by results, fund managers suffered no consequences when the pension dollars evaporated. Indeed, from 2005 to 2009, Goldman Sachs and Northern Trust charged Central States $41 million in fees while wrecking the pension fund.

Wall Street fat cats live in a different universe, Rita insists. They know nothing about what it means to depend on a pension you've spent decades earning only to see it disappear. The luxuries that investment bankers enjoy come from the sweat of people they will never meet. "How much money do you need before enough is enough?" she asks.

Do you need five houses? Do you need six? How many yachts do you need? How many cars do you need? [The] money that you have built your life around wasn't really yours. You didn't work for it. You took it from someone, a vulnerable segment of the population with no way to go back and rebuild their lives.

Those luxuries stand in stark contrast to all the sacrifices that Teamsters made in order to earn their pensions. Larissa Kammerer, one of the more vocal trucker spouses standing alongside Rita Lewis, notes that her husband Tim lost out on years of family time.

Every Sunday he worked. Every Sunday! We didn't even have Friday night together, we didn't have Sunday afternoon together. I mean, for almost thirty years, we're talking no holidays.

We didn't complain. It was . . . his job, and it was worth it because, at the end . . . I told Tim, I said that . . . You guys have your pension . . . And literally, it was promised all the time . . . Every function we went to and stuff. That's why you didn't take raises. That's why you agreed to work on holidays. And that's why you worked every Sunday. Because you can rely on this pension. It's always going to be there for you when you're going to need it.

Tim Kammerer agrees. He had kept his side of the bargain, giving up irreplaceable moments with his family. That this could be swept aside so callously has convinced Tim that there is no such thing as commitment any more. Ordinary people, the bedrock of the nation, cannot rely on anything. "If I gave somebody a promise myself, I always did what I promised them that I would do," he says. "And I just feel now that places that make promises, it doesn't mean anything. It's just gone. You cannot trust anyone that tells you anything anymore because they'll change it."

Perhaps surprisingly, for many retired Teamsters the list of untrustworthy institutions includes the unions themselves. Once upon a time they were on the side of the working man, but their leadership today is viewed by many in the rank and file as overly compliant, possibly even treasonous. While the legendary Jimmy Hoffa Sr. is remembered with respect, his son, Jimmy Hoffa Jr., the current president of the AFL-CIO, is regarded with suspicion. He was initially sympathetic to the request to cut benefits that the Central States Pension Fund sent to the Treasury, a position that stunned retirees who could not believe he was advocating against them.

In truth, all union leaders were caught in a vise, with retirees on one side and active workers—who want to ensure that some pension money is left for them in the more distant future—on the other. But this nuance was not persuasive to the retirees. As they saw it, Hoffa Jr. had only one responsibility: to fight for everyone. Eventually he came around to this view himself, becoming a critic of the MPRA and a somewhat reluctant crusader against the Central States plan to cut benefits.

Thomas Nyhan, the executive director of the Central States Pension Fund, has received especially heavy criticism from the rank and file. They are particularly bitter because Nyhan himself has a nearly $700,000 annual salary and was awarded a $32,000 bonus the year he filed for permission to slash their benefits. From the retirees' perspective, he forfeited his role as their guardian angel and instead became an instrument of their demise. "I don't understand why they took—I think it was 6 million dollars or 6.2 million dollars out of our pension fund that's already failing to pay the legal fees to fight us," says Leon Barnett with exasperation. "How could they allow that?"

It's a fair question. What was Nyhan thinking? Doubtless he, like Hoffa Jr., was trying to balance the needs of retirees against those of active workers, and did not believe that there was any hope for massive federal subsidies to correct for the losses that had accrued in the crash of 2008. Given the resources on hand, he thought he was doing his duty. The pensioners saw it as the opposite: Nyhan abrogated his responsibilities and got paid handsomely in the process.

Congressional representatives from union states came in for their share of criticism as well, and with them the entire idea of government as a force for the good. The process by which the MPRA was passed left Rita Lewis incredulous. "They snuck it through at the eleventh hour," she says, "and a lot of the congressmen and senators said they didn't even know it was in there, they didn't read [the legislation]." Leon Barnett shares her outrage. How could people charged with such important responsibilities, whose actions can make such a devastating difference in the lives of retirees, vote without being fully informed? He wishes that the congressmen who voted for the bill would try to "live on our income for a year and see how they could do it. And then talking about cutting our checks 50 percent? There's no way they could—they don't have a clue of how to live like we live."

The MPRA legislation overturned pension protections that had been in place for forty years, making it much easier for financially troubled retirement plans to cut back benefits. For the Teamsters, this showed that laws themselves are not dependable. They can be altered if special interests want them to be. Government is not to be trusted to stand by its own rules.

Because MPRA was cloaked in secrecy, buried in a huge bill whose contents were largely unknown, its passage amplified Teamster suspicions of government in general. Not only are ordinary people unable to depend on their representatives to protect their interests, it seemed, they could not even get help understanding exactly how they were screwed. "The government will not help you," says Doug Flynn. "You've got to find out for yourself. You've got to dig. You've got to scrape. You got to figure it out on your own."

THE MORAL DIMENSIONS OF THE CRISIS

The pension losses were about more than money. For the truckers, they represented an attack on the legitimacy of their life stories, on the value of supporting their families and country. The Teamsters had never been the beneficiaries of public admiration, particularly as manual labor and union solidarity seemed to fade from the economic scene. Nonetheless, the retirees viewed themselves as part of the "all American" bedrock. Having paid their dues, often first in the military and then in jobs that subjected them to social indignities and physical stress, they saw themselves as honorable if ordinary folk. Retirees who were about to lose so much identified themselves as symbolically worthy, more so than the elites who controlled their fate. As the Teamsters saw it, bankers who push paper around all day and gain financially whether or not they are performing well cannot be seen as "real Americans" in the same way.

All across the rust belt, truckers reacted to the threat as a complete affront. "I am a retiree with just over thirty years of service who may be impacted by this legislation," Joseph Rossi posted on an online board regarding MPRA. "We as retirees have contributed to society and the government for our entire lives and we are now being thrown under the bus so that well financed companies with armies of lobbyists get what they want . . . Have we lost the respect for our seniors who aren't asking for anything but to be treated like they matter or to be treated with dignity and fairly?"

The money involved was a key point of contention, but moral indignation was the more trenchant language. Retirees described themselves as having been betrayed, their families financially violated. Walking the halls of Congress and stopping anyone who would listen, mounting rallies in front of their representatives' Washington offices and stacking town hall meetings back home, the Teamsters and their families pointed to their experience as evidence of the erosion of fundamental values: sacrifice for the greater good, fidelity to one's word, and respect for self-reliance.

People who had worked for decades on the strength of the pension promise, who sacrificed wages and vacation time at critical moments to help their firms survive, were supposed to get what they had been promised. It already belonged to them. As Rita puts it, the Teamsters were not asking for any kind of handout. They were not seeking an act of charity. They just wanted what was rightfully theirs.

Critical to this moral stance is the meaning of a promise. Workers pay in; firms agree to reward them after thirty years; banks and investors do their part to make that happen. This social contract unfolds over longer time periods than many marriages or mortgages. The length of the arrangement underscores its essential quality: it is a commitment reinforced with every payroll deduction over an entire working lifetime. That is what the traditional world dictates.

In this brave new world, though, retirees discovered that the promise can evaporate because of a piece of legislation passed without debate, snuck into a gargantuan bill that no one on the floor of Congress even read. So much for lifetime commitments, retirees note. And so much for their faith in American institutions more generally. If this pledge is no longer reliable, they ask, then what pledges are? Social Security? Medicare? Anything? This is the question they raised over the course of months of protests as they took their case to the media, to the public, and to legislators.

On a sunny day in April 2016, two thousand retirees bused into Washington, DC, from all over the country, gathering to denounce the Central States application to the Treasury to cut their pensions. Some had been on the road for forty-eight hours. Teamsters who could barely walk hobbled on their crutches. Their wives lugged old coolers and umbrellas to protect against the rising heat. They raised handmade signs denouncing Congress, with drawings of coffins containing skeletons labeled "Social Security"—the next on the hit list of benefits, they said. Dozens of senators, representatives, and union leaders turned out to address the crowd, assembled on the lawn outside the main office building of the House of Representatives.

Marcy Kaptur, the Democratic congresswoman from the 9th District of Ohio (which stretches from Toledo to Cleveland), took to the microphone to condemn the way MPRA had been foisted on Congress. "You should know," she told the raucous crowd, "when the decision was made to force your pension cuts, that bill did not come up under regular order." It had never been given time for debate. "People like me weren't a part of the deal," Kaptur continued. "We never had a chance to testify against it, we never had a chance to go before the Rules Committee. The whole thing was off-kilter from the beginning. From the very beginning . . . Our government of the people, by the people, and for the people was thrown out when it came to your pensions."

Elizabeth Warren, the firebrand senator from Massachusetts, mounted the podium to the roar of the crowd. "Let's figure out how we got here," she told the protesters. The reason why Teamster pensions disappeared, she argued, lay somewhere between naked class conflict and unpunished—indeed, by some lights, rewarded—negligence.

Thanks to Washington bailouts, Wall Street is once again flying high. Corporate profits are up. The stock market is soaring. But the real victims of the financial crash—the millions of workers who lost their jobs, lost their homes, lost their retirement savings because of Wall Street's reckless greed—those victims haven't bounced back. Many of them, many, are still in trouble. And now the hard-earned pensions of 270,000 of Wall Street's victims are on the chopping block.

As the stock market recovered and indeed soared in 2017, one might imagine that those defunct pension plans could be resurrected and many retirees made whole. Yet only once in the last twenty years has a pension plan been restored when a firm came out of bankruptcy: LTV Steel, which had a single-employer plan, did the right thing. There are no other cases of companies returning to workers what they are owed. Multiemployer plans in the hands of the PBGC are already insolvent, and a stock market recovery after such insolvency is moot.[32]

Warren told the crowd that there were many historical reasons why pensions are in trouble today, especially for truckers. She drew the connection to deregulation and pointed to technological changes that make delivery of goods more efficient and require fewer workers. There have also been recessions that pummeled the economy. "But one fact is beyond dispute," she cried, pounding on the podium. "The men and women in this pension fund would be a whole lot better off today if Wall Street hadn't made the reckless bets that tanked our economy . . . Let's be clear: You didn't lose 11 billion dollars in Central States pension funds. Wall Street did."

And what did the investment bankers do when they controlled the fate of hundreds of thousands of Teamsters? "The Central States story is ugly," Warren said pointedly. Instead of doing what was best for workers, big financial institutions had invested workers' savings in subprime mortgages that were practically worthless, since the borrowers were not creditworthy. It was only a matter of time before the whole investment system crashed and burned.

Wall Street destroyed 7 trillion dollars in housing wealth. It killed 8.5 million American jobs. It gutted hundreds of pension funds like

Central States, leaving millions of retirees hung out to dry. Now Congress—this Congress—jumped in to help Wall Street. The bankers got a 700 billion dollar bailout. And what did millions of homeowners get? What did workers get? What did retirees get? They got stuck with the bill.

From 2005 to 2009, the senator noted, Goldman Sachs and Northern Trust charged Central States $41 million in fees while the pension funds they managed evaporated.

Retirees stood in the full heat of the Washington, DC, sun and cheered Warren and the other speakers until their throats were raw. Those who didn't have the energy to stand raised hand-lettered signs up over battered lawn chairs they had dragged all the way from Ohio, Kentucky, Minnesota, and Illinois. The rest chanted, "This is what democracy looks like," and clapped for their leaders, especially their beloved Rita Lewis. Taking the stage, Rita urged the crowd to follow her into the congressional office building and force their representatives to listen.

CANARIES IN THE COAL MINE

The Teamsters do not intend to go quietly. Rita Lewis insists on accountability. Nyhan and the rest of the Central States management "never expected this pushback," she told the crowd. "They thought they were gonna steamroll over us. And we were too old, or we were too ignorant, or we were too stupid—yeah. And those are fighting words for me!"

For Rita and her followers, their fate is emblematic of what will confront the rest of the country as pensions are cut and health benefits retracted. The Teamsters are the "canaries in the coal mine," she says, the everyman representatives of ordinary people being batted around by elites and at the mercy of forces larger than themselves. If people who work this hard and for this long can lose everything, Rita reminds us, then we are all at risk. Unless this attack on retirees is stopped at the outset, that's what the Central States Pension Fund retirees will represent: the first in a long line of Americans who worked for comfort in their old age but face penury instead.

What do the Teamsters think the country should do about this mess? They are particularly eager to see the enactment of a proposal put forward by 2016 presidential candidate Bernie Sanders. Sanders advocates closing a set of tax loopholes that benefit the wealthy and using the proceeds to shore up Central States and other underfunded multiemployer pension plans. In 2017, Sanders and Kaptur sponsored the Keep Our Pension Promises Act (KOPPA), which would repeal the "benefit suspension" provisions of MPRA and ensure that pensioners continue to get their full benefits.

KOPPA's most important reform lies in its use of contributions from the general tax coffers to support pension plans that are going bankrupt.[33] This would be a fundamental change in the financial structure of the Pension Benefits Guaranty Corporation, which currently is supported only by insurance premiums from member firms. It receives no revenues from taxes, and it cannot access general government funds in the event that it starts to run dry. The moral reasoning behind the proposed change was articulated by both Sanders and Warren: if we used taxpayer dollars to bail out the banks when they were in trouble, we can do the same for the Teamsters and all other workers insured by the PBGC.

The change is important because while struggling pension funds turn to the PBGC for help, the PBGC itself is a vulnerable institution that was never built to withstand a true tidal wave of demands. Indeed, as of 2016, the PBGC's multiemployer pension system faced a 43 percent chance of insolvency by 2026, and a 93 percent chance of insolvency by 2036, if the current level of participant benefits continues to be paid out.[34] Most of this problem is connected to failing multiemployer plans, though single-employer plans are also a worry. The Government Accountability Office reported that "the single-employer program, composed of about 22,200 plans, accounted for $20.6 billion of PBGC's overall deficit. The multiemployer program, composed of only about 1,400 plans, accounted for about $59 billion."[35]

Instead of hoping for KOPPA to pass, some retirees favor an

alternative that requires people in multiemployer pension funds to make a $30 monthly contribution to keep the PBGC solvent. Brad Adams, a leader of a Wisconsin Teamsters retirees association, explains the concept:

> There's millions of people in the multiemployer system, and the investment plan would involve all [of them]. That's one of the most equitable ways to fix it, because it's such a small amount. It would be approximately twenty to thirty dollars per month per person. Fix the entire pension plan and the PBGC. We'd be bailing out the government too.

Some Teamsters have given up on the idea that they will ever see their losses restored. At this point in the exhausting struggle, all they want is to reclaim a semblance of control over what is left. For these retirees, the goal is simply to get all of the people who intruded into their financial affairs out of the way. As Doug Flynn puts it, "Just give me my money. Just give me what's left." The key point for Doug is that his pension was not some abstract investment; it was his property, and he should have the opportunity to "take it back" and be left to his own devices.

But that would not be enough for Rita Lewis. She wants to see the people responsible for this nightmare punished for their sordid deeds. The CEOs of the investment firms made big money from their firms' bad investments, even as they lost the assets of the hapless Teamsters. They should not be allowed to get away with that, Rita argues. Larry Williams, the second-generation Teamster, agrees: "Wall Street keeps getting away with everything. How many days have all of these Wall Street people been in jail? I can tell you how much: zero!" It is a theme Elizabeth Warren has invoked at every turn: the little guy gets nailed, while those who have power get away with their malfeasance and even reap rewards for it.

Regulators in the Department of Labor who first acted to strip the Teamsters of control over their own pension funds are culprits in this drama as well. It was their responsibility to keep an eye on the Treasury Department, which, in turn, was supposed to exercise "good government" authority by looking out for Teamster pensioners (when their own unions were deemed too freighted with criminals to do so). Labor and Treasury were in charge for a reason: they had the knowledge, skills, and authority to steer these funds properly. It didn't work out that way.

Of course, government regulators were not themselves managing pension funds. Instead, they were supposed to be looking over the shoulders of an entirely different set of experts: Wall Street money managers. But while Goldman Sachs and Northern Trust are legendary for their prowess at making money grow, the Great Recession showed the world a different side of these institutions: their willingness to take unconscionable risks with other people's money.

Josh Gotbaum, the former director of PBGC, believes that the banks knew they were pushing products that were enormously risky, and he thinks they should have been held accountable. Bonuses should have been withheld, and the most egregious offenders should have been fired. The reason that did not happen, he says, is that for the most part, their conduct was entirely legal. "It looks like the only actual crooks were the mortgage company salespeople and their bosses," he notes. "And most of them got away with it too."

THE IMPACT OF THE CUTS

In the end, while the bankers prospered, it was the "average Joe"—the working man who thought he could rely on a promise—who was stuck with the hardship. There are thousands of stories testifying to the damage, both financial and emotional, of this abandoned pledge: more than four hundred thousand of them in the industrial Midwest alone. Butch and Rita Lewis were emblematic of the crisis, which is one reason why Butch became something of a patron saint for the Teamsters' protest movement.

In the face of proposed cuts, Butch rallied hundreds of distressed Teamster brothers. He drove all the way from Ohio to Washington, DC, several times to buttonhole Ohio representatives and implore them to insist that the Treasury Department reject Nyhan's application to slash Teamster benefits. Logging hundreds of hours all over his home state, Butch attended endless meetings, and became the spokesman for thousands of Teamsters who looked to him to voice their angry opposition to the cuts.

The burdens of leadership and worries about his family's and his fellow retirees' finances began to wear on Butch. He kept his physical problems to himself, but Rita knew him well. Something wasn't right. "The first year when he was retired," Rita recalls, "his blood pressure was great. No problems. He was happy. And after this [bad news] started to come out, he had a slight stroke in June of 2015 from the stress. Just a minor one." The stress was causing his blood pressure to rise, and he began to have sleepless nights.

In December 2015, Butch braved the winter snow on one of his many "campaign" trips to the nation's capital, but in the middle of the journey he began to experience dizzy spells. To Rita, he didn't confess anything more than general exhaustion. "I'm glad Congress is taking a break for the holidays," he told her on the phone. On New Year's Eve, he died of a massive stroke. He was sixty-four years old.

A few days later, the anniversary diamond ring that Butch bought as a holiday surprise for Rita arrived in the mail. She catches her breath every time she looks at that sparkling diamond. The pension battle "killed him," Rita insists, anger spreading over her face.

Married for more than forty years, Rita suddenly found herself alone and rudderless. It was all she could do to get out of bed in the morning, much less return to work. But within a short time, the financial pressures caused by Butch's death began to land with full force on his grieving wife. "I've taken an emotional hit, I've taken a financial hit. That's not the way it's supposed to be," she says.

As Butch's widow, Rita was entitled to 75 percent of his pension. But if the Treasury Department approved Nyhan's request to cut the Central States pensions, she stood to receive only a fraction of what she was depending on. She was getting $2,500 a month; that would be cut down to $1,400. After taxes she would be down to $1,000 a month or less. It would not be enough to keep Rita in the house in which she and Butch had lived for decades. That would have to go.

Thousands of Teamster families found themselves in similar straits. Leon and Mary Barnett were among them. Before the cuts, they could scrape by on their combined pensions, as long as they kept their spending in check. They never expected to live in luxury; modest pleasures were enough. Their first fifteen years of retirement passed by without upheavals, but then that dreaded letter from Central States appeared in their mailbox. "Thirty-one years with the same company," Leon says, shaking his head. "And now they want to cut my pension 50 percent? So what happened to thirty-one years of my life if this happens?" For Leon, the loss was more than financial; it was a sucker punch. His loyalty was worth nothing.[36] His family was disposable.

The impending cuts would be hard enough on Leon and Mary, but as with so many blue-collar families experiencing pension losses, that wasn't the end of it. Working-class families like the Barnetts pull generations close. Even when they live in separate households, their finances and personal support—from babysitting to taking care of the elderly—lace kin together. It takes that kind of "pooling" to manage, especially when incomes are unsteady or illness strikes. They don't farm out family burdens to government agencies, and they can't afford to pay for help. It's all in the family.

That's how Leon's pension problem soon became an issue for three generations of Barnetts. Leon and Mary have grandchildren, and a daughter who was diagnosed with multiple sclerosis at the age of twenty-five. "The pension Leon gets is not just for us," Mary says, twisting a piece of Kleenex in her hand. "We help our kids with it . . . you never know when some kind of illness is going to take you. And MS has no mercy. It just has no mercy. So we try to help them, all we can."

If the pension cuts proposed by Central States went through, hundreds of thousands of families would fall into a financial abyss from which many would never emerge. They would lose homes they worked for all their lives. They would find it hard to access health care and suffer further financial trouble as a result. Worry would be their constant companion. And more than a few would suffer early deaths from lack of care and high levels of stress. The men who pass away before their time would leave behind wives who are bitter about their abandonment, just as Rita Lewis is. And the kin who depended on them, from their elders to their grandchildren, would be felled by a vicious chain reaction, multiplying the damage to engulf thousands more.

A TEMPORARY REPRIEVE

Against all odds, the Central States pension cuts were rejected, at least for the moment. In the summer of 2016, Kenneth Feinberg, the special representative for the Treasury Department charged with reviewing Nyhan's application, decided that it should be turned down. He ruled that the cuts would not prevent insolvency, that they would not have been equitably distributed among the retirees, and that the fund did not notify participants in a way that was easy to understand.[37]

Feinberg's decision was hailed by the Teamster retirees, who saw it as a response to their mobilization. They praised it as evidence that democracy is still viable in the United States. Bill Ackerman spoke for many when he explained that he had "regained some confidence in the justice system." Even so, he and his fellow Teamsters know very well that this victory is limited. The investment losses are still there, and Central States has only enough money left to cover its obligations for ten more years. It is possible that the oldest of the pensioners will now live out their lives with their payouts intact. But anyone who expects more than a few years of benefits is almost certainly going to suffer dramatic losses unless Congress heeds the call of senators like Sanders and Warren.

If this tale were just about pensions, it would be sad enough. But from the Teamsters' perspective, the losses feel like attacks on their whole way of life. It is a story about the abandonment of principles, which has led to a collapse of faith in the very idea of America. The temporary reprieve of Feinberg's decision does not settle the matter, especially because the Teamsters know how close the cuts came to being enacted. Indeed, a number of Teamster locals outside of Central States, such as Local 707 in New York, have already seen dramatic cuts in pensions and health benefits because their pension funds have run dry.

What are the Teamsters left with if the nation's political class and financial overlords abandon them? Only themselves, their community, their unions, and their families. Teamsters are used to the idea that they have to pull together across generations. They have never been secure enough to stand alone. They have always shared what they have, with retirees placing their pensions in service of their grandchildren's school bills, their adult children's medical care, their aunts' and uncles' financial needs. Blue-collar workers may not have resources to protect themselves, but when the ship goes down they are all together on deck.

The bankruptcy of United Airlines landed its pension plan in the lap of the Pension Benefit Guaranty Corporation, which paid pilots and other employees only a small portion of the retirement benefits they had earned.

2

WHITE-COLLAR DAMAGE

Blue-collar workers across the nation have faced the same fate as the Teamster retirees victimized by Central States. But their white-collar, managerial counterparts never expected to find themselves in a similar bind. Many are college educated, with years of supervisory experience and specialized skills, and saw themselves as harder to replace. Their bargaining power lay not in a union card, but rather in the human capital they brought to the table.

For many years, this confidence seemed well deserved. Particularly in monopoly businesses such as the phone company, growth was robust. New commercial opportunities depended on telecommunications, and that spelled both upward mobility and financial security for the workforce. Bell Telephone Company, known as "Ma Bell," was the place to go for anyone who wanted a job for life, a solid pension, and a corporate "family."

Phone companies, electric companies, gas companies, and similar employers offered coveted jobs, especially to first-generation college students whose parents were often ensconced in the blue-collar world. Coming of age in the high-growth decades that followed World War II and lasted well into the 1970s, these students sought better lives, more prestigious careers. No frozen loading docks; no hundred-degree days shifting freight. The white-collar world of Bell Telephone and its ilk was clean, respectable, and steady. Glamour was not part of the bargain; young men and women went to work for Ma Bell because they wanted security. Having seen the ups and downs of blue-collar life up close, they were looking for managerial jobs that were more dependable.

For the more technically sophisticated students pouring out of the nation's schools of engineering, such a destiny was of no interest. Universities were pumping out thousands of highly skilled men (and women, but mostly men) to fuel new industries that drew on knowledge of computer science and aerospace, among other fields. Wartime had brought dizzying growth to the aircraft manufacturing industry, but in peace it was the expansion of domestic and international airlines that caught the fancy of many young engineers.

For the most part, technical workers weren't thinking about security, at least not in their early years. What attracted them to airline careers was the chance to be at the cutting edge of new technologies, part of the huge firms that dominated their industries. United Airlines was one of those behemoths, and it remains one of the world's most successful international carriers. Engineers who landed jobs at United's maintenance and engineering hubs in the 1960s and '70s were sitting pretty for decades, benefiting as the growing company overtook its rivals and transformed air travel from the luxury service of the postwar period to the mass travel industry we know today.

Bell Telephone and United Airlines are good places to examine if we want to know what has happened to retirement for the nation's more privileged white-collar occupations: managers, professionals, salespeople, and technical workers. A close look suggests that now they are becoming all too familiar with the disappointments of their blue-collar counterparts—a hard lesson to absorb.

SPUN OFF AND PUSHED OUT

Lisa and John Hannigan are Ma Bell sweethearts, a married couple who have both spent most of their working lives at the telephone company.

Their careers have traversed the long arc of the company's evolution from its monopoly days to the era of the "Baby Bells," when the courts broke up the system into regional companies.

At sixty-seven years old, Lisa Hannigan is still naturally stunning, her fair features and simple white sweater contrasting with the tan that comes from time on the beach in front of her home on the suburban Boston waterfront. She grew up in Randolph, Massachusetts, the oldest girl of five children on a mini-farm. Her mother stayed at home to look after the family; her father was a lifelong Teamster, a dispatcher for a trucking company.

Lisa graduated from public high school and immediately began her adult life on the right course, as an employee of the phone company in Boston. "I started out as a clerk," she recalls. "I made sixty-seven dollars a week and carpooled with someone for five dollars a week to get to work." She took a pay cut to take the job, leaving behind a summer job in a local factory. It proved to be a good move. "The factory closed down," she notes, "but the phone company kept going."

Lisa's job predated the computer revolution. It involved diving into huge files to pick out cards for Yellow Pages advertising categories like "automobiles," with subfiles such as "tires" or "car wash." From these cards, she constructed manual records of company advertising accounts that went out to the sales force. The work was tedious, but the atmosphere was friendly, not least because the employees expected to be compatriots for the rest of their working lives.

"When I first started with the phone company," Lisa reminisces, "it really was family. You knew everyone in your office, you got invited to their Christmas parties, everybody knew everyone's kids." And it stayed that way for decades, largely because the Bell system was the sole provider of telephone service and hence did not need to worry too much about wringing every last dime out of its loyal employees.

Little by little, Lisa worked her way from the clerical margins of the Yellow Pages empire and into its heartland: sales. She spent her early days selling advertising in a windowless cubbyhole that barely qualified as an office. For "smaller accounts," she recalls, "you just did it over the phone. You worked in a little cubicle and just dialed away all day long and talked to people and tried to sell them advertising."

When she was given the chance to take a personality and skills test to advance to the next level, Lisa passed and was promoted. Liberated from the cubicle, she now had the opportunity to land higher revenue for the company. She became a "premise salesperson," meaning she went out on the road to visit her customers and persuade them to take out larger ads in the Yellow Pages. For a new mother, this travel requirement was not without its complications, but it was worth it. "I sacrificed," Lisa says, "'cause I knew down the road I'd be making more money and there'd be a better future for my family."

John Hannigan's story is parallel to his wife's in many ways. At seventy-nine, with white hair and glasses, John still has the charisma of a successful salesman. A tall man, he favors golf shirts, in accordance with his favorite pastime. The oldest of seven children from a traditional Catholic family, he grew up near Canton, Massachusetts, and like his siblings served as an altar boy in the local parish church while attending parochial school.

After graduation, he followed many classmates into the Navy and served there for six years. Coming from a family of modest means, with strong blue-collar roots, John valued economic security. That meant a union job after leaving the Navy, and John started driving trucks under the aegis of Teamster Local 25. But a couple of cold winters later, he decided the white-collar world was more to his liking. So he took the Yellow Pages sales test, passed with flying colors, and three weeks later bid farewell to the Teamster world.

Like Lisa, who became his wife several years later, John traveled to clients to pitch for their business and found the social side of sales very congenial. Sadly, John's career came to an end much earlier than expected. In 1985, after sixteen years with the Yellow Pages, he had a stroke and was forced to take long-term disability at half pay. John and Lisa had two small children at the time, ages two and three, so John became "Mr. Mom" while Lisa continued to work for the phone company.

Although his illness was a shock, John and Lisa were comforted by the fact that her job was rock solid. After all, they worked for the phone company, which everyone knew was the epitome of stability. And the Yellow Pages was an American institution.

That confidence was tested a few years later, when President Bill Clinton signed into law the Telecommunications Act of 1996. To understand what that legislation meant for phone company employees like Lisa and John, a little history is in order. Ma Bell was a network of companies, led by the Bell Telephone Company and later by AT&T, that since 1877 had provided local and long-distance telephone services to much of the United States and Canada. In 1949, the Department of Justice took AT&T to court for antitrust violations, alleging that it was using its near-monopoly in telecommunications to establish an unfair advantage in related technologies. After another antitrust lawsuit, in 1974, AT&T agreed to divest itself of the Bell operating companies that provided local phone service. The divestiture meant that AT&T continued to offer long-distance service, while the newly independent Regional Bell Operating Companies, or "Baby Bells," were allowed to provide local phone service.[1]

One of these Baby Bells was NYNEX, a regional Bell operating company made up of former AT&T subsidiaries New York Telephone and New England Telephone. Starting in 1984, it served five New England states (Maine, Massachusetts, New Hampshire, Rhode Island, and Vermont), as well as most of New York State.[2] It was NYNEX that provided Lisa and John Hannigan their first jobs. The legacy of the old Ma Bell lived on through its successors, which is why NYNEX employees still felt that they had security, mobility, and a workplace family.

The Telecommunications Act of 1996 reshaped the landscape. The Federal Communications Commission stated that "the goal of this new law is to let anyone enter any communications business—to let any communications business compete in any market against any other."[3] Just a year later, NYNEX merged with Bell Atlantic, another regional Bell company, with the combined operation keeping the Bell Atlantic name.[4] In 2000, Bell Atlantic bought GTE in a $64.7 billion merger to form the firm we know today as Verizon Communications.[5]

Lisa weathered all of this organizational tumult because, through it all, she remained a valued, experienced sales representative in the Yellow Pages, the company's main advertising unit. That thick book of listings and ads, printed on yellow paper and delivered yearly to every doorstep, was the principal way that consumers found the merchants who provided the services they needed, from dog grooming to car repair.

But with the arrival of the internet and the rapid growth of Google and other electronic search engines, the print advertising that had sustained the Yellow Pages dried up and blew away. The downturn catalyzed internal changes at Verizon that were welcomed by almost no one, especially not old-timers like Lisa Hannigan. "They were bringing in people from other regions to come and take over," she recalls. "It wasn't like a family business anymore. It was more like corporate America . . . You're just a number, and it's not what you did for me last year, [but] what are you doing for me this year? And you were just a number on paper. You weren't 'Lisa.'"

She was soon to discover that when it came to loyalty, the sand was falling through the Verizon hourglass at a rapid rate. The atmosphere at work shifted from trust and benevolence to surveillance and discipline. Petty mistakes that would have gone unnoticed in the past became reasons to add a black mark to employment records. The deteriorating climate scared Lisa into leaving the company. The managers, she thought, were looking to put in "some new college kids that are hungry and want money . . . A guy I worked with, who used to be a top performer, he got fired for non-performance. And he isn't sixty-five yet, he's not even collecting his pension yet." She did not want to risk having the same thing happen to her.

Jeffrey Byrne had a similar experience. He became a chief switchman at Verizon after working for the company for ten years, and eventually he represented Verizon management in contract negotiation, arbitration, and grievance processes. As Jeffrey saw it, in the early years of his managerial career the relations between labor and management were fundamentally positive and collaborative. "We weren't mad at each other," he says. "They were trying to get the best contract that they could get, and we were trying to get the best contract we could . . . We always managed to get along."

It didn't last. By the late 1980s, after the Ma Bell breakup, cost containment and offshoring became more common and the atmosphere became notably more hostile. Upper management instructed Jeffrey to winch up the pressure on the unions. "You get someone telling you, 'Your job is to ram it down their throat,'" Jeffrey says. "That's the beginning of the downslide . . . They no longer treat[ed] people the same way they would want to be treated themselves." Jeffrey moved toward retirement in 1991 and recalls talking to a friend about how to navigate the financial options. "He told me to take the lump sum and run," Jeffrey remembers. "The company's going to hell, and it's spitting [flames]. So that's what we did."

Verizon pushed people like Lisa and Jeffrey toward retirement with a combination of carrots and sticks. Those who were already eligible to retire were offered pension increases if they pulled the trigger immediately. If they decided instead to continue working, either because they needed the income or because they weren't psychologically ready to leave the work world, their fates were potentially more problematic. The company was hovering over its older workers, pressuring them with more rigorous performance evaluations and emphasizing that if they didn't take the retirement deal they could face retractions in benefits instead.

Slightly younger employees, with less time in the company, were offered a "six and six" package. It enabled eligible workers to add six years to both their age and years of service to meet the NYNEX Pension Plan's eligibility requirements, which normally required either thirty years of service or seventy-five years of combined age and service.

From Lisa Hannigan's perspective, such sweeteners were not gestures of appreciation. They were window dressing disguising an effort to push loyal longtime workers out the door, the kind of move the old-time Ma Bell system never would have entertained. It was a message of "we don't need you, Lisa," she remembers with bitterness. "We don't care if you're sick. We don't even know your name."

It may literally be true that no one at Verizon knew Lisa's name. After most of her generation was pushed into early retirement, Verizon spun off her division, the Yellow Pages, into a new company called Idearc.[6] With that one move, Verizon removed $9.5 billion in pension-related debt from its books.

Idearc is one of those "here today, gone tomorrow" entities that many former employees believe was created just for bankruptcy. It has no history as a functioning company. It didn't exist independently before 2006. Almost immediately after it was founded, Idearc showed signs of insolvency, and within twenty-eight months it was bankrupt.[7] For retirees like Lisa, who never actually worked for Idearc, the whole arrangement seemed designed to leave her and all the other Yellow Pages veterans in a corporate never-never land. Verizon was looking to walk away from the pension obligations on its books by setting up a new set of books that weren't real.

Labor lawyers like Eddie Stone, an attorney in Connecticut who represents Verizon retirees, are wise to this strategy. "The Idearc case was an example of a merger where . . . they offloaded these liabilities, and then all of a sudden there was a bankruptcy," he says. "And a lot of benefits got lost."

Idearc's creditors—not just retirees, but lenders to whom it owed money—sued Verizon over the spinoff, arguing that the company was just trying to weasel out of debt.[8] Werner Powers, an attorney for the creditors, argued that Verizon had deliberately saddled Idearc with debt, making it so unattractive to potential buyers that it was basically "sent . . . into the market to die." Powers noted that the directory business was suffering double-digit declines in major urban markets, which was a "'canary in the mine shaft' that . . . the company hid from investors."[9] But the creditors lost the case, since the court determined that they could not prove that Idearc was insolvent at the time of the spinoff or that Verizon intended it to fail.[10]

Spinoffs like Idearc have become relatively common. In 2012 there were eighty-five of them, worth over $100 billion. According to UC Berkeley law professor Steven Davidoff Solomon, they represent an attractive way to "clean up a parent [company] balance sheet," one that doesn't require shareholder approval. It is also an easy way for those in upper management to artificially jack up earnings: they no longer have to factor in a low- or no-growth business, which is what the Yellow Pages had become.[11]

Every time such disruptions happen, retirees like the Lisa and

John Hannigan lose something tangible.[12] Retirees from other Verizon departments have also seen their retirement packages decline. In 2001, Verizon reduced medical coverage for its retirees from 95 percent to 80 percent, phased in over three years. The new retirement plan also decreased life insurance coverage from the employee's salary at retirement to a flat $10,000. A lifetime dental cap of $6,000 per family was also imposed, and the firm eliminated a special death benefit.[13]

Meanwhile, the push to get rid of older workers continued. In 2003, Verizon offered another voluntary buyout package to 74,000 management employees. It provided them two weeks of severance pay for each year of employment, as well as $15,000 to $30,000 based on management rank.

Idearc eventually emerged from bankruptcy under the name Super-Media Inc.[14] In 2012, SuperMedia jettisoned health care for Yellow Pages retirees altogether. This would be a blow to any family, but to John Hannigan, who continues to suffer the aftereffects of a serious illness, it is particularly destabilizing. "All the medicine I take is very expensive," he explains, because of the stroke he had when he was working for Verizon. But it isn't just the cost that bothers him. It's the about-face, the betrayal of a social contract.

> They said they were going to take care of [me] for the rest of my life. They just lied. Totally lied. This new young management group that they have, who think that if they make these brilliant decisions, that it's gonna boost them up the ladder somehow or other. They don't care who they walk on, who they step on. Who they cut out of the picture.

Teamster retirees are familiar with these kinds of losses, because the firms they worked for were in financial trouble and often turned to their workers for givebacks to help keep them solvent. Verizon, however, is not a struggling enterprise. It is a highly profitable firm. Other large and successful companies, like GE and IBM, have also pulled back on retirement benefits for their skilled white-collar managers.[15]

Ellen Schultz, the author of *Retirement Heist: How Companies Plunder and Profit from the Nest Eggs of American Workers*, provides a trenchant account of these rollbacks.[16] She notes that the legal rules that governed pension funds did not actually require employers to use the monies to meet retirement obligations. "By the end of the 1990s," she states, "pension plans at many large companies had such massive surpluses that the companies could have fully paid their current and future retirees' pensions, even if all of them lived to be 99 and the companies never contributed another dime." Instead, they began to "siphon billions of dollars in assets from their pension plans."

> With perfectly legal loopholes that enabled companies to tap pension plans like piggy banks, and accounting rules that rewarded employers for cutting benefits, retiree benefits plans soon morphed into profit centers, and populations of retirees essentially became portfolios of assets and debts, which passed from company to company in swirls of mergers, spin-offs and acquisitions. And with each of these restructuring deals, the subsequent owner aimed to squeeze a profit from the portfolio, always at the expense of the retirees.[17]

Schultz's account describes the history of Verizon to a tee, and indeed she points to the company as a prime example. But it was just one of many firms that took this path and left its retirees reeling. Ford, General Motors, JCPenney, Sears, Kimberly-Clark, Boeing, and many others followed suit.[18]

Besides slicing into their health insurance, Verizon also ended cost-of-living increases for its retirees, reducing the value of their pensions over time. The firm has not adjusted its defined benefit pensions since 1991, even though such an adjustment was built into the original retirement plan. Verizon never announced a change in policy; it simply stopped providing cost-of-living increases. That was one of the precipitating forces behind the formation of the Association of BellTel Retirees, which can claim some limited successes. Due to pressure from retirees, for example, in April 2000 Verizon made a one-time payment to certain former employees who had retired before 1995.[19]

For the most part, though, pensioners have simply had to make do with a lower standard of living. "I've never had a cost adjustment," longtime Yellow Pages manager Betty Eber says. "I've had the pension twenty years and it's exactly the same." She notes that the company also changed the way it calculates the pension itself. As a result, she has "a much smaller pension than I had been anticipating. It's probably close to ten thousand dollars a year less" than the money she had been expecting to receive. The financial stress has mounted over the years, particularly in periods of higher-than-average inflation.

She has one word for what Verizon has done: "Disgusting."

DERISKING

A pension was once regarded as something of a sacred bond between an employer and loyal employees. For decades, pension funds were like savings accounts, invested to grow in order to take care of retirees, who would receive monthly cash outlays. But as the long-term consequences of deregulation and globalization take hold, the concept has undergone a metamorphosis.

Verizon was one of the leaders in developing a different definition altogether: starting in 2012, the firm transformed its management pension plans into insurance annuities.[20] Group annuities are similar to defined benefit pensions, in that participants receive a fixed amount each month. But instead of being held in-house by the company where the retirees had worked, the pooled money is held by a life insurance company. And unlike in a 401(k), employees do not own individual stocks, but rather "units" of a pooled investment.

Verizon paid Prudential Financial to take over its pension liabilities for 41,000 management retirees, totaling $7.5 billion. For the firm's upper management, the move made sense because it reduced volatility and relieved Verizon of the expense of paying an annual fee or premium to the Pension Benefit Guaranty Corporation. It also means that the company does not need to concern itself with how its retirement plan is doing year after year—it no longer holds the risk involved in owing the pension money directly to its employees and retirees. Verizon is among dozens of major companies that have "derisked" their pensions in this fashion.[21]

Another result of this change, though, is that it effectively ended the protections provided under the Employee Retirement Income Security Act of 1974. ERISA requires plan managers to disclose information to beneficiaries about investment performance, establishes fiduciary responsibilities, and enables standing before the federal courts to seek remedies if these rules are abrogated. By placing their pensioners into the hands of state-supervised insurance companies, Verizon broke its link to ERISA. The move effectively stripped retirees of their rights to obtain information about their retirement plans' solvency and ability to fulfill obligations to beneficiaries.

In response, Verizon's retirees sued the company. Their suit was later dismissed by a federal judge, but in May 2016 the US Supreme Court asked a federal appeals court to review the right of Verizon to "derisk" those 41,000 pension plans.[22]

Eddie Stone, the lawyer who represents Verizon retirees, contends that Verizon's move exposes retirees to risks they would not have faced if their accounts had remained under ERISA protection. Because ERISA is a federal law, it applies regardless of the residence of a pensioner. Retirees have the same rights to know what their pensions are worth, and whether investments are keeping up with the expected returns needed to fulfill them, whether they live in Connecticut or Michigan. When Verizon replaced pensions with insurance annuities, it moved those retirement benefits entirely out of reach of federal law and placed them under the control of state laws that regulate insurance. This is not acceptable, Stone says. "Why should one person's pension be subject to the claims of creditors because they live in one state, and why should someone who moves to another state lose protection? And you know retirees like to move! They want to be with their children, their grandchildren, they go south, they go west, they go wherever they go!"

Joe Cahan, a founder of the Association of BellTel Retirees, similarly objects to the "great risk shift." "As a pensioner, you used to get an annual statement showing what's happening to your retirement fund," he points out. "The insurance companies have no obligation to do that, and they're fighting it tremendously."

For the moment, few pensioners have actually experienced losses. The annuities have held up. But under the terms of most state legal systems, retirees can no longer monitor their pensions and have no legal right to know if Prudential or anyone else is managing their money wisely. Eddie Stone sees it as his responsibility "to educate as many members of the legislature, people at the PBGC, retirees about how important it is to have transparency in these transactions." He argues that we cannot rely on the insurance industry to be candid with retirees. "'Just trust us' is a really bad answer," he says. "You're not gonna know for twenty years, and at that point if there were huge mistakes made in pricing and people do live longer and they got it wrong, it's gonna be a real problem . . . They won't have the money to pay out."

This might sound like a Chicken Little worry were it not for the lingering shadow of the Great Recession. There is no guarantee that something like it won't happen again, Stone warns.

> With all of these companies shedding their pension liabilities, who knows if they've gotten it right globally? We learned during the financial crisis, that all this stuff is related because one sells derivatives to the other . . . If there's a run on the banks and everyone wants to get out, then those long duration liabilities suddenly plummet in value, and that's the big risk that I see . . . Insurance is uniquely opaque by design, and that's something you learn the hard way.

Stable companies like Prudential are unlikely to falter too badly, but stranger things happened in the stock market crash of 2008. Another severe downturn could, at least theoretically, cause Prudential to fail and default on the annuity payments it is supposed to provide Verizon retirees. And since the strategy of moving from ERISA-regulated pensions to annuities has become something of a standard move in corporate America, Verizon pensioners are not the only ones affected. General Motors, Motorola, Kimberly-Clark, Bristol-Myers Squibb, and other large companies are among those that have followed suit, putting their retirees in the same boat.[23]

THE BANKRUPTCY OF UNITED AIRLINES

In the annals of labor history, the tale of United Airlines workers is perhaps even more troubling than the Verizon story. After all, many phone company retirees (aside from the Yellow Pages veterans spun off into Idearc) still had pensions, even if they were frozen for some workers and no longer subject to cost-of-living increases for others. In the case of United, the company's descent into bankruptcy cost hundreds of highly skilled engineers, technicians, and administrative employees their retirement security altogether.

The company's history is a good place to begin for understanding what happened to United's technical workforce. Incorporated in 1931, United signed its first collective bargaining agreement with mechanics and ground service workers in 1939.[24] It was among the most successful companies in mid-twentieth-century America.

Fast-forward four decades or so, and the story changed because of many of the same factors that roiled the trucking industry. First, in the mid-1970s, OPEC's increasing clout sent oil prices steeply upward. Any fuel-dependent industry, which included transportation both on the ground and in the air, saw its costs soar. Next, the wave of deregulation that caught the trucking companies also slammed into the airlines. The 1978 Airline Deregulation Act thrust United into an entirely different kind of marketplace. The legislation ended government oversight of airfares and quality of service, leaving only safety under federal regulation.[25]

What was originally a transportation system for businesspeople and wealthy individuals became a mass traveling experience. New landing slots were opened up at major international and regional airports, enabling the first of the low-cost carriers to sweep in and gather up customers. Today, few passengers remember People Express, but other low-cost carriers—like Southwest and Spirit Airlines—have persisted. Collectively, they were able to exert massive downward pressure on ticket prices. Airfares fell dramatically.

In time, that democratization would expand the flying public. But in the early 1980s, it led to massive overcapacity and sharply declining profits. The eleven thousand air traffic controllers who went on strike in 1981—and were fired en masse for defying the federal government—learned this lesson the hard way.[26] The controllers thought the airline companies would be their allies in an effort to improve their working conditions. Instead, the airlines were only too happy to ground most of their fleets when skeleton crews in the nation's control towers could not handle the traffic. Companies released only those planes the government gave them permission to fly, and they reveled in the fact that they were now completely full. Yet once the emergency subsided, companies like United were faced with a cost structure that was no longer so favorable. Some of the major airlines recognizable the world over, like Pan Am, went out of business entirely. Others, like United, started taking on water.

In 1985, United pilots and flight attendants, who had not been particularly sympathetic to the air traffic controllers, learned how vulnerable they themselves were to downward wage pressures brought on by competition. After bargaining failed, they went on strike for twenty-nine days over a new two-tier wage structure that would pay new pilots much less than established pilots and reduce the retirement benefits for both groups. The pilots' union eventually reached a compromise with United over the two-tier system, but many flight attendants were embittered by the way management had rewarded strikebreakers and punished those attendants who had refused to cross the picket lines.[27] United's profitability continued to wobble, and the firm once again demanded wage and benefit concessions, this time including reduced retirement contributions.

To protect their jobs, United's pilots, flight attendants, and machinists agreed to those givebacks in exchange for majority ownership of the company through an employee stock ownership plan. An ESOP is set up as a defined contribution invested by employees in company stock. Making employees into owners is intended to improve performance and keep workers personally invested in the success of the firm. (About 28 million employees nationwide participate in an employee ownership plan of this kind, which means they control about 8 percent of American corporate equity.) By December 1993, United's unions had reached a tentative agreement to buy the carrier in a $5.15 billion cash-and-concessions deal that would give them at least 53 percent owner-ship of the airline under the ESOP.

United's troubles did not end there, though. In the terrorist attacks of September 11, 2001, two of the four hijacked flights were United planes. One hit the World Trade Center; the other crashed into the ground in Shanksville, Pennsylvania. All passengers, flight attendants, and pilots on the planes perished, along with nearly three thousand people on the ground, plunging the nation into bitter mourning. As public attention focused on terrorism, 9/11 set in motion yet another downdraft for United. Eight days after the attack, the airline announced twenty thousand layoffs. On November 1, the company reported a $1.16 billion quarterly loss, the biggest in its seventy-five-year history. A few months later, United declared a $2.1 billion loss for 2001, a rec-ord for any airline.[28] By the end of the year, United had submitted an application for Chapter 11 bankruptcy, the largest filing by an airline in the industry's history.[29]

The bankruptcy process dragged on for more than three years. Busi-ness journalists characterized United's descent as "brutal." The com-pany "slashed salaries, defaulted on its corporate-pension plan, and stopped upgrading facilities and replacing planes, leaving a deeply embittered workforce and one of the oldest fleets in the business," a *Bloomberg* article noted. "Everything from baggage handling to aircraft reliability suffered."[30] Another report summed up the damage:

> United . . . now has about 30 percent fewer employees (58,000), 20 percent fewer airplanes (460) and 20 percent lower operating costs (7.5 cents per seat per mile), excluding fuel, than it did when the bank-ruptcy began on Dec. 9, 2002. Labor costs are down by more than $3 billion annually after two steep pay cuts and the elimination of defined-benefit pensions. Dozens of daily domestic flights have been eliminated.[31]

By the time the bankruptcy had been fully adjudicated, United faced a $10.2 billion shortfall in its retirement obligations. Over the objections of the unions, United received court permission to default on its four employee pension plans (for pilots, flight attendants, mechanics, and management/nonunion engineers). The ruling turned over responsibility for the plans to the PBGC, putting 134,000 United workers under the aegis of the agency.[32]

Due to the limits of the program, the PBGC paid the United retirees only $6.8 billion; employees would lose the remaining $3.4 billion worth of retirement benefits.[33] The impact on individual workers varied widely. The ones who had left United years before or had retired at an older age saw little change in their pensions. Those who had taken early retirement or were still on the job, however, faced major losses. The PBGC's maximum coverage for someone retiring at the age of sixty—the mandatory retirement age for airline pilots—was $28,000. Pilots who had been receiving the company pension of $125,000 were beside themselves.[34]

Tim Joiner, a retired United engineer, remembers that the losses gathered force gradually and for many months were opaque to the workforce. Now in his midsixties, with white hair and a round, ruddy face, Tim was a die-hard, devoted United employee from a long line of aeronautical engineers. United's bankruptcy cost veteran employees like him in many ways. "There were indicators [of the bankruptcy], but United was in denial," he recalls. It wasn't long, though, before everyone knew. "When they first declared bankruptcy," he notes, "all the employees . . . lost a full week of vacation, we lost two holidays, and we lost 20 percent of our salary."

United's engineers, who didn't enjoy the exceptional salaries of the company's pilots, waited what felt like forever to find out how their pensions would be affected by bankruptcy and the move to the PBGC. When Tim finally got the news, it was a shock: his pension was cut in half, from $30,000 a year to $15,000. "It was devastating," he says. "People couldn't believe it. Understand, I had a lot of coworkers who did not participate in a 401(k), and all their money was in that pension, and that's been cut in *half*. I didn't lose anything from the 401(k). Luckily, United couldn't touch that. If they could have, they would have. They would have brutalized that."

Fellow engineer Ted Eakins was similarly blindsided. A tall, thin man now in his early 70s, Ted was born with flight in his blood. A second-generation United employee, he followed in the footsteps of his father, George, who was also a flight engineer and a United loyalist. A good student, Ted had many options when he graduated from high school, but in the end he enrolled in the engineering school at a top public university, where he was captivated by cutting-edge applications of information science to aeronautics.

Ted's college advisor was so impressed with the simulation studies Ted did on problems of airport design, he urged the young man to go on for a PhD. But Ted was keen on a career in industry and headed to business school, figuring that the combination of engineering and management would set him up well for the future. It worked. With a second master's degree under his belt, Ted attracted United's attention and listened to his father's advice: take their offer. "I remember Dad pulling me aside and telling me, 'It's a good place to work. You'll get a guaranteed pension there.'" Ted's father assured him that "the work is really steady. They're always going to have work."

But Ted's history with United bore almost no resemblance to his father's time. Between deregulation, declining revenue, rising fuel costs, and bitter labor disputes, the economic conditions that impacted Ted's career were almost all negative. Most distressing of all was the long-term impact of the one action taken to try to restore some semblance of financial stability: the creation of United's employee stock ownership plan. ESOPs had existed since the 1950s, but in the early years of the Clinton administration the Department of Labor started pushing hard for them as a way of both increasing workers' stake in the profitability of their firms and providing much-needed working capital.[35] In United's case, the ESOP solution emerged as a means of injecting capital into a firm that was in a tailspin.

Policy makers and government officials were bullish on the idea. Farhad Manjoo at *Salon* tried to capture the spirit behind employee ownership:

In 1994, when United Airlines was on the brink of a financial crisis, the company's executives and its employees embarked on a grand experiment in corporate governance. In a marked departure from years of tension between labor and management, the parties came together to save the airline. Employees agreed to forgo billions of dollars in wages in order to keep down the airline's operational costs, so that United could more easily compete with low-cost airlines such as Southwest. In return, the airline would hand over half of the company to the workers, who would have a say in the direction of the airline and would supposedly directly benefit from its future success.[36]

United's ESOP created one of the biggest employee-owned companies in the United States; it was seen as a new opportunity for cooperation between labor and management in the airline industry. Clinton's labor secretary, Robert Reich, was an enthusiast for this form of "rescue," believing it would inject an element of democracy into the workplace. "From here on in," he proclaimed, "it will be impossible for a board of directors to not consider employee ownership as one potential business strategy." In an effort to show the public that everyone at United was now on the same page, the company changed its slogan from "Come fly the friendly skies" to "Come fly *our* friendly skies."[37]

But whether the overall idea of ESOPs was fatally flawed, or the particular circumstances of United's version doomed it, the airline's bankruptcy took the employees and their pensions down with it. Managers like Ted were given United stock in lieu of cash contributions to their pensions, but they were not permitted to sell those holdings until they quit or retired.[38] Those were the rules governing ESOPs, established to ensure that workers actually did have a degree of control over the firms of which they were now part owners. But the requirements hemmed workers in, restricting their pension investments to the company's stock. In essence, Ted was told he had to invest in a company that was wobbling and that he could not exercise the right all other stockholders have to sell.

When United implemented its ESOP, Ted recalls, "I wound up with five hundred shares of the United Airlines [stock], which was supposedly eighty-five dollars apiece, and I thought, 'Well, that's pretty good.'" But before long, the ESOP shares "didn't really have any value anymore. You couldn't sell them at the time you were granted ownership,

you [had to] own them at the point when you retired." And by the
time Ted was ready to retire, he was holding stock in a bankrupt company. It was worthless.

OUTSOURCING AND ITS DISCONTENTS

The financial losses incurred by United's skilled workforce were only
part of the downhill trajectory they endured. And while money was on
everyone's mind, working for a company with such a storied history was
its own kind of reward—until it wasn't. Just as Yellow Pages employees
at Verizon discovered that they were becoming anonymous and subject to surveillance, United engineers found that the quality of their
jobs declined alongside their retirement benefits. This rubbed salt into
their wounds: not only were they getting a raw deal financially, the
prestige of their jobs was eroding, alongside the security they had once
enjoyed as members of one of the largest and most skilled workforces
in the "new economy." In this, they were not unusual. Pension losses
almost always go hand in hand with other kinds of degradation, as
cost pressures impact working conditions, compensation, and retirement benefits at the same time.

Outsourcing work that had previously been assigned to engineers
"in house" was one cost-saving move with which United began to
experiment. And the trend was not limited to engineers. Patty Florio,
who worked in the human resources department, recalls how United
brought in office workers from India with the intention of sending all
the HR work back home with them. "My manager was told, 'We're
going to bring in the folks from India, you teach them how to do all of
your jobs, we'll send the job back to India, and then—we won't need
you.'" But it didn't work out well.

We were getting [Indian workers] that needed a job, and they knew
how to do a little something. They didn't catch on. Our system was
too complicated for them to learn in six weeks. And fair enough, it'd
be too complicated for most people to learn in six weeks . . . Then they
started doing the work and we said, "This isn't working." And the

errors that were coming back, and the time our people had to do to correct the errors.

And [we] kept telling [our managers], "It's not working, it's not working . . ." We're just cleaning up their mess. [The managers] said, "Make it work. Make it work." [whispers] "It's not working." So, finally, after a year or a year and a half, they said, "All right, we get that it's not working." And they finally abandoned the project. And let it go. It took a long time. They didn't take our word for things along the way.

The same cost pressures that prompted efforts at outsourcing also led to "RIFs"—reductions in force—through layoffs and the failure to fill vacancies. Yet the amount of work did not diminish just because there were fewer people available to do it. Management and union jobs now required more work of the survivors, even though their raises had been suspended and their benefits reduced.

Some of the biggest losses in skilled people came about because United pressured them to take early retirement. Older employees, who were often more expensive, might be told that they would have to move to another location across the country, essentially giving them a choice between upending their lives or leaving the company. Patty was eventually forced out in a different way.

Management said, "Well, now what we're going to do—all you people that've been here for ten, fifteen, thirty-five years, we're going to have you re-interview for your job." . . . These fabulous people that've been doing this wonderful job that are so dedicated, that have learned so much over these years . . . "Could you re-interview?" "Sure. Be glad to." So then we set up all the interviews, and then they had to go over who they were going to keep and not keep. And so they let people go that way.

After the interviews, a new organizational chart was unveiled in Patty's division. She scoured the diagram for her name and couldn't find it anywhere. She asked her boss what that meant, and the boss claimed not to know. Finally, she got a letter saying she was out.

Fortunately, Patty had twenty-five years of service under her belt. Between that and her age, she qualified for one of the retirement packages. She could have looked for other jobs within the company, but she didn't bother, though she was sad to leave a job she had genuinely enjoyed. United employees are "very disappointed with the company," she says. "It's not anything like the way it was twenty years ago. Just fractured. And people work together better when there's camaraderie going on. Now I think some of the energy is gone from there."

In 2006, when United's bankruptcy process was coming to a conclusion, the firm began preliminary negotiations on a merger with Continental Airlines.[39] Four years later, after looking into possible mergers with other airlines, shareholders for both firms approved a $3.22 billion fusion.[40] It was one of many marriages of convenience in the industry, designed to reduce administrative costs, increase efficiency by eliminating duplication, and create more comprehensive national and international route structures. Whatever the benefits of these amalgamations, mergers often force longtime employees to compete with similarly qualified people, since the new firm rarely needs two of everybody. Someone has to go. Alternatively, workers may be told that they can retain their jobs, but not in the location in which they have been working, because facilities are being combined to achieve efficiencies. Tim Joiner, for example, was told he could keep his job if he moved from his town to Continental's home base in Houston.

Quite apart from the disruption of moving a family, mergers place the acquired company's employees at a disadvantage compared to those with equivalent positions at the acquiring company. United employees moving into a facility dominated by Continental workers could expect—unofficially—to fall to the bottom, as Tim explains. "I'd be the new kid on the block. I'd be that outsider," he says. "And by their [scales], I was overpaid, because on average, [workers in my area] are offered about 25 to 30 percent more than the Houston people . . . You know come next round of layoffs you'd be number one on the list to be laid off."

On occasion, the transfers ran in the other direction. Continental workers came into the United facility and were placed into the local hierarchy. To Tim, it felt like an alien invasion. "They came to [our location], a much larger organization for engineering, and very well established, very well organized, very efficient—as a matter of fact that was the first thing they said to us when they came by: 'You guys are great! Oh you guys are doing such a good job!' And then they turn around and say, 'We're taking over.'"

Tim thought about hanging on for another year, even under these less-than-ideal circumstances. But he learned that if he stayed, he was risking his financial future. "Anybody that retired after the end of March [2014] was not going to get any benefits," he discovered. "And that's a huge difference. With the healthcare provision, I'd be paying 114 bucks a month. Without the healthcare provision, I'd be paying 1,500 a month! A huge difference."

Tim scrambled to retire early and ensure he could hold on to that health plan. United outsourced the personnel process, which did not make his task any easier. Instead of turning to someone he trusted—like Patty Florio—he had to run a bureaucratic gauntlet with a stranger to be sure he would get what was supposed to be coming to him.

> I luckily made sure I filled out all the paperwork, I made copies of everything, and then I submitted it. And sure enough, a month later they tried to say I was not eligible for [individual health insurance]. Again, to save money, this was being managed by a third party. They were not United employees, and so pretty much all they could do was read off the monitor. If it was not on the monitor, they didn't have a clue. And I could tell that was exactly what they were doing . . . It took weeks to resolve! And dozens of phone calls! And each time you call it in, you're put on hold for half an hour! . . . It was very stressful.

Tim persevered because there was so much at stake. He had already given up on the family health plan he would have had if United had been true to its word; he just wanted to be sure he could put his hands on his own coverage.[41] Meanwhile, Tim's pension payout was reduced because he signed up for pension benefits that will take care of his wife, who is several years younger, in the event he dies before her. This means that he receives $1,000/month now, and after he dies, his wife will receive $500/month for her share.

Under these unexpected circumstances, Tim felt he had no choice but to supplement his pension. He began to access Social Security at the age of sixty-two, the earliest year in which he was eligible, at which point the monthly payout is the lowest possible. If he had been able to wait to sixty-eight—which would have been feasible if his pension had not been impacted by United's bankruptcy—his monthly Social Security payment would have been 40 percent higher.

Patty Florio remembers that it was difficult to find out what her PBGC pension would be. She was in the dark about how sharp a reduction she faced. "They weren't going to tell us how much we were going to make" from the PBGC pension, she recalls.

> If you decided to retire, they didn't do your paperwork until your last day. Because so many people, when they found out . . . said, "Oh, I can't live on that! Never mind, I'm not retiring." So they weren't sharing enough information.
>
> And then, in 2005, they said, "Oh, you know what, you don't need as much pension as you think you need. We're going to stop the pension now. You'll be fine. You'll be fine. Now, you're going to have this opportunity to work on your 401(k) . . . You get to decide where to do it." [laughing] I said, "Wait, I don't think that's going to work out."

The pension cuts came as a shock to many United employees, who were living in one of the most expensive areas of the United States and suddenly found themselves with a fraction of the income they were expecting. As Patty points out, many of United's workers were in their prime work years; they weren't young, and they didn't have skills that could easily be absorbed in other industries. "These are airline people," she explains. "That's what they do. They don't build houses."

WHO IS TO BLAME?

To some degree, the forces descending on Verizon and United were not of their own making. Deregulation was imposed on both firms. The rising cost of fuel hit airlines just as it hit the trucking industry. Bankruptcy and mergers were also not unique to United. Yet unlike airlines like Pan Am, Eastern Air Lines, and America West, United eventually came out of bankruptcy and reestablished itself as a highly profitable company. Indeed, today its planes are packed full, its fuel costs have declined sharply, and its commanding postmerger position as one of the most powerful airlines in the world is now well established.

Verizon, for its part, never had to contend with bankruptcy and has always been highly profitable. This fact is not lost on workers who have watched their jobs migrate to India, raises disappear, and retirement benefits—especially health insurance—go the way of the dinosaurs. While unionized employees were better protected than frontline management, virtually everyone other than the very top brass saw work quality erode and long-promised retirement provisions evaporate. The two negative trends go hand in hand, since they share an originating push factor: the company's efforts to cut costs. It did so both through speeding up work—often replacing older workers with younger, cheaper ones—and reducing its pension liabilities.

While the Teamsters focused their ire on politicians, the Treasury Department, and Wall Street, Verizon and United retirees tended to direct their moral critique at company management. As outsourcing, the pressure to retire early, and reduction of retirement benefits swept through the big firms, the language of inequality became more salient in the United States. The "1 percent" started to attract attention in the news media. In this climate, Verizon and United retirees were inclined to think of themselves as victims of greed. If their companies had once been paternalistic families, they had morphed into instrumental, profit-driven institutions with executive compensation in the spotlight.

With Patty Florio's retirement benefits cratering, she watched with dismay as the CEOs floated gently to the ground strapped to golden parachutes. "Every couple of years, every CEO was going, and everyone's getting . . . whatever they needed," she says. They "literally took millions from the company . . . Do you really think that's fair? Nope. Of course we didn't think it's fair."

Ellen Shultz, author of *Retirement Heist*, thinks that this is more than the lament of an aggrieved workforce. It is an accurate view of the relationship between CEO compensation and diminished retirement plans. Cutting retirement plans increases company earnings, she explains, which is directly connected to C-suite paychecks.

> Unfortunately for employees and retirees, these newfound tricks coincided with the trend of tying executive pay to performance. Deliberately or not, the executives who green-lighted massive retiree cuts were indirectly boosting their own pay.
>
> As their pay grew, managers and officers began diverting growing amounts into deferred-compensation plans, which are unfunded and therefore create a liability. Meanwhile, their supplemental executive pensions, which are based on pay, ballooned along with their compensation. Today, it's common for a large company to owe its executives several billion dollars in pensions and deferred compensation.
>
> These growing "executive legacy liabilities" are included in the pension obligations employers report to shareholders, and account for many of the "growing pension costs" companies are complaining about. Unlike regular pensions, the growing executive liabilities are largely hidden, buried within the figures for regular pensions. So even as employers bemoaned their pension burdens, the executive pensions and deferred comp were becoming in some companies a bigger drag on profits.[42]

Schultz is pointing to a growing debt with which firms will have to reckon someday. When they promise to provide executives with "deferred compensation," usually in order to encourage them to remain at the company in the face of outside offers, they are placing a marker on the company's balance sheet without any requirement to set aside revenues to pay for it. As Schultz notes, this burden expands every year but goes largely unrecognized. Those executive payouts seem to grow in proportion to the cost reductions managers have implemented—reductions that improve the profit picture, but at the expense of ordinary workers whose jobs have become unstable and benefits unreliable.

Like many other employees, Tim Joiner thought that if and when

United emerged from bankruptcy, it would restore the benefits taken from its longtime employees. No such luck. By 2014 the company was thriving, but the cutbacks continued. He was aghast.

> This year it's expected that they'll make *4 billion* dollars in profit! Not in gross revenue—in *profit*! And they're still playing this game! Until it happened, I really thought United was, legally, obligated to fulfill its promise and pay that pension. But no, they've just bailed out. And, what was deceitful was, they knew they were gonna bail out, and they just kept it a secret until they actually did it. And, in addition to that, the senior management did not take a cut in salary or anything! They still got their full check!

Verizon, too, is a highly profitable company in a high-tech industry. It doesn't appear on the surface to have much in common with the old steel mills or auto plants, beset by foreign competition and aging production technologies. Given the phone company's modern appearance and healthy balance sheet, retirees whose benefits have been cut cannot imagine any explanation for their fate other than upper management greed. Cutting benefits was discretionary and hence avoidable. "It's a very wealthy company," remarks Amy Janowski, a veteran of the Yellow Pages. And when the upper management is making "ten, twenty, thirty times more than the average person" whose benefits are being cut, she says, "there's a resentment that comes with that . . . They don't care about you."

It all comes down to power, says the Verizon retiree association's Joe Cahan. Chief executives have the upper hand and can simply impose inequalities on employees, such as middle managers, who have no union to defend them. The only solution, he argues, is to band together. "You gotta go out with a fight. Make 'em know they're in a fight. You can't let 'em do it because they'll run over us and back up and run over us again."

Sadly, the phone company *is* actually subject to technological change and the pressure that comes with globalization. Even the most furious BellTel retiree knows this and can chart out the impact of those forces in great detail. Wireless is replacing wired phone networks. The integration of telephone and internet systems is enabling providers of the latter to gobble up the former. The pace of change has been relentless. We had the Yellow Pages for decades, until we didn't need it anymore.

Kelly Shannon, who worked for the Yellow Pages, could see the writing on the wall. "When I retired," she recalls, "my manager said, 'You did a great job.'" He told Kelly that he could surely find her more work if she wanted. But she was skeptical. "You know, computers were coming and the internet," she says. "And it was getting bigger and bigger. And I just thought, why would they want a phone book? I just thought it was odd that none of the Yellow Pages people seemed to see that." For her part, she says with a laugh, "I never use a phone book!"

Everyone wants to think that they are irreplaceable, or at least that their work is of some durable importance. Many of her coworkers thought that way, Kelly says, believing that the company "can't do away with my job." Somberly, she set them straight. "They can send it to China. They can do whatever they want."

Technological change rendered the work these people did obsolete. But that does not explain why a profitable firm would treat its loyal, longtime workers so poorly in retirement. It is one thing not to need this labor force. It is another to kick the pensioners to the curb—to create fly-by-night companies like Idearc in order to relieve Verizon of liabilities for hard-earned pensions; to jettison retirement accounts in favor of insurance annuities that are not covered by the same rules of financial transparency; to end retiree health coverage; and to show such unwillingness to even notify longtime employees that these changes are coming.

Lisa Hannigan sums it up:

> We really believed . . . when we started working for the phone company . . . it was like a career for life . . . You went there from high school to grave. [But management] politely [explained] at a corporate meeting that we don't want people to stay for life anymore. We just really want to use you for like five years and once you're burnt out, go somewhere else . . .

We showed up for work every day and we did the best job we could and were loyal to our . . . customer and to the company. And that's why we got those benefits. But . . . once we retired, they really didn't care. No one called you, no one cared if you were sick. It was like you were gone—you were history . . .

They'll tell you, "We have to show a huge profit for our shareholders." Really? How about taking care of the people that made the money that you're giving to the stockholders?

Detroit's municipal civil servants—from firefighters and police to librarians and construction inspectors—faced pension cutbacks and increased health care costs after the city's bankruptcy. Hundreds were also required to pay back pension money they had been lawfully awarded years before.

3

MUNICIPAL BLUES

You told me I work for you thirty years . . . When I get out of here, I'm supposed to have a check at the end of that time. You reneged on all of that and blamed it on *me*. That's the way I feel, and the way a lot of city retirees feel.

[This was all] because the city bankruptcy happened, but we didn't have anything to do with that! We are just city workers. We didn't have the power to vote for that. Whatever mayor or accountants, whoever, they knew back then . . . The auditor for the city said back in the 1990s that the city wasn't balancing their books. The city *never* balanced their books.

What does a city worker have to do with you not balancing your books?

—Susan Day, thirty-four-year veteran of Detroit's civil service

Private-sector pensions have been vulnerable to cutbacks for years now. The public sector was believed to be immune to that kind of insecurity. "City jobs" never paid as well, but for many decades they were free from dramatic upheavals and generally carried better benefits. Federal government jobs were similarly seen as the epitome of stability. Millions of Americans set their sights on civil service employment,

sitting for exams to qualify for jobs as maintenance engineers, emergency first responders, librarians, and the like. They knew that at the
end of a thirty- or forty-year career, they would be able to count on the
benefits they had earned. They felt sorry for autoworkers, office workers, and countless others whose jobs were cut and pensions stripped
away, but they felt certain this would not be their fate.

Then came the bankruptcy of Detroit, Michigan—the first, and still
by far the largest, municipal bankruptcy in American history.[1] When
the city filed for "Chapter 9" in 2014, it upended decades of assumptions about what a public servant could expect at the end of a working
life. At one point in the unfolding of Detroit's bankruptcy, workers were
told that if the city could not find its way back to solvency, they could
expect pension cuts of nearly 30 percent. To make matters even worse,
the bankruptcy courts insisted that retirees give back thousands of dollars in pension payouts that had already been distributed to them, in
most cases more than a decade earlier. And they hit retirees with health
insurance premium hikes that exacted yet another financial toll.

This tale is likely to be repeated in many parts of the country in the
years to come. Three California cities have already filed for bankruptcy.
Even prosperous cities like New York and Chicago are staring at large
pension liabilities for which they do not have the necessary revenues, a
fact that has not escaped the attention of bond rating agencies whose
opinions of city finances dictate the interest rates that cities have to
pay when they borrow money for construction projects or any other
needs.

There is no better place to begin understanding how the United
States got into this kind of trouble than Detroit, and no one more willing to tell the tale than the retirees who have paid the steepest price for
municipal mismanagement.

THE BLACK MIDDLE CLASS, SECOND-GENERATION IMMIGRANTS, AND THE PUBLIC SECTOR

For decades after World War II, civil service jobs were enormously
important to African American job seekers. With an implacable wall

of discrimination in the private sector, municipal jobs often represented their only hope for stable employment, and certainly their best option when it came to benefits like pensions.[2] All across the country, city jobs were a ticket to the middle class for black men and women, as well as for the children of foreign immigrants—especially Poles—whose families settled in Detroit during and after World War II.

American migrants who had come up from the Jim Crow South were particularly desirous of landing city jobs. Isabel Wilkerson's monumental chronicle of the Great Migration, *The Warmth of Other Suns*, recounts the dangerous trek that millions of black citizens undertook in hopes of leaving behind the brutality of sharecropping life in the small towns and farming regions of the Deep South.[3] Often forced to flee in the middle of the night, departing from train stations down the line so that their movements would not be detected, men, women, and children lit out for better lives in the northern cities, where war production and labor shortages held out the promise of higher wages and greater freedom.[4]

Understanding the origins of these workers creates a context for the disappointments they have experienced in the course of Detroit's bankruptcy. For many of the city's black civil servants, their family history is an intergenerational tale of escape followed by ascent into the middle class. For those who have been impacted by the city's financial woes, this upward trajectory is ending in a sorry spot.

James Edmond is an African American from a small town in Mississippi whose story could easily have been featured in Wilkerson's account of the Great Migration. After he was born in 1943, his family moved north to Detroit. There, his father landed a coveted job in a Ford Motor Company factory, helped along by one of his brothers who had gone north a few years earlier. This was the first job his father had that paid a living wage, and on its strength he could dream of buying a little house in one of the black neighborhoods burgeoning with other southerners.

Unfortunately, the good times didn't last, at least not for the Edmond family. In the 1950s, a recession led to layoffs at the plant, and James's father was not rehired for one of the high-wage union jobs. Instead, he found occasional work with parts suppliers; when that faltered, he swallowed his pride and took welfare. In the 1960s he found his way back to Ford, at a factory in the Detroit suburb of Livonia. The financial rollercoaster was difficult for the family to manage, leading as it did to bursts of optimism followed by months of scarcity. The family would have been at a loss if James's mother had not been able to find domestic work to contribute to the household budget.

All that turmoil led James to want more security in his working life. Besides, as a child of the North, he had more education than his parents. He aspired to better things than a blue-collar factory job. An excellent student, James was encouraged by his high school guidance counselor to seek a college degree, which was not the norm for black students of his generation. He won a National Merit Scholarship, which gave him the wherewithal to pursue a college education, and he enrolled in a historically black university in the South, from which he graduated in 1965.

With that diploma in hand, James could seek jobs that paid well and offered more respect than the manual labor to which his father had been confined. He was offered a supervisory position by one of the Big Three car manufacturers (General Motors, Ford, and Chrysler), James recalls. "But I didn't do college four years to be a foreman. I didn't want to be on the 'iron pile.'" So he took a job with the city, even though it meant a pay cut. "And I loved it," he says. "I stayed there three years. I was working for the Detroit Civil Service Commission, which no longer exists now. We called it management training now; [back] then they called it a technical aide."

Always looking to advance, James left civil service for an opportunity at another car company in labor relations. But racial animus was pronounced on the shop floor and in the back office.[5] From the inside of labor relations, he found that for each black worker promoted, one was demoted.

"Then came the gas shortage" of 1973, James says. "I knew they were going to cut me, and they did . . . If you were a foreman or some type of supervisor, you were safe. But if you were in the administrative level and were black in the professional level, you were cut. I knew it was coming so I prepared myself for it." The layoffs and cutbacks set James to thinking again about the enviable stability of city jobs. After achieving high scores on the civil service exams for management positions, he was hired back by Detroit, becoming the head of human resources for one of the major city departments.

Coleman Young's 1974 election as mayor of Detroit opened up interesting jobs in the political world for African Americans, who previously had been excluded from positions of authority in many city departments.[6] James took up a number of leadership positions under Young. For him this represented a huge step up in the world. He was responsible for important economic development programs and was recognized as influential in a city where his father had been relegated to the "iron pile" in the best of his years.

James is proud of his record. "I worked twenty-seven years and never took a sick day," he notes. Sadly, he got very sick in 2003, and due to his ongoing health problems decided to retire the following year at the age of sixty-two, earlier than he had anticipated. That was unfortunate, but James was not worried about his family's economic health. He knew he had a solid city pension coming to him, along with health insurance that would cover the treatment he needed. That was a lot more than his father and mother had ever been able to look forward to, and he felt secure—until the Detroit bankruptcy threw everything into upheaval.

Susan Day has a similar story. She started her professional career in the Detroit health department, where she worked as an entry-level medical technician for several years. Yet, like James, she was ambitious and always on the lookout for a better opportunity. She too was a college graduate, still unusual among African Americans of her generation, and she felt she deserved a shot at more elevated employment. Her hopes were realized when a position opened up in a Detroit city engineering lab. To her delight, Susan was hired. Some of the skills in medical lab testing were transferrable, and even though women were rarely involved in that type of work back then, she had "a bunch of cheerleaders, guys who [said], 'You can do this! You can do this!'" She got a specialized management degree and moved up the ladder until, by the end of her career, she was finally "the boss."

Over time, the civil service became an avenue of upward mobility, especially for well-educated people like Susan and James.[7] "Back in the 1960s . . . there were a lot of [black] kids who were coming up then that were the first to even go to college," James recalls. "So that was a big thing. And your community supported you, and the churches." For African Americans seeking advancement, the civil service was better than the private sector for a host of reasons. By law, the rules that governed hiring and promotion were, at least in theory, out in the open. That was hardly the case in the private sector, where black people who sought good jobs, good houses, and good schools for their children were routinely blocked. It was so hard to prove discrimination charges there that virtually no one bothered to try. But in the public sector, "good government" reforms—originally aimed at reducing corruption and patronage, rather than curing racial discrimination—led to the creation of the civil service examination system, which was supposed to be the first and last word on who was qualified. There was an orderly process of jobs postings, open competition, and lists of applicants ranked by qualifications. In practice, nothing was as fair as it was in theory. But at least there were mechanisms for challenging injustice.

Susan Day discovered how helpful those mechanisms were in bucking personal favoritism, which could be just as consequential as racism or gender bias. "At the City engineers' office, it was predominantly white and historically had been white," she recalls.

> Everybody was there for years and years. So when my group of workers came in—we were all races. But [white] people had power over your promotions and stuff, they still had their old boy network. So it was really hard to break into it. That's why we always had to do something bigger, better, longer just to prove that we could you know handle the jobs. With me, I had to do it [even] more so because I was a woman.

Civil service hiring and promotion rules enabled Susan to challenge less-qualified people who were promoted ahead of her. At one point, she applied for an inspector position along with many others. Susan passed the test, and was second or third on the list to get the promotion. It would mean a salary increase of $4,000 a year, money her family could really use. Her supervisor supported her bid. A few months later, she called City Hall to find out why she had heard nothing about the job and was told they hadn't gotten the paperwork. "I went downtown" to lodge a complaint, she says.

> As I was leaving, there was this woman there . . . who had worked in the Mayor's office. So when I was leaving the office, she was standing up at the counter and she says, "What's going on?" She saw I was really upset. She was the . . . HR person at the time, onsite. I said, "I put in this application over a year ago. They've been promoting other people ahead of me and they're not as qualified." She said, "What?" And I said, "Yeah. You know, I've taken the test, blah blah blah." I went through the whole spiel with her. She says, "Well, I'll see about that." So I left and went back to the office. A couple weeks later she calls me and says, "You've got the promotion." She went over their heads and cleared all of the stuff up.

Susan was lucky to have found a champion. Applicants who didn't have one discovered that favoritism "just went on and on and on," she says. Even though there were regulations for filling openings, the department where she worked "disregarded all of that. So they were doing the old boy network."

James Edmond saw the same problem from the inside, especially as he was often the only black person in a supervisory position in his department. "At first, I really didn't realize" that racism was a problem, he explains, "because your coworkers accept you. Really it's the superiors . . . that got the problem. I have yet to have a problem with a coworker because of race. It's either the superiors or the subordinates."

None of Detroit's African American city workers thought they had landed in heaven. But relative to what they could expect in other parts of the city's economy, they were ahead of the game. That fact was so well known that within the black community, there was plenty of friction over who had the right to those precious jobs. Tensions erupted frequently between black women and black men about who was "taking jobs" from whom. Susan can recall several occasions when one of her black male friends told her that she was taking an engineering job from a man who really needed it. She would have none of it.

> They would say stuff like, "You shouldn't be out here. You're taking a job from a man!" I said, "Well, if a man wanted this job"—and you could curse during that time—"then his ass should be out here doing this job. But I have a family to take care of too, and I don't want to hear that. So go —— yourself!" [laughing] You had to deal with them on their level.

Susan needed the job as much as any of her male neighbors. Only because she and her husband had full-time work could they put down roots in a home of their own. Together they could imagine that thirty years down the road, they would have a comfortable retirement. No one in the generations before them had ever had any such expectation; it would have been completely unthinkable. That's why the jobs were worth competing for, and why working women like Susan stuck to their guns and refused to accept the popular postwar notion that men should come first in the struggle for employment.

Aside from the money, prestige mattered too, especially for a generation that was better educated than their blue-collar parents. These college-educated children wanted jobs they could be proud of. Odette Spence had this satisfaction: as a registered nurse for an STD clinic, she was a professional with skills that saved lives. "That was the best job I ever had! I really enjoyed it," she exclaims. "I got the chance to actually work with the patients. I was able to examine the client. I drew blood . . . I was able to diagnose, then prescribe treatment."

Monique Allen, a city tax collector, found her sense of accomplishment in the way she contributed to the city's treasury. Extracting taxes from businesses that owed the city improved Detroit's bottom line. She was the person the city would send out into the field to deal with difficult cases. "I was one of the top money-getters," she notes proudly. For a woman whose father was a baggage handler in a bus station, this was upward mobility, bringing a sense of authority and self-respect.

For Susan Day, the pride was even stronger because she was a black woman in a field entirely dominated by white men. She spent every working day interacting in a very professional fashion with people who never expected someone in her demographic to be their equal. It was demanding, varied work. It wasn't perfect, of course: long before Detroit's descent into bankruptcy, it had its ups and downs. Corruption was one of the downs. People hoping to get a construction permit would offer Susan liquor and money to overlook a flaw.

> Some of the crooked inspectors—a lot of them were drunks—what they would do, when the [project manager] wanted to cheat on something, he would buy him a bottle of liquor or something . . . I went back to my car after inspecting something and here's this bottle of liquor on my driver's seat. And I don't drink liquor! So I just politely took the bottle of liquor out and said, "Hey!" and threw it on the ground. Because it's just blatant! Are you going to bribe me? With a bottle of liquor? So you can get in 1,500 dollars of work? It didn't make any sense to me.

Such corruption extended all the way to the top: several Detroit mayors and Michigan governors are serving long prison terms for their roles in various scams.

It wasn't only college graduates like Susan and James, or skilled professionals like Odette and Monique, who benefited from municipal jobs in Detroit. Grant Preston is African American, born in Detroit in 1957. At his birth, his mother was barely out of childhood herself, and he never knew his father. He was effectively raised by his grandparents, who gave him a loving home. Grant's grandma stayed home to care for him and her own children, while his grandfather worked as a supervisor in one of the Big Three car parts factories. Grant was "raised right" by an older generation that wanted to be sure he understood the meaning of hard work.

His first job was sweeping up in a shop near home for pocket change. The next year, he graduated to cleaning up after a group of retired auto mechanics, acquaintances of his grandfather. By the time he was a teenager, he had moved up to a "real job" in a convenience store around the corner. He made it through two years of college studying psychology and sociology, but then gave up on the degree in favor of making money as a truck driver with UPS, unloading freight.

Like his mother before him, Grant became a parent at a young age. It was important to him to do right by his family, so he married soon after his child was born and began looking for a job that carried health insurance. In 1977, he found what he was looking for: a city job writing parking tickets. Grant remained part of the Teamster brotherhood, since the union organized all of the transport workers in the public sector as well. For thirty years, he remained in the union and served as the shop steward.

Detroit depends on fines for a steady stream of income and the public wants streets to be safe and orderly, but nobody likes parking tickets. Occasionally, Grant would find himself helping stranded motorists, "Going to get people gas when they run out of gas . . . Or giving them a push under their hood trying to give them a boost when their car broke down." But this was a minor part of his day. Most of the time, he faced a public that was not happy to see him coming around the corner. At best, people shook their heads or muttered under their breath as he slipped tickets under their windshield wipers. At worst, the job was dangerous. "Citizens tend to disagree [about] what you just did, they're mad and they're ready to bust your head," he recalls. "When you're out there—no one wants to be told anything by the one in the blue uniform. There were repercussions all the time . . . They cut your tires, throw bricks at you, threaten you on the streets."

The night shift was the worst. When he encountered inebriated drivers coming back to cars when the party was over, he had to worry about his safety just for doing his job.

I used to get off work 10:30 at night . . . So when you're out there, and people don't think you have help . . . they're going to pull a pistol out on you, a knife and threaten you. "If I see you again in that car I'm going to blow your head off!" . . .

How do you feel about getting in that car the next day after somebody told you that? You don't want to get in that car no more. That's going to interfere with your living. How are you going to . . . pay bills and buy food with this threat? . . . You've got to be bodyguard and everything else just trying to save yourself.

James Edmond and Susan Day saw a lot of intrinsic value in the jobs they did, finding them fulfilling in their own right. Grant never felt that way; for him, the only thing worthwhile about his job was its steady salary and reliable benefits. But all three of them had seen family members go through cycles of layoffs in the automotive factories. They were all looking for something that wouldn't disappear on them. For African Americans, the civil service was one of the few places where they could lay claim to such a steady life. Detroit's European immigrants and their children came to feel much the same way, even though they were white. Not always welcome, sometimes the butt of jokes about "dumb Polacks" or "greasy Italians," these immigrants also wanted the kind of security that city jobs alone could deliver.

When Patricia Kowalski, whose parents were born in Poland, was growing up, she hoped to create her own business. But those dreams faded fast when her father died at forty-eight of a heart attack. Almost overnight, her family went into a tailspin. Her mother was not working at the time, and the large Polish Catholic family was suddenly without a breadwinner at all.

It took years to climb back to a semblance of stability, and the fear that this experience created never left Patricia. When she finished high school, the only thing she wanted was a job that could not disappear. For a young woman, that often meant teaching or nursing. In Patricia's case, it meant the Detroit public library, which is where she would work for the next thirty-five years. It was not exciting; many days were monotonous. But the paycheck that appeared every two weeks, the health insurance that never failed her, and the retirement account that she could look forward to more than made up for the shortcomings.

DETROIT IN FLAMES

Stability and security depended, first and foremost, on a tax base that could reliably pay for the services these civil servants were providing. At the height of its prosperity, the Motor City was pulling in plenty of revenue from the property and employment taxes of the auto firms, the parts suppliers, and the services sector that attended to the thousands of workers in the plants. Yet even as far back as the 1950s there were some hard times. And by the 1970s, the Big Three car manufacturers were starting to seriously feel the pinch of foreign competition.

Layoffs and callbacks were built into the work culture at Ford and Chrysler. In time the same disease spread to the public sector. Rust-belt cities throughout the Northeast saw their tax receipts decline as the middle class decamped for the burgeoning suburbs. Industry began to hear shareholder demands for increasing profit margins, and companies responded by fleeing the unionized northern industrial tier in favor of the right-to-work states, the abundant cheap labor south of the Mexican border, and eventually the Asian tigers. For Detroit, Baltimore, Gary, Youngstown, Newark, Chicago, Providence, and Washington, DC, "deindustrialization" translated into rising prosperity in the ever-whitening suburbs and deepening poverty for the people of color remaining in the cities.

The riots that would destroy Detroit in 1967 were a response to the despair of unemployment and the anger generated by police brutality. But they were the culmination of decades of grievances going back at least as far as the 1920s, when the Ku Klux Klan—which we generally associate with the Jim Crow South—launched a massive anti-Catholic, white supremacist campaign in Detroit.[8] It was an ugly time for African Americans and for Polish Catholic immigrants, who had arrived during

World War I only to be met by hostility and vigilante violence, especially from whites determined to prevent the racial integration of Detroit neighborhoods.

By the late 1940s, Detroit's black population began to expand outward beyond the city center, as an educated and business-owning black middle class flourished.[9] The region added more than 600,000 people in the ten years between 1940 and 1950; a third were African American and the vast majority were "up from the South."[10] Tom Sugrue, a noted social historian of northern race relations, describes the unremitting hostility with which they were greeted:

> White Detroiters instigated over two hundred incidents against blacks moving into formerly all-white neighborhoods, including harassment, mass demonstrations, picketing, effigy burning, window breaking, arson, vandalism, and physical attacks . . . The number of attacks peaked between 1954 and 1957, when the city's economy was buffeted by plant closings, recession, and unemployment, limiting the housing options of many white, working-class Detroiters . . .
>
> A potent mixture of fear, anger, and desperation animated whites who violently defended their neighborhoods. All but the most liberal whites who lived along the city's racial frontier believed that they had only two options. They could flee, as vast numbers of white urbanites did, or they could hold their ground and fight.[11]

Detroit endured four recessions from 1949 to 1960 alone. Major auto plant closings in the 1950s left hulking industrial carcasses behind. The taverns, laundromats, grocery stores, and barber shops that had served them closed as their customers left the neighborhoods behind. Black and working-class white workers did not have the resources or the appetite to follow those jobs.[12] For working-class African Americans, this industrial transformation had devastating consequences, as historian Kevin Boyle details in the *Washington Post*:

> From 1947 to 1967, Detroit alone lost 120,000 manufacturing jobs. In the city's ghetto, unemployment skyrocketed. Poverty intensified.

And under the strain of it all, life on the streets became more dangerous. There were 112 murders in Detroit in 1946. In 1966, there were
twice as many, a sure sign of a horribly strained social fabric.

As if that weren't bad enough, the crisis of the inner cities struck
as much of the nation's economy boomed, creating a dazzling world
of color TVs, backyard barbecues and cars the size of luxury liners.
Poor blacks could see it all on display in the new suburbs that neck-
laced central cities. But suburbia was white man's territory, and it was
fiercely defended . . . So African Americans had no choice but to stay
on the far side of the urban color line, struggling to make do while
white America made good.[13]

In the years leading up to the riots, the long-simmering anger of
black residents toward an abusive, overwhelmingly white police force
gathered into thunderclouds of anger.[14] The great majority of police
officers were white, working-class, and not well educated (about
80 percent had blue-collar jobs or served in the armed forces before
joining the force). Police officers were said to believe that Detroit's black
community was a "privileged minority" that was being treated as well
as or better than the city's white population, while the emerging civil
rights movement spoke of the police as thugs with badges.[15] The police
routinely assumed black women to be prostitutes, while regularly sub-
jecting black men to humiliating stop-and-frisk episodes, derogatory
language, and excessive physical force.

The situation exploded in July 1967, and Detroit suffered five days
of hell.[16] Arson, looting, and homemade gasoline bombs were met with
police gunfire, mass arrests, and state-sanctioned murder. Governor
George Romney ordered the Michigan National Guard into the melee
and President Lyndon Johnson followed not long after with federal
troops. Sugrue recounts the grim statistics:

After five days of violence, forty-three people were dead, thirty of
them killed by law enforcement personnel. Altogether 7,231 men and
women were arrested on riot-related charges. The property damage,
still visible in vacant lots and abandoned buildings in Detroit, was

extensive. Rioters looted and burned 2,509 buildings. $36 million in insured property was lost and undoubtedly millions more were lost by those without insurance, not to mention wages, income, and government costs.[17]

When the fires burned out, the prospects for a thriving Detroit had evaporated. The tax base necessary to sustain the city's public workforce dried up.[18] Hundreds of burned or looted businesses were never rebuilt. Tens of thousands of white Detroiters moved to the suburbs, around eighty thousand of them in 1968 alone.[19]

Fifty years later, civil service retirees recall the riots like they were yesterday. Librarian Patricia Kowalski remembers that businesses shut down and laid off everyone. "There was no work for anybody. And then they had a curfew, so even though I had a little [extra] job substituting at Hudson's department store, they couldn't call me because we all had to leave and be off the streets before nine o'clock. So I never came back." Walking her dog, she saw armed National Guard troops patrolling Eight Mile Road.

Dan Tilton, a retired police officer, remembers how the outmigration of thousands of Detroit residents in the aftermath of the riots made the city impossible to take care of. City schools, the fire department, and the police were all hit with budget cuts, and the remaining workers had to attend to half-empty blocks spread out over a vast space with a skeleton staff. Huge swaths of Motor City were now deserted.

Clyde Felton, another black civil servant, watched as black businesses all over the city closed their doors. "When I first came to Detroit it was a lot of neighborhood businesses," he recalls. "Black-owned neighborhood businesses . . . Little mom and pop grocery stores, things like that." But those all went away. Under those circumstances, competition for public employment opportunities ratcheted up even higher than it had been before. The civil service was now the only remaining option for steady employment; everything else was disappearing.

THE POLITICS OF URBAN BANKRUPTCY

It was not lost on city workers that their community's poverty was unfolding in the midst of regional affluence. The Detroit region overall remained one of the wealthiest metropolitan areas in the country, as the middle class (and its tax revenue) took up residence in the surrounding suburbs.[20] As journalist Nathan Bomey notes in his book *Detroit Resurrected: To Bankruptcy and Back*, this decline in tax revenue was a "slow bleed" that accumulated over several decades.[21] By the early twenty-first century, the financial impact on the urban core was devastating.

City services began to go downhill. Citizens soon realized that the police would not come when they called; emboldened criminals took advantage of weakened law enforcement. Fires began to burn buildings to the ground, and ambulances arrived late. There were fewer and fewer emergency responders, even as their workloads grew.[22]

Throughout the run-up to Detroit's bankruptcy, tensions rose between the state of Michigan and the city of Detroit about which government entity was responsible for the fiscal crisis. It is a story repeated in virtually every city that undergoes outmigration and depopulation, whether sparked by riots or not. The movement of the middle class—especially the white middle class—out of the city turned a government divide into a racial crisis. Would voters direct state money emanating from white suburbs to a majority black city? "Detroit is a Democratic, minority city," notes Trevor Sherman, who formerly worked for the city in the financial department. "And Michigan has a state legislature that's totally Republican. So you can get the picture."

The political finger-pointing arose from debates, complaints, and unresolved disagreements about who owed what to whom. From the city's perspective, the state of Michigan was at fault because it was not collecting the taxes that individuals and corporations were obliged to pay the city.[23] Commuters and corporations could have been asked to pay up what they legally owed to Detroit, which would have relieved some of the pressure.[24] As Frank H. Shafroth, director of the Center for State and Local Government Leadership at George Mason University, notes, "An estimated $6.6 million of municipal-income taxes on commuters who work in Detroit, $21.8 million in corporate taxes and $155 million of income taxes on residents weren't collected in 2009. That amounts to almost 50 percent of the taxes owed from people living in or working in the city." City residents who worked in the suburbs also failed to pay their fair share, Shafroth adds. "54 percent of city residents who worked outside the city didn't pay; in Michigan, employers aren't required to withhold city taxes, creating an estimated shortfall of about $142.3 million."[25]

Residents and nonresident commuters are obligated to pay city income tax whether or not their employer withholds it from their paychecks. But many commuters fail to do so because the state is not deducting those contributions to begin with and the city lacks the infrastructure to do so. Governor Rick Snyder would not commit the state to pay what it owed the city. Professor Bruce Pietrykowski, an economist at nearby University of Michigan in Dearborn, explains the situation:

> Detroit levies an income tax, but it's not collected oftentimes because there has to be the state going into the jurisdiction where people live. They'll work in Detroit, but they live in the suburbs. They still need to pay Detroit income tax, but Detroit doesn't have the resources to track them down and to make them pay, so [the city is] losing millions and millions of dollars. And the state refuses to go after them. And they could.

To make matters much worse for municipal retirees, when the state of Michigan developed fiscal problems of its own, it looked to solve them by capturing more revenue from Detroit workers. Until 2011, public-sector pensions in Michigan were exempt from income tax. But that year, the legislature came after city pensions, enacting special taxes to stream revenue back to the state coffers. The resulting three-tier tax payments were structured according to the age of the Detroit worker.[26] The youngest employees were hit hardest; instead of being allowed to exempt $47,309 in retirement income, they were now taxed fully until age sixty-seven. Thereafter, they qualified for a $20,000 exemption.[27]

Meanwhile, city officials were looking for ways to increase the money flowing into the public pension system.[28] Surprisingly, given the city's fiscal turmoil, public pensions had started to rise under Democratic mayor Dennis Archer, who took office in 1994, and continued that rise under his successor, Democrat Kwame Kilpatrick. Before this pair of mayors, the pensions had been steady and reliable but modest. The average pension for police and firefighters, who often see the most generous benefits as a reward for the hazardous nature of their jobs, was only $30,000. Many public-sector workers received much less. Now, mayors with an eye on reelection continued to try to raise pensions even as the city's finances became perilous. But municipal property taxes, business taxes, and income taxes were not providing enough revenue to sustain this more generous pension system. What the city needed, the leadership concluded, was a more aggressive investment strategy to swell the coffers and make good on those promises.

Accordingly, in 2005–6 Mayor Kwame Kilpatrick plunged the municipal funds into risky financial instruments known as interest-rate swaps.[29] Most of that investment was lost in the financial crash of 2008–9.[30] The swaps were essentially a bet that interest rates were going to rise, but with the economy tanking, rates were instead falling quickly. Detroit found itself owing $286 million to the Wall Street banks that had created the swaps, with the bad bet costing the city nearly $50 million per year.[31] In the end, the city paid another $85 million to the banks to get out of the deal.[32]

Theo Markel, a lawyer for the city, regards this sorry saga as entirely unnecessary. According to him, the pension funds were not in such bad shape that the city had to take such risks. At 75 to 80 percent funded, he notes, Detroit's funds were on solid ground, roughly on par with pension funds in most American cities, which are almost never fully funded. But instead of accepting the situation, the mayor turned to the banks and bet on the future of interest rates. He lost. "Kwame was baited to go into these interest rate swaps that we lost our shirts on," Markel says. "What Kwame didn't understand but the [banks] almost certainly understood, when the bubble burst the interest rates were going to go down to rock bottom. As the debtor on the hook, you have to pay premiums, because you lost the bet. You have to pay. It's stupid as hell."

Pundits began to mutter that something worse than stupidity was at play. In many cities, well-funded pension accounts had begun to function as piggy banks that cities could dip into when they faced budget woes like Detroit's. While conservatives railed against what they deemed to be extravagant, unaffordable pension promises, in fact city fathers were raiding those funds to pay for city services, and investment banks were all too eager to bait them with bad deals. The 2008 financial crisis only further deepened the debt of municipal pension plans around the country.[33]

Arguably, cities should have raised tax rates when the revenue they took in proved inadequate to pay for all their obligations, such as schools, hospitals, and emergency services. But this was anathema to conservatives, who argued convincingly that higher taxes would simply fuel more business departures. So where were municipalities like Detroit supposed to find the money to support public services? In many rust-belt cities, retirement accounts looked like one place they could dip into to cover the city payroll. They could worry about the retirees who were depending on those same accounts later.

An opinion piece by Roosevelt Institute fellow Saqib Bhatti makes this point in trenchant language.

> Because state and local governments did not have enough tax revenue coming in, they often opted for "pension holidays" to make ends meet, skipping payments to the pension fund. Over time, this created large unfunded pension liabilities. In effect, cities and states borrowed money from pensioners to make up for revenue shortfalls. Now austerity hawks are using these unfunded liabilities to argue for slashing pensions, even though it was their own anti-tax policies that caused the problem.[34]

Anti-government conservatives also used the lack of tax revenue as an excuse for privatizing public services. "As municipal debt exploded, from $361 billion in 1981 (about $940 billion in today's dollars) to $3.7 trillion in 2012, banks started targeting cash-strapped cities with . . . predatory finance deals," Bhatti notes. "This allowed many of the same corporations that had lobbied for lower taxes to then profit off the revenue crisis they had helped create by literally buying up public assets, such as tollways and parking meters, and then charging us to use them."[35] Conservatives portrayed privatization as more efficient than tax hikes, but as Bhatti points out, it was also quite profitable for these corporations, which now had a captive clientele—anyone who had to have garbage collected or to go to a hospital.

From some viewpoints, putting money away for retirees may appear a less urgent use for municipal funds than keeping hospitals and schools open. Cities are not raiding pension accounts for trivial reasons. Nonetheless, pensions are obligations, which can be fulfilled only if the tax revenue is there to pay for them and has not been used for something else.

In March of 2013 Michigan governor Rick Snyder appointed an emergency manager for the city of Detroit. Kevyn Orr, partner at the law firm Jones Day, was experienced with bankruptcy: he had cut his teeth on Chrysler's Chapter 11 process in 2009.[36] Orr was given enormous power to put Detroit's finances back together.[37] Under his aegis, the city filed for Chapter 9 bankruptcy in July 2013 and began the process of restructuring its finances under the watchful eye of the courts.[38]

Orr calculated that, including its pension obligations, the city's expenses exceeded its revenues by nearly $200 million for 2014. To extract itself from bankruptcy, Detroit had to show that it could close that gap.[39] From the beginning of the process, therefore, retirees were pitted against the city's bondholders. They worried bankruptcy would lead to severe cuts to their pensions.

Their fears were justified.[40] Orr's first proposal to the bankruptcy court involved imposing a cut of 26 to 34 percent on all pensioners except retired police and firefighters, who were slated to take reductions of 10 percent. On top of that, all retirees were to face 70 to 80 percent reductions in city contributions to their health care plans.[41]

THE GRAND BARGAIN

To soften the proposed cuts, the city needed to find other sources of revenue to fill the budget gap. One of the most unusual options involved auctioning off the collection of the world-renowned Detroit Institute of Arts. With an estimated value of $4.9 billion, the DIA was an appetizing target from a purely financial point of view. But it was also a treasured institution in a city whose civic reputation had already taken a beating. People worried about the blow to Detroit's status were it to let the DIA collapse. On the other hand, many retirees would have sacrificed any amount of precious art to keep the pensions that were promised to them.

In the end, the option to sell the city's artistic heritage was never tested. The idea is still remembered by many civil servants as a way out that might have spared them losses, but it fell by the wayside as another solution emerged: a "Grand Bargain" crafted by Judge Gerald Rosen, the mediator for the bankruptcy case.[42] City leaders worked with prominent nonprofit foundations in the region to collect contributions, obviating the need to sell the art collection or slash pensions as deeply as would have been necessary otherwise. The Ford Foundation, whose fortune was built off Detroit's auto industry, pledged $125 million. Another Michigan nonprofit, the Kresge Foundation, followed with $100 million. The Knight Foundation kicked in $30 million. Nine other nonprofits contributed to the pot. Altogether, between the foundations, private donors, and the state of Michigan, over $800 million was put into a rescue plan.

City pensioners would not be completely unscathed. They were asked to accept the end of health care coverage and to absorb some reductions in their pensions, albeit more modest ones than those proposed by Orr: a 4.5 percent pension cut, reduced cost-of-living (COLA) increases for police and fire retirees, and the end of COLA for the rest of the city pensions. This was certainly an improvement over the original plan, but it still hurt. Meanwhile, the agreement protected the Detroit Institute of Arts, erecting legal barriers to its collection ever becoming a financial asset, as the institute was transformed from a

municipal department to an independent charitable trust.[43] There
was resistance to these tradeoffs at first, but Judge Rosen convinced the
representatives of the key parties with an impassioned three-hour
pitch.[44]

The final proposal involved $816 million over twenty years com-
ing to the city via the Grand Bargain rescue plan, plus projections of
"potential cost savings through more efficient government operations
that could increase the reinvestment plan to $1.7 billion."[45] Local
unions would have to agree to wage cuts, and current city workers
would be forced into a hybrid pension plan, which froze the old
defined benefit pension and combined it with a new one that provided
fewer benefits.[46]

City retirees asked to vote on the proposal faced a very difficult
choice. They could accept the specified cuts or face the uncertain
prospects that would follow from rejecting the Grand Bargain. Union
leaders pushed for a "yes" vote because they were terrified of the alternative. If the deal were rejected, many members of their organizations
would be dead by the time the courts resolved the issues.

There were no forums in which retirees could voice objections. "I
think we all felt like they had us over a barrel," notes one retiree. "There
really wasn't much we could do about it. Because we really didn't get
a lot of votes on this or anything. You know, it's not like any of us ever
had to appear before Judge Rosen." Another retiree agrees: "It was
nothing I could do about it. My biggest thing was, well we'll see what
happens, we'll see what's left. Because they had made up their mind . . .
There was nothing I could do about it anyway." "When somebody
declares bankruptcy, you have no fight," laments Monique Allen, the
retired tax collector. "Union, contracts, all that went null and void. So we
were left to accept whatever they gave us. And I don't think that's fair."

Even though retirees had an up-or-down vote on the proposal, this
was not a terribly democratic process: neither the Detroit city council,
nor the mayor, nor even the governor was particularly influential in
shaping the settlement.[47] As city lawyer Theo Markel sees the situation,
it was Kevyn Orr's show from beginning to end.[48] Orr was sent in to
be the "local duke or earl or overlord. And he's [got] pull power and

he's not going to be bound by any contracts except . . . he's going to make sure the bond holders get paid no matter what." In effect, Markel says, the outside powers were telling Detroit residents, "We've redefined your governance. We've got this set of priorities, which has always been the most important set of priorities. Now we're setting aside everything, except what . . . big business [wants], neoliberal demands. And that will be our agenda."

Of course, bondholders did not actually get paid in full: they got a fraction of what they were owed. But from Markel's perspective, their interests took precedence over those of the pensioners, who were stuck with whatever they were handed.

> It was a comprehensive restructuring program. And the pensions are the most vulnerable, because how do these people fight back? Half of them are sick! They're dispersed all over the country. You're taking away their healthcare. That's the first thing they're worried about. The pensions? How do they even fight it? They barely can, so balancing the city's budget on their backs was one of the key steps . . . And that's what [the bankruptcy managers] are continuing to do.

Susan Day, of the city engineering office, likewise argues that the civil service retirees were the primary victims in this deal. She concludes that ordinary people like her should no longer put much store in agreements that are supposed to govern their futures. They don't mean much.

> They just snatched the rug out from underneath us . . . The only thing that we as retirees can do is do what we do and make the best of it. Because it's written in stone now. . . . That's always been an old saying: "Nothing is ever promised to you." They promised the pension to me and look where it got me! They just reneged.

This was a particularly bitter conclusion because if the emergency manager had sacrificed one or two paintings from the $4.6 billion holdings of the DIA, the retirees argued, they could have been spared the cuts altogether. The fact that this solution was off the table after the orchestration of the Grand Bargain led many retirees to feel that their lives were devalued. One retiree says that "the city had to choose between art and human beings . . . And the city chose art. Over human lives." Still, in the end the majority voted in favor of the pension cuts determined by the Grand Bargain.[49]

Among the most controversial provisions of the bankruptcy settlement was the requirement that retirees pay back interest earned from their optional annuity savings fund accounts. At one point, Detroit's municipal employees had been given the opportunity to put additional money—on top of their defined benefit pensions—into these accounts, and get a fixed amount each month. That amount was supposed to depend on interest earned, but for a decade the city promised them more than what the interest earnings justified, leaning on the pension accounts to make good on the deal.[50] Workers and retirees were none the wiser: they had no idea they were being overpaid, not only because they were never told, but also because the "extra" interest had been authorized by the pension board and city council under the Kilpatrick administration.[51] The exceptionally generous payouts should have triggered more scrutiny. But no one was paying attention.[52]

Now retirees were saddled with debts they had never applied for.[53] Those with sufficient reserves often chose to return the money in a lump sum. But many lacked the savings to do so, and hence had to pay monthly via pension reductions, which came to nearly 30 percent of their expected pensions.[54] Adding insult to injury, monthly payers were assessed an additional 6.75 percent in annual interest until the "debt" was cured.[55]

Patricia Kowalski, the librarian, could afford to pay back the lump sum, but she was infuriated. "That was terrible," she complains bitterly.

> That was absolute theft. I had to give them a sixty thousand dollar check or else my retirement would've been diminished by five hundred dollars a month for the rest of my life . . .
>
> I'm sixty-eight now. I should probably live another twenty-eight

years . . . And even if I don't live that long, I still have to plan as if I would. I don't want to be eighty-nine and run out of money. But I'm looking at it and thinking, "Now I'm young. Now, while I'm young, is when I want to spend money and do things and go places. So I don't want to have five hundred dollars less every single month right now." It's a lot of money. Yeah, it's a lot of money.

Patricia was furious not only about the losses she faced, but also about the fact that those who ended up penalized for the city's financial mistakes were the most prudent and blameless workers. Participants in the additional annuity savings plan were the people who had paid the most attention to preparing for retirement. These retirees were trying to ensure they could take care of themselves. Their virtue was rewarded by punishment.

For most retirees, the pension clawback was money they had already spent. "The money I get right now is short . . . almost three hundred dollars," says Paulina, another city retiree, who worked for the Department of Transportation and as a building attendant. Her annual pension was only about $30,000 before the cuts, and the clawback added more misery. "I pay interest on that as if they loaned me something. They did not lend me anything," she protests. "I'm not saying I shouldn't pay it back. However, the interest that I'm paying? I don't think I owe them any interest . . . That was my money. And if it was your money, that was not my fault . . . I didn't borrow the money."

Monique Allen, who had about $7,000 to pay back, refused the lump sum option. "I think it was just a rip-off, truthfully," she says.

How can you give somebody something and then take it back? To me, when they cut the pension, it was bad enough . . . They gave us no choice either, on the paying that money back. They take it out of your check. What if I didn't want to pay you this amount each month? Why am I obligated to pay you this amount of money each month? If you made the mistake, let me pay it back the way I want to . . . Because no, that wasn't [my] mistake. That was your mistake.

Even Susan Day, who had more savings than many of the other retirees, decided not to fork over the lump sum, opting instead to pay the monthly installments with interest. She reasoned that keeping that money under her control was worth the extra cost. After all, the city had already shown it could not be trusted to manage money properly. That could happen again. "There's no guarantee that this pension plan isn't going to collapse anyway," she notes. There were notices saying that the retirement

can only be funded until 2023 or something like that. Well, if I live longer than 2023, what am I going to do? Rely on my Social Security? They keep saying even that might not be around. So it made no sense to give them money back that I had already earned. It wasn't my fault that whoever the crooks were who swindled them out of the money and made the investments—I had no control over that. I went in good faith . . .

I think for me it was like 115,000 dollars, maybe 120,000, that they wanted me to give back. Can you imagine that? And all of the clawback is going to go to another black hole. 'Cause there's no guarantee that I'm gonna have a pension in 2023 . . . Come on, how stupid can you be?

For less-well-off retirees, such as Monique, the limited pensions mean they cannot indulge in many creature comforts. "They cut my [pension] money approximately one thousand dollars a month," Monique says. Her after-tax monthly income from the city—the base defined benefits pension plus her annuity—used to be roughly $28,800 per year. Her new pension is just $16,000 per year.

With such limited means, Monique and her retiree friends spend their days in senior centers, like the one where Monique was interviewed. Located in an old Catholic girls' school in downtown Detroit, next-door to the parish church, the senior center is a godsend to cash-strapped retirees. For $2, they can eat a fresh lunch at noon every day. For $1, they can participate in dance, yoga, a walking club, go on field trips, or take computer classes. Grateful for these "amenities,"

Monique and her friends help out by cooking and serving meals as volunteers, then head home on the bus. They were hoping for a more elevated standard of living when their working days were over. Instead, they are scrimping and making do with the help of nonprofit organizations, like the senior centers that were originally designed to help the poor.

THE HEALTH CARE DILEMMA

The financial pain of the pension reduction and the annuity clawback was compounded by a reduction that affected all city pensioners, including the police and firefighters who had been protected from pension cuts.[56] Many retirees were under sixty-five when the Detroit bankruptcy occurred. Before the bankruptcy, these younger pensioners could count on the city's retiree health insurance to cover them, an important benefit for anyone not yet eligible for Medicare. But as part of the cost reductions required by the bankruptcy settlement, that insurance plan was shuttered. Instead, the city provided a monthly cash benefit—$125 or $175, depending on prior earnings—that retirees could use to purchase whatever coverage they could find.[57]

Obamacare exchanges were open by this time and many retirees turned to them, using this substitute benefit to pay for the coverage. But it wasn't sufficient to cover their costs, so anyone who did not yet qualify for Medicare was stuck with higher health care expenses. Indeed, even retirees who were already old enough for Medicare were falling short, because rates for Medicare Advantage—the version of Medicare that entails monthly fees rather than charges for particular services—continued to climb, and "gap plans"—which supplement basic coverage when it falls short of medical expenses—were no longer in play.[58]

For pensioners like Monique, the combination of the pension clawback and the health insurance cuts created something of a financial nightmare. Frugal by nature, she had made no preparations to repay a "loan" she had never signed up for, and had no idea she would face problems maintaining her health care. "It was just a mess," she says.

"Then they cancelled our medical. I had to pay 592 dollars a month, medical, to maintain where I was."

Roberta Coleman, who had previously been a Blue Cross subscriber, found that the only insurance she could now afford was a less expensive, inadequate Humana plan. Her longtime doctor refused that insurance given its low reimbursement rates, effectively exiling her. While it may seem a small matter, for people with persistent health concerns the sudden loss of a trusted physician is a blow that compounds pressures they are already feeling from reduced income and rising expenses.

Retired police officers and firefighters were particularly troubled by the health care cuts. In their working days, these civil servants had full health coverage with neither deductibles nor copays. Because they faced mandatory retirement at age sixty, five years short of the finish line for Medicare eligibility, the city's bankruptcy terms placed a big financial burden on their shoulders. Neither firefighters nor police participate in Social Security, so they could not turn to that solution to cover unanticipated costs. As retired cop Dan Tilton explains, the hit to the pocketbook was no joke.

> If you're married, that's 1,600 dollars a month that you're going to pay that you didn't pay before. My wife didn't work and was under sixty-five. So she didn't get [Medicare]. So up until this year . . . her [insurance] was 835 dollars a month. Plus I was paying the Medicare. So we went from paying nothing to paying 1,600. But others was worse than us.

Those "others" included retirees whose dependents needed medical care that was no longer covered by insurance at all. One of Susan Day's close friends, a fellow civil servant who had decided to leave due to a very difficult work environment under the Kilpatrick administration, faced exactly this situation. "She had two years to go before she reached her thirty" years of service, Susan says.

> She could not take it anymore. So she quit and she had two years before she could get health insurance. Meanwhile, her husband is sick

and they're saying he needs a heart transplant . . . So for two years, she had to pay every month 1,500 dollars out of her pension to provide health insurance to keep her husband alive. Now what kind of crap is that? . . . Then this bankruptcy starts up and she's still not sixty-five. So now she's got to keep paying.

Many Detroit retirees worry that even if they can find a way to adjust to their current circumstances, they will have to adapt to something even worse in the coming years. Fundamentally, they no longer trust what they are being told about their future. The pressure became far more pronounced with the election of President Trump and the concerted effort to destroy the Affordable Care Act. Periodic attempts to privatize Medicare are also particularly worrying, especially since so many younger pensioners limped across the age of sixty-five to qualify for Medicare.

And the concerns are not short-term. They are not going to disappear one day when Detroit magically recovers its financial footing. Indeed, as Susan Day points out, it could get much worse, without much warning. Her pension could need to stretch much further than it does now. "Suppose one of us has to go into long-term care. What are we going to do? Go to one of these state-run facilities that's going to shorten your life?" That's why every dollar counts, now and forever. "It's never going to get any better, because you're on a fixed income," she says.

DOES DETROIT'S CIVIL SERVICE HAVE A FUTURE?

Every city needs a backbone of workers to staff its schools, hospitals, clinics, and bus lines. For decades, these jobs have been sought after, especially by African Americans in cities like Detroit. They provided decent though not extravagant wages, and the stability of a paycheck on which one could depend most of the time. As Trevor Sherman sees it, this was city workers' own little bargain, and one well worth protecting. "City employees didn't make big salaries," he points out. "Average salary was anywhere from thirty to sixty thousand a year. They had a job, they got a check every week, they got vacation time, and they were happy. Worked hard, came to work every day. Did their job, retired, hoped to get a pension."

These days, the sheen is off the civil service. It does not hold the attraction it once did, though it still may be better than many private-sector jobs, where vulnerability to downsizing has become routine. Trevor can see how the change over time has cut into the city's health and the retirees' security. The Detroit municipal workforce "is reduced to under five thousand employees, and it used to be upwards of fifteen thousand employees back in the '70s and '80s," he says. "It's really declined. It's bare bones. And an employee today can't retire, or they can retire but they have to find another job. They can't afford [Obamacare], they don't have enough income to pay it. Even with a subsidy . . . It's a real crisis."

Dan Tilton, the retired cop, wonders whether anyone in their right mind will follow in his footsteps. "They're not going to get reliable people that are going to train and stay," he predicts. "Why would you stay at a department where the pensions are not good anymore and they don't get healthcare when they [retire] . . . There's no real advantage to working with the city of Detroit anymore. You have no future with them. You've got to find something else."

James Edmond is exactly the kind of person who wanted a life in the municipal work force. A veteran of several city agencies, and the chief personnel officer of one of them, he had a successful management career by any measure. But he wouldn't repeat that experience under the current circumstances. "I couldn't work for the city right now," he says sadly. "We have two names for the city right now: Detroit Incorporated, because it's like a big business, and Plantation North." He explains:

> Plantation North because for all intents and purposes, it's a plantation. Employees have no rights. [Management] could walk tomorrow and tell you, "Adios!" They don't have to give a reason. You're an at-will employee.
>
> Detroit Inc. because this is the way corporate does it. Ford used to be the master of hiring employees as contract employees. Not Ford

employees, *contract* employees. The city is trying to do the same thing.
At one point there were thirty thousand city employees. If you eliminate police and fire right now, it's less than five thousand. Everyone
else is a contract employee.

What is really dying here is more than an employment system. We are
losing the municipal job as a model of security for ordinary people,
and with it the very idea that working people deserve such a rock to
stand on.

City workers once knew they could become homeowners, with modest savings accounts and a reliable pension on which they could depend
to protect the economic stability of their loved ones. Today, they see
themselves as dinosaurs, the last generation to have this sanctuary from
market forces. In its place is a world that fluctuates without warning,
an economy that puts the onus on individuals to manage for themselves
and subjects them to unexpected downturns. As one retired water
department worker put it, "You have to now be responsible for yourself. Pensions are no longer there, 401(k)s have stopped because they
aren't working anymore, healthcare is gone, it's taking them ten times
longer to find a job if they can find a job, and if they do it's not at the
level that they left . . . It's just one horrendous story after another. And
it's not going to get any better."

As she sees it, responsible parents must now make sure their children
understand that there is no safe haven, no protection. "The children
coming up now, should have alternate plans of how they're going to
get through life. They aren't going to have the same advantages that
we had. They're not going to have people watching out for their pensions and watching out for their healthcare. You have to sit down and
train these children now how to take care of themselves." We are all on
our own.

THE SPREAD OF MUNICIPAL BANKRUPTCY

The Grand Bargain was intended to put Detroit back on a solid fiscal
footing.[59] The extent to which it accomplishes that goal depends

critically on whether the municipal budget comes back into balance. That future is questionable, according to *New York Times* investigative reporter Mary Williams Walsh, because the liabilities that loom ahead are still much greater than the treasury can bear. And the investment performance of the pension fund will have to be much stronger than any current interest rates would seem to permit.

> Even after the benefit cuts, the city's 32,000 current and future retirees are entitled to pensions worth more than $500 million a year— more than twice the city's annual municipal income-tax receipts in recent years. Contributions to the system will not be nearly enough to cover these payouts, so success depends on strong, consistent investment returns, averaging at least 6.75 percent a year for the next 10 years. Any shortfall will have to ultimately be covered by the taxpayers.[60]

Detroit is a cautionary tale, but it is no longer unique. Harrisburg, Pennsylvania, the state capital, sought bankruptcy in 2011 after being "plagued by the financial fallout from privatizing an incinerator decades ago and subsequent mistakes." (The bankruptcy was blocked by the state legislature.)[61] In May 2017, Puerto Rico became the largest public bankruptcy filing in US history: it owes $74 billion in bond debt and $49 billion in pension obligations, for a total of $123 billion in debt.[62] Other cities look at these cases and shudder because they face similar vulnerabilities.

The details matter, to be sure. For example, many would declare Baltimore similar to Detroit in its precariousness. Baltimore too has experienced the loss of manufacturing firms, high rates of urban poverty, and even higher rates of violent crime. It too had major riots that left a trail of destruction in the 1960s. Yet it has lost only a third of its population since World War II, while Detroit's exodus was twice that. Baltimore also has a thriving tourist industry that Detroit lacks. Visitors to Charm City spend money in restaurants and museums, which adds to the municipal treasury (even as it does little for the blighted neighborhoods of East and West Baltimore).

Most of all, Baltimore is fortunate to be located close enough to Washington, DC, to enable residents to commute to what has become one of the most expensive real estate markets in the country. This is helping to attract taxpaying families to the city. Through prudent management, Baltimore also achieved a balanced operating budget in 2013, the year before Detroit's descent to bankruptcy. This has given Baltimore a stronger bond rating, which eases the costs of borrowing for construction and the like.[63] Nonetheless, in that same year, Baltimore had $3 billion in unfunded liabilities for its municipal retirees.[64] That will exert drag on the city's prosperity, just as it has in other parts of the country.

Even in cities with no history of deindustrialization, underfunded retiree pension and health care obligations are nipping at their heels, leading them to warn retirees of cuts to come. Dallas, Texas, for example, seems like an unlikely case for fiscal distress; Mary Williams Walsh notes that it has "the fastest economic growth of the nation's 13 largest cities." But the city was still threatened with bankruptcy, because its pension fund for its police and firefighters was near collapse.[65] Due to concerns about these pension obligations, Dallas saw its bond ratings go down for several years.[66] Fiscal mismanagement and bad investments seem to have contributed, and the mayor has ordered an investigation.[67]

Some of the largest American cities are nowhere near insolvency, but nonetheless have underfunded pension plans and other retiree obligations. Chicago, for example, is in big trouble on this score. As reported by *Business Insider*, "the city's Municipal Employees' Annuity and Benefit Fund (MEABF) reported $4.7 billion in assets and $14.7 billion of actuarially accrued liabilities at the end of 2015, representing a funded ratio of just 33 percent."[68] New York City, meanwhile, brings in an enormous amount of revenue but spends almost as much as it collects, resulting in a significant debt burden.[69] The Big Apple faces even more difficult financial issues when it comes to health care and other post-employment benefits: in 2015, that price tag was $85 billion.[70] These are monstrously large amounts, and they could easily undo the municipal finances of Chicago and New York.

Fear of the consequences is leading many American cities, including New York and Chicago, to seek higher investment returns to try to catch up. A number of cities are turning to pension obligation bonds as the instrument, enabling Wall Street firms to gamble with their money in an attempt to increase the funds they have and cure their debts.[71] The strategy works well if the investments in stocks, bonds, or real estate markets pay off. But there is no guarantee, and knowledgeable financial analysts worry about what could happen if this move goes awry.[72]

GRANT PRESTON, WHO braved threats of violence to issue Detroit's parking tickets, and his wife have been married for decades. Sadly, she now has diabetes and kidney disease, requiring constant care from Grant. His thirty-three-year-old daughter has epilepsy, which has left her disabled. As a consequence, she has moved in with her parents and brought her three children, ages three to twelve, with her. "They're all just sick and need a little help, man," Grant sighs. And he is the person best positioned to help. The financial pressure never lets up.

> You pay all your bills that you have [with that pension check], period. That's it! You don't have extras. You're not going to have extras . . . What do you do when you need something or need some help? Some people wouldn't think of helping you when you're down and out . . . That's what you have to deal with. Every day.
>
> You're broke all the time trying to pay . . . Every time you go to the doctor and you go home, you get another bill in the mail a couple days after that office visit. I don't care what doctor you go to, you're getting a bill in the mail. It discourages you from going.

Grant has been a hardworking man his entire life. He has never asked for anything from anyone. Today, though, his retirement losses have translated into impossible bills. Debt collectors are circling him like sharks.

You can't pay the bill. Then you get the phone call with the harassment. "Pay the bill!" from the bill collector. It's a new world for poor people who can't pay. It's almost as if no one cares anymore. You're down and out and it's almost like rather than somebody helps you, they would rather come up and give you a kick. So how do you handle that? How do you deal with that on an everyday basis?

This is not the retirement experience Grant anticipated. It is far from what the civil service promised back in the day. There seems to be no safe haven anymore.

ROSA IRENE BETANCOURT / ALAMY

The proportion of Americans over sixty-five who are working has doubled since the year 2000. More than 26 percent of the country's seniors are now back in the labor force or were never able to leave it in the first place. But the jobs most older workers find pay less, and carry less prestige, than the jobs they held during their prime working years.

4

GRAY LABOR

Seventy years ago, Americans typically ventured into the labor market in their teens, worked for one or two companies until they hit their sixties, then headed for the door. They gathered the grandchildren around and spent their remaining years in retirement. It wasn't a very comfortable existence for the elders: many were poor and often dependent on the generosity of their adult children. Older women took their places in extended households, helping their sons and daughters with the chores and childcare. Older men didn't live very long beyond the end of their workdays. As recently as 1960, their average life expectancy was under seventy-eight years.[1]

Today's demographics are fundamentally different. Sixty is the new fifty. The baby boom generation is reluctant to leave the workplace, in large part because we are living much longer and enjoying better health into our mature years. Most of us no longer have backbreaking jobs; if anything, many of us have to watch our waistlines because for forty years of work we have only exerted our fingers on keyboards, and that's not much in the way of exercise. Overall, though, we are healthier for a longer period of time.

That's the good news. The bad news is that our retirement systems were not built for this new demography.[2] Experts agree that the "replacement rate"—the percentage of a person's preretirement income retained during retirement—is dropping precipitously.[3] Retirement planners argue that people need 70 to 80 percent of preretirement earnings when they stop working, and previous generations of workers were able to do that. However, millions of baby boomers will replace less than this amount; one in five will receive less than 50 percent.[4] Their resources will be further strained because many are turning to Social Security as soon as they can, lowering their monthly benefit payouts. For someone who starts taking Social Security at sixty-two, the earliest age allowed, the monthly amount is less than 60 percent of what it would be if the recipient waited until seventy.[5]

In response, millions of Americans are joining the "gray labor force."[6] The easiest way to measure this change is to look at the workforce participation among those who are between sixty-four and seventy-five years old.[7] Surprisingly, employees over the age of sixty-five constitute the fastest growing segment of US workers.[8] After three decades of decline, the percentage of older workers began to rise sharply in the 1980s, a period marked by pronounced unemployment and rising inequality.[9] By 2000, 13 percent of people over sixty-five were working. Just fourteen years later, the number was up to 26 percent.[10] And these elders are not just dabbling in work: in 2007, the majority of the gray labor force was on the job full-time. That represents a doubling of the proportion of older workers who were full-time employees in the space of only a decade.[11]

What is propelling this growth of the gray labor force? At least four factors are in play.[12]

- **Longer lifespans.** According to data from the Centers for Disease Control and Prevention, "In 2014, Americans at age 65 could expect to live an additional 19.3 years . . . or until about age 84. That's up about 3 years since 1980."[13]
- **The demise of the defined benefit pension system.** As recently as 1980, some 38 percent of Americans working in the private sec-

tor had company-provided pensions, often pegged to their length of service and their final salary.[14] By 2015, only 8 percent were lucky enough to be covered in such a plan.[15] Everyone else was either absorbed into the dubious world of 401(k) plans or had no employer-provided retirement plan at all.

- **Rising age threshold for Social Security benefits.** As the US Department of Labor notes, "The age to receive full Social Security benefits was raised in 1983, grows higher according to year of birth, and is currently 67 years of age for those born in 1960 or after. Benefits are even higher if one waits until age 70 to retire."[16] Among people born between 1943 and 1954, those who can wait to the age of seventy to start accessing Social Security will receive 132 percent of the standard monthly payment for the rest of their lives.

- **Decades of stagnant or declining wages** even as the cost of living has continued to rise. According to the Economic Policy Institute, "Despite increasing economy-wide productivity, wages for the vast majority of American workers have either stagnated or declined since 1979, and this weak wage growth extends even to those with a college degree."[17] The wage problem worsens with age. After forty-five, wages stop increasing, and from age forty-five to fifty-five, average wages *decrease* by 9 percent. From fifty-five to sixty-five, workers get hit by another 9 percent drop.[18]

For those who enjoy what they do for a living and cannot see any reason to stand aside, remaining on the job is a pleasure.[19] In a society that values employment above almost all other aspects of identity, work protects Americans from feeling that they are no longer important. Even people who don't particularly like the jobs they do can feel lonely without coworkers. Remaining in their presence provides a sense of continuity, and even reduces a worker's sense that he or she is actually aging. As anthropologists have often observed, age per se is not especially revealing as a social marker, but all of the status changes that go with it are very consequential. For instance, as young people delay marriage and childbirth, their parents delay entry into grandparenthood—and the longer they go without that marked change in their roles, the less they feel sociologically old.[20] Leaving the work world is another one of those markers, and for that reason the prospect of retirement often makes people scared about feeling isolated or left on the shelf.

Positive motivations for remaining in the workforce are most likely to accrue to upper-middle-class professionals. For them, the workplace is a source of fulfillment, whatever its daily stresses might be. But manifestly, this is not how Teamsters feel about driving long-haul trucks. And it isn't how Detroit firefighters feel about their jobs either—especially once their numbers were trimmed back even as the phone rang off the hook with fires and medical assistance calls, leaving them exhausted. Any job that demands physical strength is going to take its toll on the body, and easing off is one of the privileges that is supposed to follow from a life of hard work.

The distribution of advantaged and disadvantaged participants in the gray labor force is a function of inequalities that build up over a lifetime. The most privileged older workers are well educated, earned high incomes, lived in pleasant communities, had consistent access to health care, and as a result, enjoy good health for their age. They can hold on to their jobs as lawyers, professors, teachers, doctors, and the like, or they can participate in the labor market in other capacities that are similar to (though perhaps less pressured than) what they did during their "real" work lives.

Conversely, workers who are not well educated, have endured lower-status jobs and the more modest salaries that come with them, live in dicey neighborhoods, and have had to deal with erratic access to health care usually come to sixty-five wanting nothing more than to put their feet up. If they are forced to continue earning, the jobs available to them often offer only minimum wage and irregular hours—the hallmarks of work typically given to teens and other new entrants to the labor market. Even if the workers are skilled, age discrimination may mean that they cannot capitalize on their experience, but instead are channeled into jobs that they feel are below them. Yet they cannot simply quit those jobs either. As pension problems mount, the inadequacies of

401(k) plans begin to register, and Social Security becomes too meager to make up for what has been lost, many find it necessary to stick with the work world past normal retirement age just to make ends meet.[21]

IRVING AND LESLIE LERNER

Forty miles west of New York City, suburbia extends far and wide. Once upon a time, the small towns built here as bedroom communities for urban centers held millions of young families, for whom modest house prices and decent schools were a big draw. Today, these regions are aging. Affluent baby boomers and ambitious millennials are migrating back into the cities; elders of modest income are often stuck in place.

Irving and Leslie Lerner have lived in their small suburban New Jersey town for the better part of forty-four years. They like their home and community, and have never given serious thought to leaving it, though the need to economize pushed them to move from a single-family house to a less expensive townhouse in 1978. The area is mainly residential; the downtown, such as it is, is very small, with a few Italian restaurants by a lake. Irving and Leslie drive to Safeway or ShopRite to buy groceries and light bulbs. They are not big spenders, especially recently, so they avoid the pricier malls and consider the decline in gas prices a godsend.

Frugal by habit, both Irving and Leslie came up the hard way. Neither went to college: back in the day, that wasn't needed to lay claim to a decent job. A trade school education, which is what Irving pursued after trying college for one week, was good enough. It qualified him for a good job as a skilled printer, and that became his occupation for nearly thirty years.

Irving was born in 1946 in suburban New Jersey, just across the river from New York. When he was growing up, his parents owned a luncheonette, and he was a loyal worker in the family business. He spent many hours doing dishes, cleaning windows, handling a cash register, and bantering with customers. "I hated working in the store," he recalls, but all the long hours he put into it would pay off later in life

when he went into business for himself. "I knew how to treat a customer," he says.

First, though, Irving found employment as "a four-color stripper"—a
skilled printer—working for a large commercial firm in New York City.
It made for a steady career until the 1990s, when waves of technological change began to wash over the industry and the older tradition of
setting type was replaced entirely by computers. "Everything I did
was all handwork on a light table. Now everything's done on a key-
board," Irving notes. "And they're not going to train someone my age
to learn the programs, to do what they do now." The attitude is dis-
missive, he says: "Oh, you're an old fart. One day you're just going to
come into work, and you'll . . . kick the bucket. And we'll have spent
all this time training you." Irving's friends in the trades—not just printing, but old skilled trades of all kinds—have the same problem.
He visited a print shop recently and was amazed to see how much of
the work has been shifted over to computers, with virtually nothing
done manually.

Seeing the writing on the wall, Irving realized he had to find another
way to make a living. He fancied having a little business of his own, just
as his parents had before him. Furniture repair seemed like a reasonable
bet for a man who was good with his hands. Treasured chairs, worn
couches, broken side tables, and the like could be restored to new life.
Irving invested some of the family savings into a furniture repair franchise, which made him a small business owner connected to a larger
national company. His customers lived within twenty miles of his shop,
and he came to know them personally through repeat business. He was
valued because he could save an heirloom or brighten someone's home
without too much expense.

But the work was physically taxing. Furniture is heavy and bulky,
and every piece had to be transported to Irving's shop if it needed to
be reupholstered or to have new parts installed. A low-margin business
has to hold down its labor costs, so Irving did almost everything himself. For an aging man, this wasn't getting any easier. At one point, when
Irving was in his early sixties, he was hired to fix more than thirty beds
in a nearby nursing home. Taking all the beds apart, moving them to

the cellar, repairing them, and hauling each one back up to the first and second floors nearly broke him.

That nursing home job was one of his last weeks in the business—partly because Irving simply couldn't maintain the pace, but also because his shop was starting to lose money. Furniture manufacturers didn't like the expensive rates charged by the national repair franchise and began looking for local shops, which undercut the franchisees. And business from the hospitality industry, such as hotels and conference venues, started to dry up in the Great Recession, as companies cut back on travel and turned to teleconferencing instead. "It almost seemed as if one day, the business disappeared," Irving says. He estimates that he lost about half of his commercial work and 85 percent of his residential customers.

As his franchise revenue dwindled, Irving realized he was going to need another source of employment. If being a hard worker with a reliable track record mattered, the job hunt should have been simple. He had a thirty-five-year history of solid, dependable performance. But he found the search difficult, the possibilities slim to none. "It took three years to find a job," he remembers. "The economy was lousy, and my age had everything to do" with the lack of success.

Older workers face a wall of barriers when it comes to landing jobs.[22] A 2009 report by the American Association of Retired Persons points to durable prejudice against hiring people of retirement age. "Hiring managers at state agencies listed a litany of stereotypes to explain why they tend to reject older job seekers: They felt these applicants were more likely to be burned-out, resistant to new technologies, absent due to illness, poor at working with younger supervisors and reluctant to travel. Other studies have shown that employers assume older applicants are less creative, less productive, slower mentally and more expensive to employ than early- or midcareer employees."[23]

Not surprisingly, it takes older workers much longer to find a new job than it does their younger counterparts.[24] That trend was even more pronounced during the Great Recession, when Irving was trying to find a job. Before the recession, job seekers over the age of fifty-five typically had to look for ten weeks to find a job. That was only one week more than the average worker aged twenty-five to fifty-four. But by 2011, according to the US Government Accountability Office, "the median duration of unemployment for older job seekers had increased to 35 weeks compared with 26 weeks for younger job seekers."[25]

In Irving's case, his prolonged employment search resulted only in a low-wage job at QuickChek. He bounced from there to a similar position at ShopRite, then finally landed the job he has now, at the age of seventy: a cashier at a national café chain location in a nearby mall.

Irving's wife of many years, Leslie, took a different route to her gray labor job. Leslie was born in a small town in New Jersey in 1951. Like Irving's parents, Leslie's father was the owner of a small business, in his case a dry cleaner. "A lot of times in the summer I would go and help him out," she recalls.

> You know, when he had to do deliveries or something, I ran the cash register. Which I absolutely hated [laughs], because I'm not good with math. I remember once a man came in and he gave me exact change and I freaked out . . . I'm like, "Dad, I'm not doing this anymore." I knew how to sew. And I knew how to hem. I would help him out that way. I would do the alterations for him.

Irving and Leslie met because her stepmother worked at his family's luncheonette. He used to do photography, and he took pictures of Leslie when she went to her junior prom. The following year, when Leslie was at a loss for a senior prom date, her father said: "Why don't you ask Irving?" She was initially hesitant because Irving was four years older, but she went ahead with it and they became a couple. "I promised my dad I wouldn't get married until I was twenty-one," she says, "so we had—I guess it was about a fifteen-month engagement."

When Leslie finished high school, her father insisted that she had to go to some kind of college or trade school. "We had a big argument," she recalls, "because I knew some of my friends, after they graduated high school, went right out to work. And here I am, I have to go eighteen months to [this] business college. Meanwhile, their salary increased and here I am not making any money." From her perspective, making money was the whole point. At eighteen, she expected to be able to make her own way in life, and she chafed at the dependence of being in school. That was not the working-class way.

It didn't take long after finishing her secretarial course for Leslie to find a clerical job, in a warehouse owned by a company that distributed grooming products, over-the-counter pharmaceuticals, and deodorants. Her boss warned her it would be something of a foul-mouthed environment. "We walked through the warehouse and he said, 'I'm going to tell you, you're going to be working with all men. Truck drivers are going to be coming in. The language that they use is—I want you to know—it's not just going to be simple little words.'" Leslie replied, "'Well, that's okay, you mean like [swear word]' and I said the word. He goes, 'You're hired!'"

To handle the blue-collar man's world, Leslie developed a comic touch. The truckers would hang around her desk and banter with her to make the time pass. One of them asked Leslie, "Why don't you go out with me?" She recalls, "I just turned around real quick at that point and said, 'Because I already have a grandfather.' All the rest of the truckers just cracked up. It put him right in his place."

Leslie loved the job. "It was just totally amazing. To this day I miss it," she says. The truckers, who were something of a hard-bitten crowd, developed a soft spot for this young lady. "The men that I worked with were so friendly. It was one big joke. It was just so much fun I can't even describe." And she liked her work duties. "I used to schedule the vacations for the warehouse workers and do all of the shipping documents and whatever. And I really felt worth it . . . I really felt responsible for things."

Leslie's ambition was to become an executive secretary in the company, the classic "pink collar" trajectory of her time. When she got pregnant, shortly before her ten-year anniversary with the company, she had every intention of going back to work after the child arrived.[26] But her son was premature and spent six and a half months in the hospital. "So that blew that idea," she says. "I decided it was more important for me to stay home with him . . . He came home on oxygen. And there was no way I was going to go back to work and leave him like that."

Leslie and Irving were not rich enough to do without her income. If they were going to keep their home (and its mortgage), she had to find a way to earn some money while taking care of her infant. "So I took in childcare," she says. She started an in-home daycare program, and it became the center of her work life for the next twenty-two years.

Most of the children in the daycare were from the neighborhood, and the mothers tended to be, like Leslie herself, clerical workers with blue-collar spouses. Some were single moms. She loved the children, was close to their parents, and saw herself as a member of their extended families. Leslie was particularly enthusiastic about working with toddlers because they could talk, which made them feel like real—albeit little—people. She saw them go through innumerable milestones and felt she was part of what made them thrive.

The parents, in turn, were grateful to her. Leslie was the reason they could relax, at least as far as the well-being of their kids was concerned. At the end of the day, she would have an anecdote or two about Suzie's wobbly steps or Jeremy's masterpiece scribbles. She hugged the little ones and cuddled them on her couch. Over the years, they would graduate to kindergarten, only to be replaced by siblings and cousins.

While Leslie was a young mother, this arrangement worked out well. She could take care of her premature baby, who eventually outgrew the difficult circumstances of his birth, and she was making enough money to complement Irving's earnings as a typesetter. But being self-employed meant that she didn't get employer-paid health care or retirement benefits. And because the business was "off the books," paid for in cash only, the many years she spent working in childcare did not build up her Social Security account. In this, Leslie's setup was not unusual. In 1981, around the time when she was starting her home daycare business, childcare was the third-largest sector in the informal—meaning untaxed and unregistered—economy, after home repair and food services.[27] A little piece of that was in Leslie's purse.

Many other women in Leslie's generation, whether or not they were running an informal business, found themselves similarly lacking retirement benefits and Social Security deductions. In those days (and, to an extent, now as well), women were far more likely than men to take time off to raise children and do other unpaid family work. Such interruptions in earnings over the course of their lives, combined with gendered wage discrepancies, add up over time.[28] Those twin features of women's biographies have left millions with a fragile economic base for retirement. In addition, women like Leslie who leave salaried positions in their thirties lose out on wages more than those who take time off early on, in their twenties.[29]

As she entered her fifties, Leslie started to worry more about the financial implications of losing out on Social Security. What's more, she hadn't had a proper vacation in years, since her daycare could never really close down. Perhaps if she could find an official job in a proper licensed childcare facility, she thought, she could have the best of both worlds. So after more than two decades of working out of her own home, Leslie went looking for a job that would pay her for the occasional day off, give her benefits, and enroll her in Social Security.

Given her experience, it didn't take long to find a daycare center that would hire her. But it was tough leaving her business—not because of the autonomy or the pay, but because it was hard to let go of the kids she had grown to love. "That was the absolute worst day of my life," Leslie says, "saying good-bye to all these children that I essentially raised. Spent more time with them than their parents did. And it was like saying good-bye to this one. And then the next day it was saying good-bye to the other one . . ." She still gets choked up thinking about it.

Still, the new job had its advantages. Her wages weren't high, but they were steady. "It was nice because you knew you were going to get a paycheck every other week," she remembers with a smile. "You had that money to depend on." She also got two weeks' vacation time, and the ability to take a sick day when necessary without inconveniencing anybody. She liked the new place, too. "It was a small school. We got very, very friendly with everybody who worked there. It became a family. As far as watching the children, I enjoyed the toddlers. They were at the age where they loved learning."

Unfortunately, the daycare industry is volatile, since it is sensitive to the ability of parents to pay. In 2008, when unemployment spread far and wide, many families couldn't afford childcare and pulled their kids out of school. At Leslie's new place of work, hard times spelled erratic paychecks. The company was running out of money, and the management didn't seem altogether trustworthy.

Daycare companies are born and then they die, and the retirement prospects of their employees expire with them. One day, Leslie's manager shut the door and let everyone go. She went home to recover from the shock and thought maybe she'd just stay there. But watching TV, checking out senior citizen activities, and waiting for Irving to come home at the end of the day left her monumentally bored. Besides, she had worked "on the books" for such a short time that her Social Security—which is set up to reward the consistently employed breadwinner—amounted to almost nothing.[30] So, at the age of sixty-four, when many Americans are contemplating stretching out in the easy chair, Leslie hit the pavement to find a new job.

But now she was just a bit older than during her last search, and it seemed a little harder to find a decent job. Leslie was starting to get discouraged when a parent she had kept in touch with from her old daycare business put in a word with a corporate childcare center. To her relief, Leslie landed the job. The center assigned her to look after the babies, the six-month to one-year group.

WORKING IN THE SUNSET YEARS

Irving and Leslie became part of the large and growing gray labor force, the set of Americans who have either returned to work after retirement or who never left the working world because they couldn't afford to. For the gray labor employees on the job out of necessity, the likelihood of finding work that is as enjoyable as the jobs they held during their prime employment years is low. Age prejudice catches up to people and reduces their choices in the job market.

In the case of Irving and Leslie, they had spent most of their working lives in companies that provided them with a degree of personal pleasure. They made friends in the workplace. People were lighthearted, celebrated birthdays together, had the occasional drink after work. Work life wasn't perfect, but it wasn't cold or terribly pressured. The jobs they have now bear none of these human qualities. Work is very much at the mercy of impersonal bureaucracies, with a fair amount of surveillance and control. Mistakes result in reprimands or docked pay. Their bosses are more imperious, in part because they too are being measured and benchmarked, and the pressure trickles down to lower-level workers like Irving and Leslie.

Irving first experienced this atmosphere at QuickChek and Shop-Rite, the two cut-rate stores where he initially worked after his furniture repair franchise went south. He detested the lingo of corporate human resources management, the way he would be described as some kind of a partner in the operation, as if the job were elevated above the entry level. "'Associates'—that's another great term that I just love," Irving says, his voice dripping with sarcasm. "[Management thinks] it makes you want to work, which to me is a lot of crap, excuse the language." If the company really treated its workers as well as it claims to, he says, it wouldn't need "all these cutesy phrases and terms and all, to make you feel like 'Wow, I'm part of a great organization.'"

What Irving really wanted was to be respected for what he could do, or at least not be demeaned in the course of the workday, as if being an older worker meant he should expect to be ridiculed. "I mean, I don't think that's asking a lot," he says. "And, if you treat people that way, and pay them decent, you'll keep them." Reducing turnover is not a high priority at these companies, though. They invest little in training, which means their workers are disposable because it takes so little time to bring a new person on board. According to Irving, QuickChek told him they spent just $500 per person for training, running classes with over two dozen people in them at a time.

To use an old phrase from labor history, jobs in places like Quick-Chek have been "deskilled," broken into component parts so that inexperienced new hires can learn what they need to know in just a few hours. In periods of high unemployment, older workers like Irving have no choice but to swallow their pride and live with this workplace culture, even if they find it distasteful. "The way it is today," Irving says, "there's a thousand people in line for a job. 'Well, you don't like it? Take a hike. We've got, you know, Joe Blow and his two kids looking for that same job. We'll train him.' . . . I don't know how many training classes they go through, 'cause [the way] they go through help, it's amazing. It's a revolving door."

Leslie's new job is less routinized, since she has little babies to care for. Yet it is a far less personal or intimate version of the childcare industry than what she had when she worked for herself. There is a lot of paperwork. "I hate it. I do," she says. "It's corporate-run, and they have all these crazy paperwork things that you have to do . . . I want to be there with the children. Not filling out paperwork about what time they got there, what time they left, what time we changed their diaper." The paper trail is meant to increase safety and to satisfy working parents, who appreciate a record of what their little ones were doing all day. Nonetheless, the ambience of rules and regulations bothers Leslie, who prefers the personal touch. "It's a cold atmosphere," she complains.

The same sense of distance permeates the feeling on the "shop floor" as well—which, in her case, is an actual floor with little kids crawling around, playing with toys, and occasionally knocking into each other. The babies are there from early morning to late at night, and Leslie has responsibility for four little ones at a time. Unlike at her own childcare business, where she could watch children grow and learn over time, here she sees the kids only when they are in the prelingual phase. There is no one to communicate with, except in the baby-talk way that grownups use with little kids. This kind of "age grading" may be helpful in some ways for the children, especially if their teachers develop specializations that meet their cognitive needs. But for the teacher, this setup represents a kind of industrial model of childcare that, for Leslie at least, is alienating. "I get them at six months and then I watch them until they turn a year. And then they move on," she says. "They're cute. They crawl. You watch the stages as they're learning to walk, but it's not challenging."

The sense of distance Leslie feels on the job shapes her perspective about the value of daycare as it's practiced in the corporate sector, catering to hardworking parents who are themselves run ragged at work. Leslie has her doubts about whether this is good for either parent or child. "You feel bad for the kids," she declares. "They . . . come in at

6:30 and leave at 6:30 and have a nanny pick up some of them. So you figure they go home, get chicken nuggets thrown at them, and then they go to sleep." That's not how childhood used to be, she says.

Aside from their dissatisfaction with the deskilled, assembly-line nature of their work, both Leslie and Irving have issues with their managers. Bosses are a real problem for Irving in particular. In his opinion, they have no respect for older workers and wouldn't recognize their talents or contributions if they were the last employees standing. Irving takes pride in the good work he does as a café cashier: even in the midst of a rather impersonal environment, where customers typically don't interact much with the workers behind the counter, he has occasionally been the recipient of unsolicited appreciation. Irving beams when he recalls the praise, but he feels downcast when thinking about how little it mattered.

In a span of two weeks I had two separate customers pay me a nice compliment. And I made the mistake of telling them to talk to the manager and let the manager know of their experience, since [the company] is very conscious of compliments and complaints, and they [the company] love compliments.

The first instance, one of our assistant managers was working. It was at lunch time. And the lady [says], "I'd like to tell someone." I showed her where the manager was. She told the manager and she came back to me. She says, "I let the manager know." I never heard anything else. The manager never came back to me and said, "Irving, you got a nice compliment. Thank you!" So I figured well, that's the way she is, it's no big deal.

The following week I had another couple I interacted with for about five minutes at the register, which is a big "no-no" at our store. And they said the same thing: "Is there anybody we can let them know about our experience?" I said, "The store manager. The head honcho is at the other end. Let him know." The lady came back to me, she said, "I told him about my experience and he said, 'Did Irving send you to me?'" . . . That was his remark. He didn't want to hear it. It was like she interrupted him with a compliment about me.

At a café chain that claims to care about customer sentiment, Irving was taken aback to discover that his manager considered these episodes to be bothersome and annoying, rather than evidence that Irving is a good worker.

Irving never discussed the situation with his boss, and it is always possible that he misinterpreted the signals. He admits to being sensitive about how his age affects the way he is perceived at work. Rightly or not, he is convinced that older workers are not really welcome at the café. When his manager rebuffed the customers' compliments about him, he says, he felt insulted, and his attitude about the store changed.

> I thought, "If I'm nice to customers and they like what I do, I think a manager should know it. I would think a manager would really want to know it." In [my] case they don't. I've had other customers pay me compliments, [and] I just tell them, "Thank you for the compliment, but please don't tell the manager, because they don't want to know about my experience with you." They all give me a look like they're surprised. That's the way it is here. And it's sad.

If the café were the only workplace where he had experienced such treatment, Irving could just chalk it up to a manager with bad people skills. But it is part of a pattern dating back to QuickChek, where he was the oldest worker at the store. "I got treated the same way, and it was terrible," he says. "And I've talked to people [who work] in the store I'm at now, about the way I'm treated, and they agree with me. I thought maybe it was just me, [but] they could see what's going on." He objects to the snubbing not only on his own account, but because it's bad for morale and business in general. "I think it's terrible . . . to do it to anyone," he says, "'cause that's not the way you're going to get people to really want to work."

Irving knows full well that low-wage jobs like his are not grooming employees for a corner office, perhaps not even for a long-term stint. It matters to him, though, that he not be demeaned. And he suspects that the management regards him as a second-class citizen on account of his age. "I don't want to be on a pedestal," he says. But "you know that

I come in every day. You know that I'm not lazy. You know I don't turn work down. So, to be treated that way . . . is just not fair, because you're not going to find a lot of people" with the same solid work ethic that he brings to every job.

There is also other, more tangible evidence that Leslie and Irving point to as evidence of the low worth that managers assign to them. They are not seen as people with a future, workers who deserve a chance to rise within their organizations. Raises are meager when they happen at all. Irving notes that in his two and a half years at the café, his wages have only gone up from $9.10 to $11.03 per hour. If the much-discussed $15-an-hour "living wage" becomes law, he thinks the company will "reluctantly pay it," but then cut his hours to compensate.

Leslie's managers resisted paying her more than her coworkers, even though she had more than two decades of experience in the field. When she insisted, they gave in and made her salary $13.65 an hour. That's quite a bit more than Irving earns, no doubt because the work is more skilled. Still, they both feel it's an inadequate wage. "I wish she would go somewhere else," Irving confides. He doesn't think this daycare center will ever pay her much more than it does now. "Even when they hired her, they complained about her rate."

Leslie is unusual in earning more than her husband. Within the gray labor force, it is not the norm for women to earn more than men. The reverse is usually the case, because women are often restricted to pink-collar jobs that carry lower wages. Secretaries and administrative assistants, maids and house cleaners, personal and home care aides, cashiers, cooks, and retail salespersons—these are the jobs that women typically hold in their sunset years. The wages are better for low-wage jobs typically held by men, including janitors, laborers, and stock movers.[31]

According to the federal Bureau of Labor Statistics, in 2015 women over the age of sixty-five who were in the workforce earned an average of $740 a week, while men in the same age group averaged $1,003, a very significant gap.[32] Indeed, it is in this age group that the divergence between men and women is largest overall.[33] In part, these facts are born of a particular generational experience in the labor market. Among couples in Irving and Leslie's generation, typically men outearned women across their entire lives. "Women born in the late 1940s over their lifetime are estimated to have earned roughly 40 percent of men's lifetime earnings," the BLS report notes. "For women born during the 1960s the gap is smaller, but still average earnings for women are estimated at less than 60 percent of men's."[34]

Going forward, this pattern may not hold. Today women outnumber men in getting higher education degrees, and the wage gap has narrowed considerably. It is not hard to imagine that for the baby boom generation, and gen X behind them, something closer to parity will be achieved. But for the moment, Leslie and Irving are a bit of an anomaly, mainly because Irving's lack of education foreclosed the possibility of jobs that paid better.

Irving's job at the café is nonstop, which he doesn't mind. "It's a very busy store," he says. "We're at the mall, so we get a lot of movie theater people. People shopping. I like it that it's busy. Most cases it's busy, those [days] seem to flow a lot faster. At a slow store, no matter what kind of store, the day'll drag on, and it'll make it that much more unbearable to be at work." But though a busy store makes the day feel shorter, it also makes work difficult for older employees. Even the healthiest of gray labor workers are likely to find their jobs physically straining at times. Demands that would have been simple to meet ten years earlier become harder to manage.

Employers know this, and justify their reluctance to hire from the gray labor force on the grounds that illness or lack of stamina will make even a desk job harder to maintain, to say nothing of more physically intense tasks. Irving believes his presence is an asset to his employer, and that he is actually one of their most dedicated workers because he really needs this job. But working the cash register isn't easy. "It's standing all day long," he says, and his scoliosis makes that a problem. Moving around doesn't bother him as much. "But standing in one spot for too long is agonizing sometimes . . . I mean, it's not going to kill me. I'm not bent over like an old guy, and I don't have to take pills for it. But it's a cement floor so that doesn't help. And they're not going to get mats for people to stand on to make it easier for you." How

long Irving can tolerate this discomfort is a question he doesn't like to
think about, because this is the only job he could find and he needs
the income.

Childcare is not easy on the body either. Leslie's responsibilities
unfold on the floor, sitting with babies who are crawling around on
mats or learning to walk in their own wobbly way. The very youngest
children don't require close surveillance, but they do need their diapers
changed, most often on mats on the floor. The one-year-olds require
someone to spot them as they pull themselves up on furniture and learn
to launch their first steps. Irving knows that his wife feels fatigued at
the end of the day. At sixty-seven, it isn't easy to do this much physical
work. "It's tough for her," he notes in a worried tone. "She's on the
floor all the time, and she's back to changing diapers every day . . .
That's the job that was offered her, and she knew she had no choice
but to take it."

Leslie doesn't want Irving to worry, but in her private moments she
confesses that she is having a hard time keeping up.

> Some days are fine. Some days it's like, "I can't wait to get home."
> With the babies, I'm on the floor with them. And this franchise doesn't
> want them to have any swings. No jumping chairs. Just the teachers
> are supposed to be on the floor with the babies all the time, unless
> you're changing them or doing paperwork or whatever. So it's a lot
> of up and down and up and down, lifting and carrying . . . I didn't
> know if I could make it from the building to my car to go to the park-
> ing lot. That's how tired I was.

If she could make some friends on the job, Leslie's workday would
be more pleasurable, and she might be able to set those aches and pains
aside. But as with many other members of the gray labor force, decades
separate Leslie from the other employees in her workplace. Very few
women in their late sixties take (or keep) such exhausting positions.
Leslie feels isolated. Her job gets her out of the house, but it doesn't
surround her with friends, because there aren't any at her job. The management is "kind of cold," Leslie says. "And I haven't really formed a

friendship with anybody there. They're just coworkers . . . It's tolerable. It's not what it could be."

As for Irving, his café is a haven for new entrants to the labor market. Most of his fellow workers are eighteen to twenty-five, and while they are nice enough, they have little in common with a man in his seventies. The most affectionate of them call him their "work grandfather," which surprised and pleased him. But the impersonal nature of a semi–fast food restaurant barely generates social bonds even between people of the same age. It's asking too much for the "kids" to reach common ground with Irving.

Instead, Irving humanizes the workday by being friendly with the people who come in for a meal. "I really enjoy it 'cause I can talk to my customers," he says, and that helps to pass the time. For him, customer satisfaction comes from the chatter over the counter.

> I'm the only one in the store that actually gets the customers to laugh.
> I like to tell them jokes, make fun of me, make fun of the company . . .
> And that's the part I enjoy. I really do . . . I've had people tell me I'm
> a cantankerous S.O.B., and—be that as it may, I enjoy what I do.
> I enjoy talking to the public. I got that from my father. And I enjoyed
> it when I had the [furniture repair] franchise.

The Lerners want to stay busy. Neither Leslie nor Irving finds the prospect of sitting around doing nothing very appetizing. And they recognize that many younger employees are also forced to adapt to stressful schedules and unsympathetic supervisors. Yet those workers (who no doubt also complain about their jobs) have many decades of work ahead of them, and the fortunate ones will "graduate" to something better. For Irving and Leslie, that's not a likely prospect. They are not trying to build toward some imagined future career, in which their poor working conditions give way to more elevated work. Instead, they are just trying to cope with their current situation, which is "over the top" busy and too taxing from a physical standpoint.

The notion of working fewer hours while staying active in the work world appeals to them. But they would lose the jobs they have right now if they insisted on that accommodation, and they worry that they would find very little "out there" if they went on the job market again at their age. They play with the idea of other jobs—Leslie, for instance, likes the notion of being a home shopper at Walmart, getting away from working with children for a change. But these conversations never really go anywhere. For now they are stuck working at places where they are unhappy. And they have no idea when they'll be able to stop.

"I wouldn't mind going down to four days a week," Irving muses.

> But in reality, I don't know if that's going to happen for a while. Unless we sell our townhouse and move into something smaller. And right now, that's not in the future. It really isn't [possible], especially in New Jersey, to do that. So I don't know what's going to happen down the road . . . At my age, I'm relegated to the sweeping of floors. They look at you like you're dragging your coffin behind you, and one of these days the lid's going to open up and you're going to fall in.

That's how hiring managers looked at him when he was sixty-four and interviewing for the job. Today he is seventy. He would like to think his experience counts for something, but he knows it doesn't: "You're old, and companies don't care about what you do, what you've done, what you grew up doing."

To be sure, millions of American workers of all ages have to work for high-turnover businesses. Millions are routinely subjected to the coldness of corporate environments. Plenty of younger low-wage workers also have impersonal or officious bosses. Those workers, too, wish for a more humane work world, and often find that the opportunities for something better are not there—for reasons ranging from high unemployment to discrimination to simply the limited set of options for entry-level employees. Still, their work lives tend to improve when unemployment declines and they can be choosier about their jobs, or when antidiscrimination laws are more rigorously enforced, opening up better opportunities. Most commonly, the younger workers pile up experience and maturity and move into an entirely different segment of the labor market, where respect is more plentiful or autonomy more likely. That's the sequence Irving and Leslie themselves experienced in the work world during their prime working years, with Irving moving up from his family's luncheonette and Leslie from her father's dry-cleaning business.

But it is not what Leslie and Irving expected to contend with at the end of their careers, and it's not what they had prepared for in this "encore period." They feel they have earned a degree of respect and the right to a better work experience over the many years they have been in the labor force. It has been a rude shock to recognize that their years of experience entitle them to virtually nothing. They are beggars who cannot be choosers, and no amount of experience relieves them from this fate.

THE BOTTOM OF THE BARREL

As it happens, Irving and Leslie are not at the bottom of the gray labor barrel. There are thousands in their cohort who are far more disadvantaged, particularly low-wage workers who cannot rely on the support of a spouse. This is often the lot of women who have spent much of their lives at home or in minimum-wage jobs and now find themselves divorced or widowed, single and in financial distress.[35]

Marissa Romano is Italian American, thin, white, with short dyed-blond hair. She is seventy-two years old, lives on Staten Island, and works thirty hours a week cleaning houses. Marissa grew up in Brooklyn, attending high school until her sophomore year ended with the birth of a child. She had four children altogether, was married for twenty years, then got divorced in the late 1970s.

While she was married, Marissa had stayed home with the children. Her husband was a police officer, but after the divorce it was hard to secure child support. When she finally extracted something from him, it wasn't much: $100 a week, which barely covered food for the family. So she was forced into the labor market with very little to bank on in terms of skills, and went into housecleaning. "That's all I knew how to do," she says. "I never had the chance to go back to school, so I didn't have a career. I think it was my husband . . . who said—do what you do best. Clean." She worked for a cleaning company and did other housecleaning on the side.

When Marissa first started working for the cleaning service, she had only ten hours a week there. For the rest, she was paid off the books and hence, like Leslie, accrued no Social Security, was not covered by workman's compensation, and had no other benefits. And even with the side work, the money wasn't enough. Between the insecurity of her family finances and the blossoming of a new relationship, Marissa decided she should move her family in with her new boyfriend, Jorge, who was married but separated from his wife. By moving in together, they could share expenses and spend more time with each other. Sadly, Jorge passed away in 1991, after he and Marissa had spent twelve years as a couple. Because he had never formally divorced, his wife retained all of the benefits due to his widow when he died. Marissa received nothing.

The cumulative effect of Marissa's history—a divorced woman who has spent many years working at least partially off the books—has been to leave her in financial straits. Her housecleaning job is taxing: she has to bend to lift mattresses, haul heavy vacuum cleaners, and be on her feet all day. At the age of seventy-two, she works six days a week. She starts early in the morning and puts in eight hours straight. Her financial survival depends on the hours she can work, because she is paid by the hour. One house gets her around $135 to $150. "Sometimes it's overwhelming when it's a big mess," she says. "I get, like, anxiety or something. But then after a while I calm down."

To help with the mounting bills, Marissa began to take Social Security when she turned sixty-five. It covers part of the rent and some of her other bills, like cable, gas, and electricity. At one point she was paying about $500 a month for Medicare supplemental coverage, but she dropped that and just started covering the copayments herself. She's also on food stamps. Still, the expenses keep piling up: car insurance, the water bill, and so on. "The rents are bigger," she adds with a laugh. "Not thirty dollars, or two hundred. Big!" She has to hope she can continue to work, because only by drawing on all of her resources can she make ends meet. At her age, though, there is always a risk she won't be able to continue. Marissa says she'll work until "my health fails," or until she just comes to the point of "no I can't do it anymore. Whichever comes first."

On occasion, Marissa's sister, who works as a police department administrator, helps her with finances. She comes by on the weekends, looks over Marissa's bills, and encourages her to economize. In return, she gets a good meal. On occasion the sister also offers a loan or a gift that helps Marissa get by. "Thank God, I have a sister who helps me," Marissa says. "It's a lot of work, but she helps me. And I have a son who helps me also, sometimes. He'll surprise me and he'll pay my rent." Marissa's daughter, too, pitches in from time to time. Another one of Marissa's sons is in bad shape and has been hospitalized on and off; she went to see him every day after working long hours cleaning houses. Her ex-husband helped, at least, by paying more for that son's bills.

Carol Stack's classic book *All Our Kin* focuses on the social organization of poor black families in "the Flats" in Illinois. Stack describes the way multigenerational families upend traditional notions of parenthood. They rely on sharing networks, borrowing and repaying, scraping by from all sources. Stack's account traces the importance of these networks for the support of children.[36] Marissa represents a grandmother in the same story, except now it is she who needs help rather than the adult children or grandchildren. She calls on the same reciprocities that enabled her to raise her children and help others in her extended networks. In her elder years, Marissa would not be able to manage without the occasional contributions of her sister and adult children, just as they needed her when she was younger.

There is a gendered aspect to Marissa's story. Both men and women are working longer these days, swelling the ranks of the gray labor force. In general, men leave the working world later than women do. But the largest *increase* in the labor force participation of the population aged sixty-five and over is coming from women. According to the US Department of Labor, for women over sixty-five the labor force participation rate was "8.1 percent in 1980, 14.4 percent in 2012, and is expected to be 19.2 percent in 2020. For men, the rate was 19.0 percent in 1980, 23.6 percent in 2012, and is expected to be 26.7 percent in 2020."[37]

The same Department of Labor report also points out that "women are more likely than men to leave and re-enter the workforce, leaving them with significantly less Social Security income since periods of non-work are not credited to individuals' Social Security accounts."[38] This is certainly a factor in Marissa's case: she spent years raising her kids, a long stretch when she was not earning any income. And because of her divorce, she does not have a spouse to rely on today.

Marissa is also in a tough spot because she has very little formal education, which makes it hard for her to land a better job. In 2011, 20 percent of women over sixty-five had not finished high school; another 40 percent had only a high school diploma. Generational trends in education will make this less of a problem in the future. Younger women have spent more time in higher education, and will accrue more human capital they can trade for better jobs.[39] Even a less physically taxing job than what Leslie or Marissa do for a living, however, can be a source of stress for an older woman. If she is the only employed person in the household, and losing that job could push the family even deeper into trouble, she will worry about any mistakes she makes that might subject her to dismissal.

Women in "pink collar" jobs often become the mainstays of their household income because they are married to blue-collar men whose jobs are too punishing to readily continue into old age. For those blue-collar men, complete retirement is always the desirable end point, because their jobs are so hard on their bodies and their family lives. They work in the "encore" period only if their families would suffer if they didn't.

James Miller is a retired Teamster from Milwaukee. He had a long and tiring career as a long-haul trucker. Yet at the age of seventy-three, he is still at work, driving a school bus twenty-two hours a week. A heavy-set man with white hair and a white beard, James came up the hard way. As a youth, he worked as a machine setup man in a manufacturing plant. He went from that plant to driving a city bus in Milwaukee, a job he landed courtesy of his father, a supervisor for a city agency.

After a few years he gave up the municipal job and started driving trucks because the pay was better. He has been with the Teamsters since 1970, first driving for a gas company, then doing various temporary jobs.[40] In 1980 he went to work in a warehouse for a grocery store chain, which was part of the Central States pension fund.

After twenty-four years in the warehouse, James retired because the chain moved out of town and he couldn't face the thirty-eight-mile commute to keep his job and seniority. When he left the warehouse job, he intended to take a part-time position. He was not yet eligible for Medicare, and hence needed a job to cover the cost of the $500/month health care premium for himself and his wife. She was still working at the time but didn't have health care benefits.

James liked golf, and he heard about a position selling permits for players to tee up on the golf course. But the job turned out to be too taxing. James had to get up at 4:30 a.m. to be there to open the golf course at 6:00 a.m. He wanted to work only twenty hours a week, but the employers pushed him up to thirty-five, which made him feel like he was going back to the grind of full-time work. So he quit to take care of his daughter's children, and sandwiched in a job as a school crossing guard and a second part-time position working at a friend's liquor store. Eventually he went back to driving, for a company that manages a fleet of school buses. That has been his life from age sixty-four to seventy-three and counting.

James would really love to just retire and be done with the work world. He has been in the labor force since he was eighteen, and he's had enough. But the press of family obligations keeps him on the job. James has always been there for his family. When his daughter's husband lost his job, James took out a home equity loan and supported his son-in-law with that money. Then another daughter was widowed unexpectedly. She went looking for a job but had a hard time finding one, and on top of it all her car broke down. James had to step in and take care of her too. His whole adult life has been devoted to the good of his family. They are "number one," he says, his voice quivering. "And I have missed a lot because I had to work."

Beyond his family's needs, the perilous state of the Central States pension fund has James worried about future pension cuts. He is a tired man who resents the hours he has to spend away from his wife and the rest of the family. He has twin grandsons who are sixteen years old and growing up fast; he wants to have some time with them before they are out of the nest. However, if his pension gets cut, it will go from $2,600 to $1,300 per month. If James quits his school bus job, that would mean the loss of another $1,000 a month. And he cannot afford a $2,300 cut in his monthly income.

THE BRIGHTER SIDE OF THE GRAY LABOR FORCE

James, Marissa, Leslie, and Irving do not represent the entirety of the gray labor force. Remaining on the job in one's later years isn't always a matter of necessity. A growing number of Americans regard being employed as a crucial part of what it means to be a productive member of society.[41] For those fortunate to have socially valued jobs, stepping away from the work world is not an appetizing prospect. At the same time, the pressure and long hours of many high-end jobs can become too much to manage as time goes on, even for people who are in good shape for their age. They often look for alternatives too, but hope to find work that is socially satisfying and a positive anchor to their identities.

For millions of Americans, especially in the baby boom generation, moving from the stressful and unforgiving world of the private sector into a lower-paid but good position at a foundation, a university, or in government is just the ticket. In a 2005 survey, more than one in five boomers said they wanted to pursue work in education, health care, and social services. By 2013, the nonprofit sector consisted of 14.4 million workers (10.6 percent of the US workforce) and contributed $634 billion in wages and salaries.[42] As the MetLife Foundation found, "a significant segment of Americans moving toward their 60s and 70s wants something distinct from a retail or fast-food work experience. They want to focus their accumulated time, talent, and experience on work that directly contributes to social renewal."[43]

Virginia Parker, a sixty-eight-year-old who lives in suburban New

Jersey, is a good example of this trend toward work that matters. Originally from a middle-class family in the Midwest, she graduated from
an excellent college and showed a zeal for work. Beginning in her mid-
twenties, Virginia devoted thirty years to retail management positions,
starting in intimate apparel at Macy's and working her way up to the
management ranks of department stores in Chicago, Florida, and New
York. "I loved what I did in retail," she says. "I liked the excitement,
I like numbers, I like putting a big-picture plan together and then exe-
cuting it . . . I liked the sense of power, of dealing with a 60 million dollar
budget."

Along the way, Virginia married and then divorced. Like many
women who have gone down this path, she found herself in search of
additional income when the settlement left her with fewer resources
than she needed in middle age. "The divorce really wiped out all my
assets," she explains. Her strategy was to move up in the retail hierarchy, a plan that required her to return to school for an MBA so she
could try to reenter the profession at a higher level. At first she thought
she might feel awkward being back in school, especially since her classmates were considerably younger. But Virginia quickly discovered she
had already done many of the things her classes were designed to teach,
and that gave her an edge.

The MBA did indeed translate into a more responsible position in
another name-brand retail empire. But as Virginia worked eighty-hour
weeks at this company, a lament gathered in her mind that fans of the
television series *Mad Men* will recognize. Retail is fickle, she says: customers change their minds, fall in love with new brands, and leave companies to sink or swim in the midst of that volatility. By 2008, the
country was in the midst of the Great Recession, and the whole retail
world was reeling from declining demand, plus the challenges posed
by online shopping. Virginia's firm was sold to a French company, and
her job disappeared. "What am I going to do?" she remembers thinking. "The job market was horrendous. And, in retail particularly, there
is clearly a bias against anybody over forty . . . You have to be young
and hip to understand trends in business."

She decided that she would leave the apparel merchandising business altogether. "I probably wouldn't have made the shift if I didn't have to," she admits. "But I really was in a position where I had to. And, in 2008, so many retail jobs were lost that I just knew that it didn't make sense for me to be spending my energies trying to get back into that field."

Virginia is pragmatic. She can stand back from the situation, assess her prospects, and pivot toward a different future. Unlike Irving or Marissa, she had a robust network of contacts and impressive credentials (both in terms of experience and education) to lean on. Even so, the change was difficult. She had to spend down her retirement savings while she looked for a new job. She put the house she loved up for sale and reconciled herself to a more modest standard of living. Now in her early seventies, she gave herself a deadline to rearrange her life—and, to her credit, managed to pull off a remarkable transition.

She started by opening a consulting service for nonprofits. As that business grew, Virginia built her networks in an entirely new field. Within a couple of years, she landed the job she has now, in a nonprofit organization supporting survivors of domestic violence. The mission is very meaningful to her. Virginia speaks of it as her "calling"—an expression of her devotion to the organization and her embrace of its intrinsic value. She is in charge of the nonprofit's fund-raising and communications, which makes her vital to its success.

Virginia enjoys her new job in a very different way than she did her life in retail. Her skills transferred to something that most of society appreciates as a contribution to the greater good (not so true of underwear sales). She has also been able to stabilize her financial situation, if not at the level where she once was then at least in a fashion she has learned to accept. "I'm not looking for something to provide extra income," she says. "I want to work in a professional job where I feel challenged and like I'm doing something and have an impact, and I want to be compensated for it." She is not on easy street, but she is in a position she feels good about. She's had to combine several sources of income—Social Security, a small pension from her retail job, and her salary at the nonprofit—but with all of those put together, she says, "I'm okay."

The biggest pluses of her work are no longer financial. They are emotional and social. Virginia really appreciates how professional her coworkers are. She marvels at how warm they are as people, something that the more competitive world of retail did not encourage. The range of ages in her nonprofit is considerable, and that's a strength. Her own age is not an issue; she is valued for her experience.

Larry Kraft made a similar move from the competitive, for-profit sector to the more laid-back nonprofit world. He worked in various jobs before getting a position in advertising sales with a tourist company in Boston, a post that he held for twenty years. "My clients were major airlines and hotels and restaurants and anyone in the meeting business or tourism business," he explains. "It was very lucrative. I worked solely on commission." Eventually, however, the company contracted with an outside vendor rather than continue to house his division, and Larry was laid off at the age of sixty-four. "I thought for a while about suing for age discrimination," he says, but that is "a very difficult thing to prove. And can be costly." Instead, he took their severance package and cashed in his 401(k).

Looking for a new play, Larry took some stockbroker exams, but he soon realized he wasn't as keen on the business world as he had been earlier in his career. Like Virginia, he wanted to find a job that would use his skills but also enable him to contribute to the well-being of others. Larry could set himself on that course because he could rely on a modest cushion in his wife's steady job. She works full-time for the state of Massachusetts and is active in her union. "She's my Norma Rae," he says. "She gets a lot of accolades and kudos. She's really passionate about what she does."

Unlike Irving, who had to take whatever job was available and cannot afford to rock the boat by demanding higher wages, Larry could take some time to invest in his skills. He also had a chance to find his way without as much financial pressure as less-skilled workers or single/divorced workers like Virginia. And he could more easily afford to take a job that does not carry the salary he once had. Even if he doesn't get paid a lot, Larry's wife not only earns a decent living, but she also has a secure pension and health care through her government job.

After patches of unemployment, Larry was able to find work at a nonprofit organization teaching low-income seniors about nutrition and financial literacy. It helped that he has some finance background from his stockbroker education. The organization was also starting a new bilingual program, and Larry speaks Spanish.

Like Virginia, Larry sees his work as a "calling," because it makes a difference for people who need help. "I [am] lucky . . . to be in a position where I can have that kind of impact on people's lives," he says. Some of the seniors in the program, he notes, have been able to "cut back on their meds because they started adhering to health practices and healthy eating and exercise. It was a very motivating and stimulating program for a lot of these older people to get up and do stuff."

The modest salary does give Larry pause. He believes he is worth more than he gets. "It's a great place to work for except their compensation is horrible. I am making next to nothing," he says. "And even though I really like what I am doing and think I am making an impact on people and people's lives, you know in the background it always rankles me that I am making what I am making." In the best of all possible worlds, he would be able to keep a meaningful job and still get paid a salary commensurate with his skills. For now, though, he is thankful that he has made an honorable career transition in his later life. "Senior power!" he says with a laugh. "I'm happily employed and hopefully will [stay that way] for the next couple of years . . . You don't have to accept being a greeter at Walmart if you have more in you as far as education and experience and everything else."

Alison Berkowitz has a similar attitude. She is seventy years old, white, and petite in stature, with graying brown hair and glasses. A college-educated woman, she lives in Cambridge, Massachusetts. For years, Alison worked in public relations, writing for medical services and nonprofit organizations. Much of what she did was temporary consulting work, which was enjoyable but never provided benefits. And it was often hard to collect on what she was owed. "I made a fair amount an hour but it was very frustrating," she says. "Even though I had a regular contract [stating that] I was supposed to get paid in thirty days, sometimes it would take months . . . So I said, 'Why am I doing this?' I just decided I was going to quit."

When she turned sixty-five, she elected to leave that world behind and start something entirely new. Being an animal lover, she chose to capitalize on her passion by creating a pet-sitting and dog-walking business. "It was a really hard decision because my identity was changing," she admits. "If you say 'I have a pet-sitting service,' you don't have the same status." It took a while to overcome the stigma, but one day Alison said to herself, "Too bad, I don't care."

In making her career switch, Alison was building on a hobby she had already cultivated. "In 2002, I started working and volunteering at the Animal Rescue League," she recalls. "I did that for three and a half years and I loved it." The rescue league had a lot of intimidating dog breeds, and as Alison saw it, "if I can handle a Rottweiler or a pit bull, I can handle anything." Eventually, the hobby became more important to her than her formal job, and she thought, "Why don't I start a business?" She began putting up flyers on the street.

In retrospect, she thinks this might be her true vocation. "I think I'm better at animals than I was at writing," she muses. She now works fifteen to sixteen hours a week and enjoys a lot of flexibility in her schedule, though she has to be there consistently for her clients year-round, regardless of the weather. She takes off only one week per year. "You can't run this business if you're always on vacation."

Alison lives mostly off of her savings, and her lifestyle is frugal. Dog walking provides enough for modest pleasures. Once a year, in September, she takes a bus and ferry to an island off the coast of Maine for her vacation. That is the limit of her indulgences. Still, she appreciates that her business does pay enough for her to afford the travel. "If I gave up the dog walking I would have to be really careful," she says. "Even though I don't make a huge amount, it makes a huge difference."

AMERICANS ARE LIVING longer and healthier lives now than at any time in our history. That demographic fact has enormous implications for our economic security in later life. Our social institutions—especially

Social Security—were not designed with this kind of longevity in mind. They were created when Americans died in their late sixties, and hence had perhaps ten years at most to survive on their retirement resources. Even if we implemented some of the policy fixes that have been recommended, from raising the retirement age to lifting the "cap" on income subject to Social Security payroll tax, those of us who are living to a ripe old age would find the Social Security "replacement rate"—the percentage of our preretirement income that is replaced by Social Security checks—too low.

When we add the unstable nature of private pensions to the mix, we can easily understand why so many American workers can no longer rely on their retirement benefits. The combination of these trends has left many feeling that the only action they can take (besides drastically cutting back on expenses) is to keep the income flowing. Hence they return to work, or stay on the job for many more years than they had planned.

As long as we are blessed with good health, there are many advantages to becoming part of the gray labor force. Aging is a social process, and staving off the less-pleasant aspects—including isolation or a sense that we no longer matter in the eyes of society—helps to protect valued parts of our identities. This course of action is particularly ideal for well-educated middle-class workers, who may even discover that the postretirement jobs they land are, at least for a while, more enjoyable than the better-paid employment of their prime working years. These jobs are much less appealing for blue-collar workers like James, who is truly exhausted and feels that he is being robbed of precious time with his family by the necessity of working.

Above all, the growth of gray labor is not a sustainable solution to the erosion of pension benefits or the slow bleeding of Social Security. Should these dismal trends be matched by a future attack on Medicare spending, we will have an even bigger catastrophe on our hands.

Striking telephone workers protest in front of Verizon headquarters during contract negotiations. Younger workers complain that they are hit harder by benefit cuts than more senior workers and retirees, a common experience in two-tiered agreements that favor older generations.

5

TWO-TIERED AGREEMENTS AND
THE DILEMMAS OF GEN X

Retirement insecurity is a topic typically associated with the elderly. We imagine retirees trying to scrape together the money for the gas bill, or older workers struggling to stay on the job because they won't be able to manage on reduced pensions. There are indeed plenty of Americans in exactly this situation, and millions more will follow.

Yet if a crisis is afoot now, the generations coming up behind the baby boomers may be in for even more serious trouble. Generation X—Americans born roughly between 1965 and 1980—have about ten to twenty-five years to go before their retirement. In particular, for those on the leading edge of gen X—now well into their fifties—there is not enough time left to make up for what they have lost through pension erosion, the collapse of property values in the Great Recession, and the slow growth of wages. They are caught on the horns of a historical dilemma that is not of their making, but will surely be their problem.

Gen X began entering the labor market in the mid-1980s. The United States was still recovering from double-digit unemployment that developed in the wake of steep increases in oil prices, high interest rates, and President Reagan's decisive slowdown of government spending.

Meanwhile, housing markets climbed so high, so fast, that gen Xers were unable to access home ownership until they were much older than earlier generations. A *Boston Globe* report notes that they are "still paying off student loans while raising families on wages that have barely budged in recent years . . . Thirty-eight percent have more debt than savings, more than any other generation."[1]

Sandwiched between two much larger generations (the boomers and their echo, the millennials), gen Xers attract less attention. But there are over 82 million of them, and their retirement dilemmas will be quite serious.[2] One reason is that many gen X workers have been subject to "two-tiered" retirement agreements, an instrument of collective bargaining that evolved as organized labor found itself in an increasingly weak position.

In all three groups of workers we have looked at thus far—blue-collar Teamsters, white-collar workers at Verizon and United Airlines, and public-sector workers in Detroit—the fate of the gen Xers in their ranks is different in important ways from that of the older workers, who are mostly baby boomers. Understanding the nuances of the gen Xers' particular situation makes it clear that the "retirement crisis" is not a problem for just a single cohort of Americans; it is everyone's problem. If anything, it is only getting worse as we descend down the generations currently in the active labor market.

THINNING THE RANKS OF THE UNIONS

The origin of gen X's retirement problems is intertwined with a broader problem in the labor market: declining union density and weakening bargaining power for organized labor. As their clout receded, unions were up against continual pressure to "give back" benefits. The alternative was to risk plant closings and the flight of well-paid blue-collar jobs from the northern industrial tier to southern "right to work" states and ultimately overseas. The givebacks focused on costly benefits, including pensions. The losses accruing to union workers would ramify throughout the economy to impact nonunion labor as well.

The proposals met with immediate anger and active resistance. In response, employers often looked for a compromise that would cut costs but minimize blowback. Two-tiered retirement agreements were one of those measures of convenience. Such contracts shield the oldest workers in a union—those who are already retired or on the cusp of retirement—and let the axe fall on younger workers, by cutting their pensions, extending the years they have to work before they qualify for retirement, retracting their postretirement health care benefits, and eliminating provisions that cover their family members. These changes represent dramatic downturns in the standard of living, but they do not kick in right away. Instead, the shock will be felt down the line, once gen Xers reach retirement age. That delay has created a period in which employers could begin to cut their costs without, they hoped, alarming those most affected by the two-tier arrangements, since those victims are years away from the impact point.

Such a move was only possible because union strength is withering. That trend is easily seen in the context of the trucking industry, where unionized workers are becoming an endangered species. Membership in the International Brotherhood of Teamsters peaked in 1978, when over 50 percent of transportation workers were unionized, and started dropping steadily after deregulation.[3] By 2017, union membership in the transportation and warehousing sector was down to 17.3 percent.[4]

There has been a much greater decline in the number of active Teamsters in the Central States pension fund specifically, since one of its largest founding unions, United Parcel Service, pulled 44,000 members out in December 2007. While the number of retirees remained at around 212,000 from 2002 to 2009, the number of contributors fell from "185,000 in 1999 to 77,000 in 2009, a loss of well over 100,000 participants to the fund."[5] The gen Xers in the trucking industry are therefore much less likely to be covered by defined benefit pensions, which are generally union benefits.

According to Thomas Nyhan, the director of the Central States Pension fund, without government funding the amount of money in the fund will be down to "virtually nothing" for both current and future retirees.[6] That is why he proposed to reduce benefits for thousands of active employees, who are almost all gen X workers.[7]

Though Nyhan's original proposal to reduce benefits for retirees was rejected for now, most experts realize that there will be a day of reckoning eventually. Central States simply doesn't have the resources to continue paying out the benefits it owes. Trucking firms all over the country anticipate the same outcome, and are cutting back on pensions promised to current workers in gen X. For example, earlier generations of truckers at YRC Worldwide, a major freight firm, could retire long before the age of sixty-five and maintain generous pensions. The company's gen X employees, on the other hand, will be hit hard in the pocketbook unless they wait to retire until after sixty-five.[8]

Teamster union leaders are well aware of the impact of two-tier labor agreements on the ability of the brotherhood to pull together. Pitting the interests of different generations against one another is a sure-fire way to blunt the solidarity the union needs to speak for the needs of all Teamsters. Tim Davis, a leader in a local Teamsters union in Wisconsin, is caught trying to balance the needs of his members who are still on the job with the concerns of retirees. Perhaps because he is in his early sixties, he often feels conflicted.

Tim's leadership role gives him an insider view into the impact of two-tier agreements. The active Teamsters in Central States resent the retirees for not having supported them when changes to their future benefits were under consideration. They don't understand why retirees were only yelling about benefit cuts they were threatened with, and were not focusing just as hard on the cuts that future generations— those still on the job—were going to experience. "The guys that are active [keep] saying, 'I want something to be there when I get there, so, they should fix it,'" Tim notes. The retirees, on the other hand, are worried about managing on reduced pensions in the here and now. They take the view that active workers have other options, such as staying longer on the job, while the "old men" are in no condition to do so.

Each generation is focused on its own problems; few can see the whole picture, the entire union dilemma. It is a case of every generation for itself. "These retirees are wondering why there's not more active guys involved in the movement" to save the retirees' pensions—but on the other hand, "the retirees weren't there when the changes were made to [current workers'] pensions." "That's not the essence of unionism," Tim reminds us. He is left trying to navigate between age-based factions, neither of which has sufficient power in an era when the proportion of unionized truckers shrinks every year.

Sebastian Cataldo is retired from United Parcel Service, but he remains a leader of a Teamster local in Ohio. Youthful for his age, with dark brown hair, he is a bit older than the gen X group, and hence can understand the arguments on both sides. He himself is one of the thousands of Central States retirees staring down the barrel of the significant pension cuts proposed by Central States director Thomas Nyhan—in Sebastian's case, from $2,800 to $1,700 a month. He laments that instead of being able to band together as brothers, the Central States truckers are divided by age.

> What Central States has tried to do is pit the workers against the retirees. And some of the [active workers] have taken the bait. In our own e-board, this last month, I put a resolution in to give a thousand dollars to these guys [the retirees] so that [Rita Lewis] could go up to DC to speak, which was a very important opportunity . . .
>
> The guys in the room, a couple of [active Teamsters] that are in Central States, argued that we should not be supporting these retirees because if they do not take the cuts now, then there'll be no money left for them later. Which is kind of what Nyhan has said in his letters, threatening that we must take the cuts now or there will be no money left.
>
> So these guys, they bit on the bait. They've taken it. They believe that it's us or them. And that's not the case. And what I try to explain to people is that, if they get the cuts now, there's going to be more cuts later.

What Sebastian wants his younger union friends to understand is that they are perched on the top of the same slippery slope. If they cannot block cuts to the pensions of retirees, the losses will continue to hurt everyone. It will not end here unless they organize to stop the bleeding. The proposal for cuts that Nyhan submitted to the Treasury Department "does not rescue the pension. It's just going to prolong it for ten years," Sebastian says. "Well, what's going to happen in ten years? They're going to ask for more cuts.

"It's the oldest ploy in the world," Sebastian notes, his contempt barely disguised. "Divide and conquer. And the only thing the union's ever had in its power is unity and solidarity . . . Back in the days there was a lot of solidarity. Right now there's not. Right now it seems more and more like every man for himself. Even within the union, [active Teamsters] don't understand the power of the unity. That's the problem . . . You either feel it or you don't."

If he has to choose sides, Sebastian's sympathies lie more with the current retirees, who can do so little to help themselves. At least people his age have the physical wherewithal to continue earning. Retirees who are sick and worn out would just be devastated with no way to fix the situation. "The fact that they would take money from widows, from guys who have disabilities . . . You know, it doesn't make sense to me," he says.

THE WHITE-COLLAR GEN X EXPERIENCE

Gabriel Jones is in his forties, with short black hair and tan skin. His parents moved to New York City from the Caribbean before he was born, and raised Gabriel and his two younger siblings there. When the family first immigrated to the United States, his dad worked in a factory. A few years later, he bought a dry-cleaning business, then traded in real estate, purchased a grocery store, and ultimately drove a livery cab for about fifteen years before retiring on Social Security. Despite this record of entrepreneurship, his family was always pressed for money. In response, Gabriel's mother went out to work as well, first in a factory where English was not required, then as a home attendant. She finally retired on a small pension and began to collect her own Social Security payments.

When he first went out into the job market, Gabriel was looking for a place where he could work toward the financial security his immigrant parents never really achieved. He took a position with NYNEX, the successor to Bell Telephone New York, deciding to go for the safety of a monopoly industry known for cradle-to-grave employment. "If you have responsibilities and you have things that you have to take care of, it's not about you anymore," he says.

> It's about your family. You need to focus on creating security, creating stability. So bouncing from position to position, department to department, company to company, really wasn't ideal when you have people that you're responsible for. People that are basically looking to you to create stability in their lives . . . Like, okay, I'm going to take this job, and I'm going to do my best, and hopefully if nothing else changes, at the very least I'll have created the stability that my daughter will need to be okay.

The NYNEX that Gabriel signed up with was a company that would have seen him over that goal line. But Verizon, the company that emerged from the tumultuous growth, deregulation, and competition of the 1990s, was a different animal. It took advantage of gen X workers, exposing employees like Gabriel to an uncertain future that is far from the old "Ma Bell" model.

At the time of our conversation, unionized Verizon employees like Gabriel were on strike. Verizon wanted the union to agree that its members could be redeployed at will, sent away from their home base locations for up to two months at a time regardless of their skill set or seniority. The company insisted that there could be no limits to the number of times they could be temporarily transferred.

To the union, this potential upheaval seemed to be a strategy to put pressure on gen X workers to quit. Gabriel understood exactly what the arrangement could mean for him some day.

> If I were transferred, let's say, to Virginia for two months, and then upon return transferred to Rhode Island for two months, and then upon return transferred to Massachusetts for two months—I would probably have to quit at some point. And I'm not retirement

eligible. So, even though I'm vested, the pension would be frozen in a sense and I wouldn't have access to it until I'm a certain age.

As Gabriel explains, Verizon requires a worker's "combination of years of service and age to reach the number seventy-five" for retirement eligibility. "Basically, you have to have at least twenty years of service and be fifty-five years old to be able to retire." Being forced to quit the company at an earlier age puts that in jeopardy.

No Verizon worker in the baby boom generation was faced with a threat like this. Instead, it was Gabriel's cohort that had to face what this transfer policy could do to a worker's family life, and the threat it posed to his pension. In 2016, Verizon strikers—mainly gen X employees—took to the streets in New York, Boston, and around the country in an attempt to force the company to abandon its plan. The strike was ultimately successful, and for now Verizon workers will not need to worry about being transferred or forced into early retirement. But Gabriel worries that it is but a matter of time before these demands resurface.

He needs only look at what has happened to Verizon's gen X managers, who have no union protection and have suffered tremendous losses in their pension and health care benefits. Vincent Pagini is one of these managers. Like Gabriel, Vincent was born into an immigrant family; both his parents "came up off the boat." He learned the value of hard work and upward mobility from his father. Vincent's dad "was a bricklayer, then went into construction . . . Then shortly after that he opened up his own construction business." By the time Vincent was nine, the family had moved to a house in Queens.

Vincent took a more conventional route to success by going to college. When NYNEX put out the call for temp workers, he jumped at the chance, and landed a unionized job as a repairman. In 2000, he was offered what appeared to be a great opportunity to join Verizon's management team. "At that time, it was a smart choice," he says. "It had a lot of great benefits to become management. A huge raise, pension was better . . . And [the company] was still paying managers overtime."

Carlos Moretti had much the same experience as Vincent. Thin and small in stature, Carlos has salt-and-pepper hair, but actually looks younger than his fifty years. After graduating high school, Carlos went to a technical school for a year, then got a bachelor's in business management. After college, he worked for a bit in sales and electronics, did some work for a fire alarm company, and had a few other short-term jobs just to make ends meet. But he was looking for something more secure and was delighted to get a permanent position at Verizon in 1994. "You know, I might have a career here, this is where I'm going to stay," he recalls thinking.

After eight years in ordinary line jobs, he was approached about becoming a manager. It looked like a prudent decision at the time. "The benefits were very good," Vincent says. "I had full medical coverage, I had a pension, I had a 401(k). Overtime was one and a half pay." Compared to his unionized position, "The pension was better; the 401(k) was better. The healthcare and benefits was the same."

Yet it didn't take long before the vulnerabilities of being a gen X manager began to plague both Vincent and Carlos. Without the protection of the union, they were unable to block the cuts that came down. As Carlos recalled, "Right away, overtime got cut from time and a half and double time down to just regular pay. And not too long after that, we started paying into our medical. It started to change almost right after I took the job."

Verizon was also one of the first financially successful firms to invoke pension freezes and other changes to defined benefit pension plans. Such changes have been spreading among corporate employers since the mid-2000s. The Pension Rights Center in Washington, DC, has identified a host of them, including "plan terminations, plan freezes for new and/or current employees, and changes to the formula by which pension benefits are calculated." Companies as prominent as IBM, Motorola, 3M, Boeing, FedEx, Hewlett-Packard, and dozens more have gone down the same path.[9]

The impact of such modifications has been felt by everyone in these firms, but the consequences differ by generation. Retirees from New York and New Jersey (aside from those who worked for the Yellow Pages) still have their health care coverage, for example. For them, the main impact on pensions has been the conversion of their original contracts into annuities, and the loss of cost-of-living adjustments. Because of Verizon's changes, their pensions will not keep up with rising costs, especially if inflation begins to raise its head in the future.

For Verizon's gen X managers, though, the long-range consequences are more profound. Active workers in Verizon's management ranks not only lost all health care they expected to receive in retirement, but were also switched over to a 401(k) plan with only a fraction of the defined benefit pension they thought they would have.[10] As the *New York Times* reported in 2005,

> Verizon Communications, the nation's second-largest telephone company, said . . . that it would freeze the guaranteed pension plan covering 50,000 of its managers and expand their 401(k) plans instead. In freezing the plan, the company will pay workers the benefits they have already earned but will not let them build additional benefits. Verizon said that it would also contribute less to the health care benefits of the managers when they retire. Over all, the company hopes to save about $3 billion over the next decade by taking the steps.[11]

To be fair, Verizon took some of those savings and invested them in sweetening the match they provide to those 401(k) plans. That arrangement—providing 150 percent of employee contributions on the first 6 percent of pay, with additional contributions depending on company performance—was more generous than that of many large firms.[12] Indeed, dozens of large employers suspended their 401(k) match programs altogether following the 2008 financial crash.[13]

Still, the generational impact is significant. Verizon's retirees and workers with long service records got to keep their health care coverage, while anyone with less than fifteen years of service lost out on the company's generous subsidies of insurance premiums. Once the plan was implemented in 2006, anyone in a managerial position who had not been working at NYNEX/Bell Atlantic/Verizon since at least 1991 lost all health care coverage in retirement.[14]

The drumbeat of reductions, coupled with job losses to outsourcing, made younger workers at Verizon feel trapped. Vincent Pagini watched the company trim away his benefits and privileges, one cut at a time. By the time he was in management, a good retirement was a thing of the past. He didn't even realize how much he was being affected until he woke up one morning to find his retirement health insurance gone and his inadequate pension frozen. Vincent knows that when a company chips away at benefits bit by bit rather than letting the hammer fall all at once, people are less likely to be alarmed. But at the end of the day, a loss is a loss.

> They say that if you take a pot of boiling water and you throw a frog right into it, it'll jump right out. But if you put a frog in a pot of water and bring it to a boil with the frog in it, he'll stay in there and die. [The company] takes a little bit at a time and before you know it, they've taken everything . . . So they started off with a little overtime, telling us to work a little more hours before you're getting more overtime, then taking overtime totally away. Pay a little bit for your benefits, pay a little bit more for your benefits, pay a little more, 'til you pay an extreme amount.

Before management pensions were frozen in 2006, they were essentially structured to reward decades of loyalty to the company. The pension would only become a substantial sum once a worker had spent many years at Verizon. But the reductions put an end to this relationship between commitment and reward. Younger managers who were moving up in Verizon, who walked away from the security of union protection in favor of upward mobility, were hit hardest by the transformation of benefits.

The highest levels of Verizon management were not affected by the changes: they were protected by individual agreements, golden parachutes, and other lucrative benefits. Lower and middle managers have none of these perks and, by definition, none of the protections afforded by collective bargaining. As Carlos Moretti notes, this means that the richest managers got away scot-free while others, like him, were hammered by losses. "They make a lot of money . . . Our CEO has a pension. That's messed up. That's the worst part about it," he says. "If it's for everybody and the company needs it, you say, 'Okay, fine, I can live with it.' But when everybody else has it, it's just you, how do you justify it?"

Unionized gen X workers at Verizon have fared better, at least for now: they still get a defined benefit pension. However, union contract negotiations with the company in 2012 produced a two-tiered agreement that turns the tables on the millennials coming up behind the gen X workers: "Future hires covered by the contracts would no longer receive traditional pensions and would instead have 401(k) accounts with a substantial company match."[15] It was the beginning of more efforts to cut the pensions back for everyone. In 2016, Verizon again tried to roll back pension benefits for unionized workers, with proposals including "a cap on the accrual of pension benefits after 30 years of service."[16] The unions defeated the proposed cuts, but pensions remain a battleground.

It is not surprising then that Gabriel Jones, who went on strike against Verizon's plan to move employees around at will, is certain that union workers of his generation are going to be on the losing end of some future contract. He has no plans to become a manager, but he is convinced the company will try to dismantle the unions, retract the benefits the strikers were campaigning to preserve, and leave them just as naked as the managers are. "You can't go to a unionized workforce and demand retrogressive changes that will create an even wider gap between the workers and management," he argues. To get around that, he says, the company is first worsening the work-life balance and imposing benefit reductions on the managers, who have no union protection. Then it can "turn around and say [to unionized workers], 'Well, we just want to put you in line with what everyone else is getting.'"

Verizon seems to be pushing everyone of Gabriel's age into the same ditch. Not only will their benefits decline, but the form in which they are provided will expose the workers to more risk.[17] Gabriel has enough of an understanding of financial markets to recognize what this means for his generation. "Secure retirement is being replaced with securitized retirement," he says—as in, a retirement funded by stocks in a 401(k). "Basically, they want people to invest their own money into the market." But that's no panacea, he explains; it is just the opposite. It's a gift to the investment banks who are reaping huge transaction fees as money flows into stocks. Gabriel has the somewhat conspiracy-minded view that this is why we see "such a big push from the government to go to 401(k)s and to go to individual IRAs and Roth IRAs . . . They want us to support the financial system. They want to transfer that cost onto the employee. They don't want to absorb that cost."

Gabriel often wishes he had extracted himself from Verizon when he was much younger. Now in his early forties, he feels stuck, not only because he needs to protect what he still has with Verizon but because his wife's health problems have made it hard for her to work consistently. She has been a substitute mail carrier, waiting for seniority to kick in, but for the foreseeable future lacks a position with benefits. Given her health problems, Gabriel has to hold on to his family insurance plan to cover her.

He might feel a greater degree of sympathy for Verizon if it were under a financial gun. But it is not a company in trouble. There are no shareholders breathing down Verizon's neck demanding stronger performance and a higher stock price. From Gabriel's perspective, Verizon could well afford to be more generous to gen X employees; it just refuses to look at the world through that lens. "This is not the struggle of the UAW against the Detroit automakers" when the car companies were broke, he says.

> This is an immensely profitable company. You don't even have to go to the extreme of bankruptcy, or potential bankruptcy. A company that's financially maybe not as solvent as they would want to be would be well within their rights to request changes to a union contract that doesn't benefit the company, and by extension doesn't benefit the stockholders. Our struggle is a little different. This company, in spite of everything that they're asking for, they're profitable beyond measure . . . They're paying out record dividends to their stockholders.[18]

Yet amidst these profits, Verizon is laying a pathway into a future where its workforce will no longer have anything remotely like the defined benefit pension and health benefits for which the company was famous when Gabriel began working for them. Every generation since the era of the Ma Bell monopoly days has fared worse on this score.

Carlos Moretti is at the "leading edge" of gen X. At the age of fifty, he has spent over twenty years with Verizon. If he had his way, he would eventually take his pension, retire, and find a job closer to home so he could spend time with his family. But he no longer has this option. As he sees it, his particular generation got screwed because they missed out on the benefits that came to older generations yet didn't know what they were getting into.

> When they stopped everything, there was a cut-off. You had to have a certain amount of years in the company. I think it was fifteen or something like that. I think I missed it by like a year and a half. So now I have no [defined benefit] pension and no [retirement] medical plan. Meanwhile, all the [older] managers got it, and I guess if you're a new manager coming in, you know what you're getting. This is the job you applied for. When I applied for the job, [the better package] is what was promised to me, and then they just took it away.

Verizon employees working side by side now have different prospects for a secure retirement, according to arbitrary features like their age and their status as management or union. It drives suboptimal decisions. Gabriel has intelligence, desire, and drive; he could have gotten an MBA and worked his way into management. Instead, because he was concerned about his family's security, he had to set that ambition aside and work at a position for which he was overqualified. Instead of feeling committed to Verizon and enthusiastic about contributing, he feels hostile toward a firm to which he has given almost his entire working career so far.

The story is much the same at United Airlines. When they started out, United's gen X workers were told they would have a defined benefit pension when they retired. They stayed loyal for ten, fifteen, twenty years, only to find themselves losing just about everything.[19] In May 2005, as part of its bankruptcy proceedings, United announced its plans to default on its employee pension plans and "switch its current employees from . . . defined-benefit plans to defined-contribution plans like 401(k) programs." The Pension Benefit Guaranty Corporation had to assume responsibility for the 134,000 workers covered in the terminated plans.[20]

All the way around, United employees were truly damaged by the change. But the most disadvantaged were gen X managers like Jerry Donegan, an engineer who had already put in many years when the company went bankrupt. A tall white man with brown hair, glasses, and ruddy cheeks, Jerry was born in 1964 in the Pacific Northwest. Jerry's father owned a small business; his mother was a homemaker. After studying engineering in college, Jerry worked for several years as a contractor in the defense industry. In the early 1990s, he joined United. For the first few years the company put him in airplane maintenance operations, then moved him to the interior of the airplane, and finally to the structure of the planes.

When United terminated its pension plans, the company's retirees in their sixties and early seventies lost 20 to 50 percent of their pensions. Jerry, on the other hand, forfeited two-thirds of his retirement money. It was a shock that unfolded in confusion. As the bankruptcy dragged on, most workers didn't understand the process. And even though the company is now largely profitable, Jerry's money is not coming back.

"Before I came in, I just presumed that management would be given the best of all worlds," he says. The managers are not allowed to organize, but there is an implicit message of "we will take care of you." As it turns out, Jerry says,

> It's really not true at all. We don't receive the same vacation benefits that [union] groups get, we do not get the same health insurance plans that other groups get, and we're always the first to take a pay cut. "To lead by example" is the statement always given, and our pay increases don't match pay increases of the represented groups.

So the company is profitable, but then it has to decide where it puts those profits. And we are usually near the end of the list for that.

GEN XERS IN DETROIT'S BANKRUPTCY

In Detroit, unionized city employees still on the job are in a worse "tier" when it comes to retirement benefits than their predecessors who are already retired. This is part of a larger trend nationally, as younger employees in the public sector are being offered weaker retirement packages than the generations before them.[21] After the city's bankruptcy, employees in Detroit are required to contribute a percentage of their base salaries to the pension plan (which feels like a pay cut), and they will have no health care coverage when they retire. As one librarian explained, "nobody knows" exactly how much more the pension could end up being reduced by the time they are ready for the easy chair.

On July 1, 2014, Detroit's city workers (except the police and firefighters) were switched over to a "hybrid" pension plan. Their "legacy" pensions were frozen, and the "hybrid" plan that replaced them for active employees and future hires is considerably less generous. It is still a defined benefit plan, but now there is an age restriction on retirement. The old plan enabled people to retire at any age after thirty years of service; under the new plan, gen X civil servants have a minimum retirement age of sixty-two, with at least ten years of service. Workers who are fifty-five and older and have already clocked thirty years can still retire, but they don't get full benefits until they are sixty-two.[22]

There are other losses, too. Traditionally, pensions have been set by multiplying the total years of service by the final salary, times a "multiplier" that usually ranges from 1 to 2.5 percent. More generous pensions are in the higher end of this range. The older generation of Detroit civil servants could look forward to a multiplier of 1.6 to 2.2 percent, but gen X workers are allowed only a 1.5 percent rate. Banked sick leave—which once counted toward the pension—is no longer included in the calculation. And then there is the required salary contribution, with gen X workers now giving 4 percent of their base compensation to the plan each year.[23]

Detroit workers who were too young to retire in 2014 also won't get the negotiated health benefits offered to people old enough to retire during or soon after the bankruptcy. As librarian Lily Hunter points out, "If you got out, and you retired before December of 2014, you would get benefits of . . . a hundred and something dollars a month *for life* towards your Medicare supplement. But if [you] stayed on, [you] lost that completely." People who retired after 2014 only got "a small annual healthcare stipend for five years . . . And who knows if in the next contract we can negotiate that, but odds are pretty slim we will."

Because of the changes, workers are now going to delay taking their retirement if possible. They need to work longer to build up their pensions and get closer to the age of Medicare eligibility. Ray Fox, a Detroit firefighter in his fifties, says the cuts to the pension plan coupled with the loss of health care coverage in retirement mean he will retire five years later than he would have otherwise. If he retired at this point, he would be responsible for his nineteen-year-old daughter's health insurance, which he cannot afford. "I'm looking at doing thirty years to try to offset or make up what I lost," he says. "I mentally psych myself up by using this saying: 'If I wasn't used to something, how do I know I'm missing it?' Are you gonna miss [the better retirement plan]? I don't know, because I never had it."

Demand is heavy for the fire engines in Ray's company. Overtime is a constant, and his schedule is unpredictable. At times he puts in twenty-four hours straight, then takes a day off. The work is physically stressful. "I'm not trying to live like a millionaire" after retirement, Ray says. He just wants to take care of his mortgage and health insurance for his family.

Health coverage is an important variable for firefighters, given how hard they push their bodies. If that were to be cut, it would put all of Ray's future plans in jeopardy. "I'm going to need the healthcare *more* when I retire than I did when I started," he says with conviction. "With the two knee surgeries I have had, the torn ligaments in the ankle, the shoulder, how many times [something] has fallen on my head or whatever. I'm more than certain that I'm going to need everything I have when I do finally say 'Okay, this is it. I'm done.'"

Ray wants to retire at fifty-five, which was routine for the firemen in the generation before the Grand Bargain. For Ray, it won't be so easy.

> When I came on, the only thing that we were paying into was the Medicare tax, and that allows us to get on Medicare when we turn sixty-five. But see, at thirty years [of service], I'm going to be fifty-five years old. I will have a whole ten years [before I can get in Medicare]. Even if it's 1,000 dollars a month when I retire, that is 12,000 dollars a year. So in that ten years I would have to pay 120,000 dollars . . .
>
> If I have an annuity when I leave here . . . and I only have 120,000 dollars in there, I would have to dedicate that, truly, just for [health care]. With thirty years [in the fire department], me and [my wife] would be married thirty-two years. It's time to take her on a trip, because she earned it. She's been supportive of me every day. But guess what? I'm in the mindset that I got to save this money to pay for healthcare, because [that coverage] is no longer there.

To a degree, all civil servants see themselves in a noble light. They don't wear this sentiment on their sleeves, but as librarians, firefighters, hospital workers, teachers, and bus drivers, they understand their work as a civic contribution. What they do every day makes other people's lives more comfortable, more rewarding, safer. Given this self-understanding, gen X civil servants bridle at the notion that taxpayers might think of them more like parasites.

THE DECLINE OF JOB QUALITY

Anthony French is a tall, broad-shouldered white man with a strong chin line, neatly cut black hair, pale skin, and dark eyebrows. Trucking runs in his family: his stepfather is also a retired Teamster, living in a nursing home out West, where Anthony's mother watches over him and struggles with the cuts to the pension fund.

Originally, Anthony expected much more from the Teamsters. Even though he could see the impact deregulation was having on the industry, he thought there would still be the benefits from the multiemployer pension system, even if individual companies failed. "It's my career," he thought. "I'm gonna retire from here. Get a full pension from here." But for younger Teamsters like Anthony, those who came into trucking in the 2000s and beyond, retirement is more elusive than it was for earlier generations. The pension fund for active Teamsters in New York is already insolvent and in the hands of the PBGC.

One might imagine that Anthony's bankrupt pension plan reflects the decline of his industry. Not so. Trucks still move roughly 70 percent of the nation's goods. In 2016, the trucking industry earned $738.9 billion in gross freight revenues, an amount representing 81.5 percent of the nation's total freight bill. There were 3.5 million truck drivers in the United States in 2015, and 7.4 million people employed in jobs that related to trucking, not counting the self-employed.[24] According to the Bureau of Labor Statistics, jobs in "transportation and material moving occupations" actually saw a modest increase between 2004 and 2014, and are expected to grow even more in the following decade.[25] More specifically, heavy and tractor-trailer drivers are expected to see 6 percent growth from 2016 to 2026, which is about average for all industries. Demand for goods continues to increase, and the aging driver population will need to be replaced, unless driverless trucks get here first.[26]

But while there may be jobs, they aren't as good as they once were, and those who hold them—gen Xers like Anthony and their younger counterparts—are significantly less likely to be unionized. Worker turnover has jumped, according to University of Pennsylvania sociologist Steve Viscelli, who took a temporary job as a truck driver himself to better understand the industry. His book *The Big Rig: Trucking and the Decline of the American Dream* documents how today's trucking jobs are much worse than those enjoyed by older Teamsters in terms of wages, hours, and work conditions. It is a portrait of a degrading work environment. Today's contracted-out owner-operators do not have better conditions than unionized employees, Viscelli argues, even as they have become a larger proportion of truckers due to deregulation.[27]

Two-tier labor agreements that impact pensions are only part of a more general decline in the quality of jobs that younger workers like Anthony hold.[28] He is part of a "swing" generation, familiar with the more comfortable version of his job that used to exist but subject to the erosion of job quality that he must now live with. He is out on the road for longer periods of time, earns less than earlier generations, has lost much of his pension, and will have to cover his own medical care when he retires. Teamsters like Anthony have to compete against non-union labor in their own industry to a much greater degree than in the past, and that exerts continuous downward pressure on his working conditions. The bargaining clout that unions can deliver now is only a pale imitation of what it once had been.

Among firefighters in Detroit, the generation gap in work conditions is most evident in the increasing number of fires with which younger employees have to cope every day. With many fire stations closed as a cost-cutting measure, firefighters still on the job have to do more than ever before. "We could have a day where we have thirteen, fourteen runs before midnight," Ray Fox explains. "And then we could be quiet the rest of the night, or we could have another three or four runs after midnight. There have been days where we can have up to twenty runs. And that's in a twenty-four-hour period."

Ray and his engine company have also increasingly been called on to substitute for emergency medical squads in ambulances. "When I hired on, I hired to fight fires, save lives, and protect property," he notes with exasperation. But with a shortage of ambulance staff, Detroit firefighters are now working as medics as well, coping with life-threatening emergencies. They're doing all this even though their own staff numbers have been cut and the pay has gone down.

Albert Kaminski protests under his breath about how the city planned to "get our department down to a thousand members from almost 1,300. You can't run this department [that way]. Well, they did. We're down to 835. Unbelievable! And the work has not changed." The smaller number of firefighters still has to cover the same ground, attending to tasks such as flushing hydrants. "Let's say there's 25,000 hydrants in the city and the city is 139 square miles," Albert explains. "Whether you have a hundred or fifty people, that area still has to be covered. None of that changed. Square footage didn't change. Hydrants that needed to be checked didn't change . . . You still have to get them."

At times, Albert and his crew are so worn out by the extra work that they can hardly manage. "Now people are falling asleep in chairs," he says. "The workload is tremendously heavier." Firefighters are sup- posed to get a twenty- to thirty-minute break after a fire, he points out, but management knows that if another engine company calls for assistance, the exhausted firefighters will respond anyway. "It's always been like that. It's the nature of this thing. I know this man. I'm not going to let him call the radio for help and not go. They know it."

Albert would feel a bit better if all the extra effort were at least rec- ognized for what it is: employees who are working until they are ready to drop. Instead, he feels firefighters are being criticized for not work- ing as hard as the earlier generations, who had a full complement of employees. "They took four hundred people away," he recalls, "and the mayor came and said, 'We expected a seven-minute addition to response time and it didn't happen.' And instead of saying 'these guys are wonderful,' they're like, 'they must not have been doing shit to begin with.' That's the incredible thing."

Verizon managers have similarly seen the workload increase in their generation even though the staff has been cut back. "When I started managing, I had twelve people on the team. I'm up to thirty-six now!" Carlos Moretti says incredulously. He has ten repair jobs around New York City that he has to get to every day. "Can you imagine what that's like?" he asks, laughing but also upset. "It drives you nuts! You can't get everywhere! It's not possible! It's crazy!"

For United engineers, the change in job quality has been largely a function of outsourcing. To an extent, this was an issue for the older generation of workers as well. But for gen X employees like Jerry Donegan, the change is far more palpable. Instead of being able to manage a large maintenance operation themselves, United professionals are now forced to rely on other people. "After bankruptcy, our model for maintenance was largely to contract to third parties," Jerry says.

> It required a lot more travel, to these different facilities that did the work on our aircraft. It required more management of these vendors. [Their] priority is really making profit for themselves . . . Things that are important to them don't necessarily match up with what we need.
>
> In the old days, if you took a part off the airplane, [our shop] could fix it while the airplane was in the hangar and bring it back—you didn't need a spare. Now you might need two or three spares to fit into the supply chain and be back—so that you would have a serviceable spare ready when the airplane came in . . . That is a constant problem, the need for more parts, but the desire not to spend more money.

The huge space where Jerry works, adjacent to the airport, used to be a bustling facility full of parts ready to be repaired. Now it is largely empty. When Jerry remembers his earliest days with the company, he recalls "a dynamic facility with large-scale employment" for what used to be the largest employer in the region.

> We did all of our work internally. The airplanes would pull up to the back of the building, we'd bring them in, put scaffolding around the building, airplanes would be opened up, all of the components and the engines that we needed to work on removed, and sent to . . . shops within this facility. And they would be overhauled and returned to the airplane and the airplane would be put back into service. And it stayed largely like that until we went into bankruptcy.

What has disappeared from Jerry's perspective is pride in the scale and importance of what United engineers actually do. They feel diminished by the reduction of the whole facility and think that the work done by others, the recipients of outsourcing contracts, is neither as good nor as efficient for the company than the old method of in-house maintenance.

A similar sense of diminishment has hit librarians in Detroit. The city's libraries, once social gathering points in neighborhoods around the city, are now operating on a shoestring. Their hours have been cut, and open access to them—which was a real point of pride—is increasingly restricted. For librarians like Carter White, raised with the notion that libraries are supposed to be free and accessible, the new atmosphere is uncomfortably restrictive. It used to be that anyone with a Michigan state ID could get in, he says. "Now you have to be a resident of Detroit to use the library . . . you can't check anything out, you can't use the computers" if you are not a resident. "I think that was shortsighted," Carter laments. "I understand why—if you're not giving us [tax] money, you can't use it—but at the same time we shot ourselves in the foot. We cut off 75 percent of the people who use the library. I'm a Detroiter, I'm not disparaging Detroiters, but people from all over the state [used to come]."

Detroit librarians also complain that they are not appreciated by the administrators (who, they admit, are facing pressures of their own). "It doesn't take a lot to keep me," Carter says.

> But I wish this situation was better. It really seems like we're undervalued here. They don't want us here. I really feel unwanted by the administration. I think they'd be happier if I just retired. I think that's why they keep giving us these incentives. "If you retire before the end of 2017, we'll give you this little bit of money towards healthcare." I mean, isn't that saying, "Get out the door?"

Gen X workers everywhere are seeing the consequences of cost pressures that are producing a thinning workforce, a speedup for those who remain, and a degraded quality of work due to outsourcing or the replacement of experienced union labor with inexperienced, cheaper, nonunion employees. The combination has had a toxic impact on work satisfaction. Nationally, the younger the workers, the less satisfied they are, with "82 percent of Baby Boomers reporting they are happy in their field whereas only 74 percent of Millennials agree."[29] According to a March 2017 Gallup poll, as described by a CBS journalist, "Of the country's approximately 100 million full-time employees, 51 percent aren't engaged at work—meaning they feel no real connection to their jobs, and thus they tend to do the bare minimum. Another 16 percent are 'actively disengaged'—they resent their jobs, tend to gripe to co-workers and drag down office morale as a result."[30]

THE CONSEQUENCES OF LOW MORALE

Gen X workers have many, many years to go before they can retire. Working in a company or municipal office where no one likes what they do for a living is not a pleasant way to spend a few decades.

What is the consequence of a workforce that feels less loyal, less valued, and less dedicated? Companies lose out on the innovation, drive, and commitment that drive productivity. When workers who have so many years to go before they do retire start to merely punch the clock, there are hidden costs to the firm. The work still gets done, but in a minimalistic "work to rule" fashion, which does not produce the kind of payoff that a committed, appreciated, enthusiastic workforce can give.

Anthony French, the second-generation Teamster, captures this mentality well, though he is not proud of his own sentiments. "You think I really care what happens here?" he asks. "That's everyone's attitude. That's what I tell my boss. 'You really think I care? Just give me my work and leave me alone. I'll do what I'm supposed to do.' There's no enthusiasm . . . I'm not going to give the extra push for you, no way . . . You're [paying] 30 percent less wage? I'll give you 30 percent less production."

Jerry Donegan was very proud of being a highly qualified engineer. He saw United as something of a colossus, and that too was a source of satisfaction. But he doesn't rejoice in the work anymore. United's bankruptcy "was a life-changing morale event . . . for just about everybody involved," he says.

> While you may still work here, you'll never forget that it happened. And you'll never forget [how] you were shorted . . . Post-bankruptcy,

there's been a series of attempts [by my bosses] to say, "Okay, let's just forget about this and move on." But it's very hard to forget about something that changes your life. You can't just say, "Oh well, that was one of those things." It was a serious thing. If the shoe was on the other foot and I had done that to the company, I would've been terminated on the spot.

The whole experience has left a bad taste in Jerry's mouth. If the higher-ups don't have loyalty to him, he doesn't think he should feel much of it toward them either. "At large corporations like United," he remarks, "the people running it have no founding interest in the company."

It would not be surprising, under these circumstances, if gen X workers started looking for new jobs, seeking companies and industries where they might find better pensions or greater appreciation for their contributions. Many do try, but fewer succeed than we might imagine. Gen X employees have been in their lines of work for so long that moving to a new industry is difficult. Yet they have enough time left on the clock that their dissatisfaction is consequential.

Blue-collar workers like Anthony feel trapped and discontent. "The guys in their fifties? They're all screwed," he says. "You put twenty years in a company, twenty-five years. What [are you] going to get out of it? Nothing, pretty much. Every giveback is for the company." White-collar workers with more education are, in theory, more mobile. Yet for United engineers, this is not really true either. Their skills are very firm-specific and would not necessarily transfer to another company, at least not at the level of seniority or pay they have at United.

Vincent Pagini similarly feels little loyalty to Verizon, but he worries that it would be hard on his family if he quit. "The job is a well-paying job, and it still has good benefits compared to a lot of things," he notes. "You say 'Oh well, it's your choice, why don't you just leave?' But that's not fair either, to say I gotta pack it up. My wife stays home to take care of the children. It's not easy for me to say, 'Okay, I'm just going to start something new,' when I have three people depending on me."

Carter White, for his part, would like to leave the Detroit public library, but the job market is not in his favor. "I really wish I could retire," he says, with a laugh. "[But] I would have to get another job, [and] I don't see that I can with the way the job market is. I know so many people that graduated from library school, they can't find a job. If you look at jobs for librarians, it's all part-time."

Albert Kaminsky knows that younger people are avoiding the civil service, heading for the private sector instead. But Detroit firefighters in their fifties have put in a lot of years and can't easily find other employment. For the past ten years, he says, people have been asking him, "What are you doing here? Why don't you go somewhere else?" But getting out is "not that easy. You can't pass a physical after this job. You do eight years on this job, you're not passing a physical for some other department. Because you can't walk. You're taking Advil. You're taking Aleve . . . 'Go apply for another job!' I can't. I've got a bad back. I'm too close to the end. It's too late for me."

Gen X workers are also old enough to face significant family entanglements, which often make holding onto jobs they no longer particularly enjoy (and in companies they don't respect) a necessity. Their children need support for a college education. Their spouses have jobs that they couldn't easily replace if the family uproots, and the need for dual incomes is pressing. Should they ignore those aching backs and stay at the firehouse to make sure their children's tuition can be paid? Should husbands urge their wives to work for a longer period? While these dilemmas are shared by millions of Americans of other generations as well, they are felt in perhaps more powerful ways by the "in-between" gen X workers, because they spent so many years of their work lives in the rosier circumstances of the past while so much of the future is conditioned by the rougher arrangements that have now become the norm.

Vincent Pagini, the Verizon manager, is not sure in which direction to turn. He had thought he could live off of his pension, he says, "and use my 401(k) to pay for college for my children." Except now, "my 401(k) *is* my pension. So yeah, now, it affects my kids." Carlos Moretti, his fellow Verizon manager, would like to spend more time with his family, something he would do if he could afford to retire in eighteen months, as he had originally planned. But now, "I can't do that," he notes, shaking his head. "I have to stay here; I have no choice. And that sucks."

Pressures of this magnitude often strain personal relationships. More than one gen X marriage has foundered as the insecurities associated with pension losses or the tensions that come with cutting back on a family's standard of living take their toll. In Albert's family, the cutbacks affecting firefighters forced his family to economize: No HBO subscription. Stick to used cars. Eventually, Detroit's financial slide proved too much for his marriage. He had told his wife not to worry, that everything would be okay. But as time went on, nothing was.

> I was reassuring my wife, "Detroit's not going to go bankrupt. They're not going to let this happen." Yeah, the talk starts coming up . . . My wife has lupus. [She said] "We've got these issues. We can't go without health coverage. And it's only going to get worse the older I get." [I said] "Listen, you need to trust me."

History turned out otherwise. "I was all wrong," Albert says ruefully.

> The bankruptcy . . . the arguments. [My wife said] "You should've left that fire department. That fucking city." At least we got a pension [whistling sound—like it was flying away]. Now I'm a dumbass and I don't know what I'm talking about. [My wife said] "What [were you] thinking? All these times I listened to you and you don't know what you're talking about. You are a dumbass. And you just fucked everything up for us."

The financial strains have been particularly trying because of some accidents of history. Homeowners in their forties and fifties lost out the most when the Great Recession landed on them. That housing crisis caused a significant number of middle-aged people in gen X to go into foreclosure, lose their equity, and be forced back into the rental market.[31] Librarian Carter White had just bought a house in the suburbs when the Detroit annuity clawback was announced. He is struggling to make ends meet.

Gen Xers are also still paying off loans for their own schooling expenses, as well as for their kids' education. That problem will only grow for future retirees because the cost of education has gone up dramatically in recent decades. Even Social Security recipients are being affected by student loan debt.[32] The number of Social Security beneficiaries with student loan debt has quadrupled in the last decade, and the average amount of debt doubled during that time. A United Press International report notes that according to the Consumer Finance Protection Bureau, "people over 60 are the fastest growing demographic borrowing money for school, currently carrying about $66.7 billion in student loans—6.4 percent of all student debt, more than double the 2.7 percent it was in 2005." Parents and grandparents who cosigned loans to help millennials are feeling the pinch as rates of default climb.[33]

At the same time, stock market fluctuations make it harder for gen Xers to know what their retirement assets really are. What will their 401(k) plans be worth in the future? In the past, much of the risk was on the shoulders of the companies they worked for. Now it's the workers' problem.

GENERATIONAL DIVIDES

> Both sides are right, and then both sides are wrong. You know, to come to a retiree meeting and have a retiree say to me, "What do I care if the fund goes broke? I'll be dead in ten years!" And I don't know what to say to the guy. I said, "Are you a union guy? That's not brotherhood. What about this guy? What about that guy? What about me?"
>
> —Tim Davis, local Teamsters leader, Wisconsin

Veteran *New York Times* reporter Louis Uchitelle covered manufacturing and labor markets for the better part of forty years. He has looked carefully into the consequences of shrinkage in the ranks of organized labor and the resulting erosion in bargaining clout. Two-tier agreements are a telltale sign of that declining power. In theory, younger employees have more time to make up lost ground. In practice, they never will. The wages of gen X workers have been cut, their benefits slashed, and, absent a resurgent union movement, they will not recover what they have lost. It is all part of a "retreat from the middle-class status that unions conferred on so many blue-collar workers," Uchitelle notes.

> Two-tier schemes, which began to spread in the 1980s, are part of that retreat, undermining union solidarity by separating one generation from another. Older union members acquiesced partly to preserve their own pay and benefits and partly to avoid layoffs. The lower tier would be temporary, they rationalized, and in those early days almost every contract included a sunset provision that brought a flight attendant's pay, for example, up to the standard wage rate after a certain period.[34]

Unfortunately, that reconciling never seems to arrive anymore, as the "temporary" wage cuts become permanent. Of course, it could be worse: in some contract negotiations, whole groups of employees are excluded from the benefits that remain. Verizon left its unionized labor largely untouched, for example, but it gutted the benefits available to lower management. And firms that turn to outsourcing never provide the benefits to contract workers that they do for their core labor force.

In some cases, the whole structure of the job has changed, as the permanent worker morphs into a short-term employee. At those workplaces, Uchitelle reports, "the second tier consists of temporary workers brought in for months at a time to replace higher-paid union regulars who have left or retired. "Perma-temps," as they are sometimes called, earn permanently less in wages and benefits than regular employees."[35]

The "perma-temp" approach is already becoming the norm in European nations that are not among the region's rich social democracies. Short-term, fixed-contract jobs now account for nearly 95 percent of job growth in Spain, for example. New employees, which mainly means young people, have no employment security. They can be laid off whenever management is so inclined, cannot rely on a minimum number of hours, and hence have no way to forecast their earnings.[36] "Precarity"—a word we rarely use in the United States but which has become part of the European lexicon—is spreading, especially for new entrants to the labor market.

In countries like Spain, Italy, and Portugal, the employment prospects of young workers are so weak that they are pushed back into states of adolescence, living with their parents well into their forties.[37] While "accordion families" of this kind are becoming more common in the United States as well, we are still a long way from the situation in the southern European countries or Japan, where long-term dependence of adults on their parents is epidemic.

Rather, the upshot of labor market changes in the United States has been to radically disadvantage gen X workers. They were already in rocky financial shape, as the Insured Retirement Institute has documented. In 2012, it records, "only 65% of GenXers reported having money saved for retirement. As one might expect, and in-line with broader research findings on retirement savings, the GenXers most likely to currently have retirement savings are Older GenXers (73%), those with income of $75,000 and above (85%), those who are married (70%), and those who are employed (69%)."[38] For gen X workers outside those categories, the picture is even bleaker.

Cash savings are only one potential source of retirement support. Another critical resource is home equity, which typically grows over the course of the prime working years. But gen Xers have been advancing slowly into the property market. Moreover, those who did get in were hit hard by the equity losses of the Great Recession. As a consequence, most simply lack the savings that baby boomers have amassed. The damage is striking. According to a 2015 study by J.P. Morgan Asset Management, "Those younger Gen Xers who are 35 to 44 years old today have a median net worth of approximately $47,000, compared with $102,000 for those of a similar age 25 years ago."[39]

The stark disadvantages accruing to gen X workers have not gone unnoticed by the workers themselves. They know they are in bad shape. All across the country, people in their forties and fifties see storm clouds ahead. Almost half of all US employees say that they will have to work longer than their parents did.[40] But those in this middle age group are among the most worried of all American working people.[41]

They are right to be concerned. An arbitrary fact—their birth year—has put them in harm's way. Their generation just happened to coincide with a complete sea change in how American firms conceive of their obligations to provide for retirement.[42] Gen X is not happy about it. Not at all.

A tribute to 9/11 and a Confederate flag fly at a Mardi Gras celebration in Opelousas, Louisiana, which has the highest rate of elder poverty in the nation.

6

RETIRING ON NEXT TO NOTHING

The Mardi Gras parade in Opelousas lasts for about thirty minutes. It is a poor cousin to the flamboyant, two-week-long extravaganza in New Orleans, but it provides a welcome respite from the harder realities of poverty in this largely African American town in southern Louisiana. Residents drive or walk over to the parade route, gathering to chat on the broad sidewalks that flank State Highway 190. March is Mardi Gras month, but already the heat and humidity are mounting. When the thermometer hits 85 degrees, the men on the sidewalk start mopping their brows and women begin waving their hands like fans to cool the sweat.

Spectators wolf down local fare from restaurants that line the parade route: Mama's, a fried chicken place; Frank's, a po'boy take-out shop; and Billy's, which sells "boudin balls," breaded and fried balls of pork sausage and rice. They hoist their children in the air so they can see the high-stepping Opelousas High School drum majors and the loud horn players. A float passes by with an all-female dance group whose members are decked out in black crop tops, leggings embroidered with blue sequins, and white gloves, proudly performing hip hop and step dances.

The boisterous crowd waves at the riders on the floats, and the children shout up to them, "Throw me something, mister!"—a traditional Mardi Gras demand for the golden, purple, and green beads that the float masters toss to the crowds.

The sidewalk crowd is integrated, but the floats are segregated, their occupants either all black or all white. A pickup truck decorated with fake flowers, bearing the image of a car emblazoned with the name and phone number of a local auto repair shop, pulls a float whose African American riders of all ages are busy hurling beads. An all-white Cajun zydeco band rides on the back of a green tractor wrapped in paper and plastic in Mardi Gras colors. Behind the zydeco band is a school bus with two large flags sticking out the front. One is the confederate standard, with the words "Rebel Flag" printed over it. The other is an American flag, emblazoned with a bald eagle and the twin towers from the 9/11 attacks. A hand-lettered "Happy Mardi Gras" banner is attached to the front of the bus, as is another advertising a cookout.

A town of about eighteen thousand, Opelousas is a thirty-minute drive from the nearest big city, Lafayette, and a little over an hour from the state capital, Baton Rouge. It is one of the poorest cities in Louisiana, a state saddled with extremely high levels of income inequality. The gap between rich and poor is wider here than in almost any other state in the country: in terms of income inequality, it ranks forty-seventh among the fifty states. That has implications for anyone struggling at the bottom, since high levels of inequality generally go hand in hand with low-wage job markets, meager social benefits, and the persistent poverty that results.

It is harder to pull out of poverty in a state like this, since people here tend to "stick" at the opposite ends of the income spectrum: the poor stay poor and the rich stay rich across the generations. The "Great Gatsby Curve," an observation from economists that inequality results in lower levels of social mobility, has an unfortunate corollary for the elderly: if you have spent your life as one of the working poor, you will almost inevitably be poor in your old age.[1] A lifetime of poverty never translates into what the rest of the country defines as true retirement. Instead, the working poor stay on the job until they are ready to drop.

The whole concept of a pension is foreign, or amounts to nothing more than what they can garner from Social Security. Beyond that, survival depends on what family and church will provide, because employers in these parts don't offer the benefits that more advantaged workers have: pensions or 401(k) plans, health insurance, dental benefits, child-care reimbursements. Those cushions help middle-class workers save for their old age or live more comfortably once they can no longer work. They are largely absent in Opelousas.

Visitors tend to pass through Opelousas rather than stop over. It has been off the beaten path for decades. The surrounding farmland that can be seen from the highway was once the economic mainstay of the region. Older residents of the town know those fields well because they worked in them as children; their own parents were sharecroppers and farmers. Downtown Opelousas is walkable, but people who can afford cars drive straight through town. Those who do not have cars ride their bikes or walk—sometimes for two or three hours—to get to a store, because there is no public transit to speak of in this part of Louisiana.

The town's stately historic district dates back to the early 1700s. The heart of old Opelousas is a small, sleepy square with a grassy center and a tree-shaded park surrounding the county courthouse, a well-made limestone structure. The former federal building, with its large brick arches, lends the town center an air of gravitas. On the back corner of the square, what was once city hall has been converted into a jail annex. The sheriff's headquarters are next door to the venerable Delta Grand Theatre, a restored concert venue and arts and event space. It is rarely used these days, but occasionally it opens up for zydeco concerts that are now the main reason for tourists to visit the area, one of the few attractions that bring in a multiracial audience.

Humble residential districts spread out in all directions from downtown Opelousas. Single-story detached homes made of wood or covered in vinyl siding line the streets. Some of the homes are in decent shape, but others are visibly sagging, with holes in the siding and broken windows peeking through plastic sheeting. Even the most dilapidated houses tend to be raised at least a foot off the ground, to protect them from the flooding that comes with hurricane season. Cars parked on the street range from barely drivable clunkers to full-size pickup trucks and SUVs that have seen better days.

Just outside of town, next to Interstate 49, is the Evangeline Downs Racetrack and Casino. It is one of the few commercial establishments that draw a crowd of customers, attracting retirees from the town and surrounding parishes. Evangeline Downs is hardly Atlantic City, though. The casino, which operates 24/7, consists entirely of whirring slot machines. To encourage folks to stay a long time and spend a lot of money, it is home to an all-you-can-eat buffet—especially popular on Monday evenings, when the price drops to $6.99.

A brightly painted mural facing the main Opelousas square displays a pastoral coastal scene, with a church, farmhouse, animals, ships on the water, several dozen farmers and townsfolk, and an Acadian flag. It celebrates the arrival of French-speaking refugees from Canada in the 1750s. Every face in the mural is white, with just two exceptions: a Native American and a man of color. A caption reads, in French, "We are proud to be Acadian, with faith in the Good Lord, Family, and Country."

Although Opelousas was settled by both white Acadians and mixed-race French Creoles, few descendants of those Cajuns live in Opelousas today. They long ago migrated to other parts of St. Landry Parish.[2] Opelousas is poorer than those areas, and a much higher proportion of its population is black. Indeed, over 75 percent of Opelousas residents are African American; only about a fifth are white. In 2017, per capita income in the town was only $15,489 a year, and 43 percent of its population was living in poverty.[3] That is a catastrophically high poverty rate, higher than that of the poorest neighborhoods in many of America's biggest cities.[4]

The paucity of economic opportunity has left its traces in the lives of the elderly, which is why Opelousas is the best place in the country to examine if we want to know what it means to retire into hardship.[5] According to the most recent decennial census, 9 percent of the US population over sixty-five lived in poverty in 2010. But that year, the Opelousas-Eunice statistical area had an elder poverty rate of 28.4 percent, the highest proportion of people over sixty-five living below the poverty line in the entire United States.[6] To understand how it got so bad, we need to back up and look at the region's past.

HISTORY OF OPELOUSAS

In 1803, the territory of Orleans—later to become the state of Louisiana—was added to the United States as part of the Louisiana Purchase. It was divided into twelve counties, including Opelousas. Four years later, the Orleans territory was additionally divided into nineteen parishes, with the town of Opelousas designated as the seat of St. Landry Parish. The county divisions were abolished in 1845, leaving Louisiana as the only state with parishes as its primary political subdivisions.[7]

By 1850, ten years before the outbreak of the Civil War, St. Landry Parish had Louisiana's second-largest population of *gens de couleur libre*—free persons of color—who occupied a social position midway between black and white populations. They could own property, and indeed held about a quarter of the real estate in Opelousas before the war; some even owned slaves. Nonetheless, as people of color, they were denied the social privileges of whites.[8]

The Civil War brought dramatic changes to Opelousas. A market in the central square of the town notes with some pride that in 1862, when the Union army seized Baton Rouge, Opelousas was temporarily designated the capital of confederate Louisiana.[9] After the war, St. Landry Parish was a prime example of the political and racial turmoil that developed during Reconstruction. The town's population was majority black, but whites refused to yield political power to them. When black residents stood up to white mobs looking to disenfranchise African American voters and intimidate a white "carpetbagger" from Ohio, somewhere between fifty and three hundred black citizens were murdered, depending on whose account one believes. After the initial riots, fifteen freedmen were arrested, then taken out of the local jail in the dead of night and lynched. Historians consider the Opelousas Massacre to be one of the worst examples of Reconstruction violence in the South.[10]

In the Jim Crow era that followed, blatant, legally sanctioned

patterns of racial segregation in housing, schools, and retail establishments became entrenched.[11] Opelousas didn't elect its first black mayor,
John W. Joseph, until 1986. Even then, his candidacy was greeted by
death threats.[12]

Seventy-one-year-old John Jarvis remembers growing up in Opelousas with his mother, uncle, and grandmother. John's mother worked
split shifts, looking after an elderly woman who was homebound; she
died of cancer when John was a teenager. John's father didn't live with
the family because he had another family somewhere else. When the
local schools started integrating, John remembers, the white kids didn't
stick around for very long. "They started putting them all in private
school," he says. "They could do that. And my mama couldn't put me
in no private school. So we had to shoot our best shot." It didn't work
out too well for John; he quit school after eighth grade, "and that's when
I went on my own. I didn't even go to the ninth."

Patterns of segregation, the poor quality of schools left for black
residents, and racial animus sealed them into low-paying occupations.
People like John were destined to be the working poor, because they
were never provided with opportunities to do anything else. That was
no accident: separate was never equal in Opelousas.

The Louisiana economy experienced tremendous instability in the
second half of the twentieth century. With its dependence on the oil and
gas industry, the state is vulnerable to energy price fluctuations. While
the rest of the country lamented the oil embargo and the astronomical
price increases at the pump that went with it, the 1970s were saw wealth
grow in Louisiana. Conversely, the oil bust of 1985 hit the Louisiana
economy hard. One in eight workers was out of work, the highest
unemployment rate in the nation.[13] Many workers migrated to richer
cities like Dallas or Atlanta in search of jobs.

The Opelousas region has been a fertile agricultural community for
much of its history. Although farming is not as dominant as it once was,
to this day St. Landry Parish produces rice, corn, sweet potatoes, pecans,
okra, tomatoes, onions, peppers, and cabbage. It remains one of the
leading agricultural parishes in the state, and small-scale agriculture is
visible across the landscape.[14] Driving ten minutes in any direction from
Opelousas on any road other than the interstate, one sees small and

medium-sized family farms adjacent to modest homes with chicken coops and rusted-out vehicles. Cattle and horses roam and graze nearby. A bit farther from town, crawfish farms are embedded in flooded rice fields.

Farming does not make for an easy life. And it certainly doesn't provide for living wages. Fluctuating commodity prices, declining land values, and periodic flooding wreak havoc on the most industrious of farmers.[15] Ginger LeCompte, the executive director of St. Landry–Evangeline United Way, has watched the economy change over the years. "Those farms have been divvied up and divided up into smaller parcels of land," she observes. "Farming is not as big as it once was."

In 1992, in his last term as governor of Louisiana, conservative Democrat Edwin Edwards hatched the notion that Louisiana needed an economic boost, and he pushed through laws that enabled the growth of casinos.[16] That initiative accounts for the presence of Evangeline Downs Racetrack and Casino in St. Landry Parish, which has brought modest employment opportunities to Opelousas. Ginning up the tourist business, a successful strategy in the jazz capital of New Orleans, was another attempt to diversify the region's economy. Since the early 1980s, Opelousas has hosted a large annual Southwest Louisiana Zydeco festival in the neighboring community of Plaisance, in the hope that it would attract large crowds of music lovers. So far, however, it too has brought only modest income to the area.[17]

Local jobs, based as they were on farming and service industries, never provided much in the way of pensions or retiree health care. Ginger LeCompte notes that Opelousans don't work for companies that feel this kind of obligation toward their employees. Farming and service industries are notorious for low wages and high turnover, and people in them spend most of their lives in working poverty. It doesn't matter whether they are black or white; when it comes to retirement, virtually everyone is at a loss in Opelousas. "We have a lot of poverty," Ginger notes.

> This is a very rural area . . . not a lot of industry. Not a lot of high
> tech. And so those who are retiring are maybe farmers, maybe people
> that have lived here all their lives, have never moved from here, and

sometimes they'd live in the same home that they were raised in . . .
A lot of people depended on the oil industry. So those companies and
businesses that relied in an indirect way on the oil industry, they're
suffering . . . But even before . . . it was a poor community already.

Arnold Ledoux is a good example of the ways in which a life in
farming, with all of its hardships and insecurities, translates into a difficult retirement. Arnold is seventy-eight years old now and lives in public
housing for the elderly poor. He was the youngest child in the family;
his parents were farmers who grew cotton, sweet potatoes, and pea-
nuts. He went to school in Opelousas up to the eleventh grade, but
had to drop out to manage the farm when his father fell ill. The rest of
the Ledoux siblings were living in Texas by that time, so Arnold was
left to shoulder a mountain of responsibility. It was the 1950s, but it
may as well have been the 1850s. "I was farming with mules," he recalls.
"I had no tractor."

There was very little money to spare, especially after Hurricane
Audrey ravaged Opelousas in 1957. "That hurricane took a big toll on
the farm," Arnold remembers. They couldn't afford to repair what was
lost. "After then, I didn't have no kind of money to continue." So Arnold
had to find another way to earn a living. With no experience to speak
of outside of farming, his options were limited. "Yeah, so I went to
work by the day. A laborer." He took unskilled jobs in construction,
working out of Baton Rouge, building freeways for a private company.
The trajectory from this job to a retirement in poverty was almost inev-
itable. Arnold had no real options for a better deal.

As farming has declined as a source of employment in St. Landry
Parish, other industries have become more important to those people
who can find work, especially women with skills. Opelousas General
Hospital has more employees than any other local concern except for
Walmart: over 1,100 workers are on the hospital payroll, and they ben-
efit from relatively generous pay and retirement contributions.[18] It is
the key hospital for all of St. Landry Parish and the surrounding areas.[19]
(Many small towns in southern Louisiana have no hospitals at all.)[20]
Lafayette remains the regional medical hub where one would access

specialists, but it is over an hour away, which is too far for many families to go for emergencies or routine care.

Some Opelousans commute about an hour to work in Baton Rouge, where there are a number of large employers in heavy construction, civil engineering, and structural road and bridge repair. The pay is markedly better in construction than in service industries.[21] Jobs in oil and gas similarly require a long commute or a move, and many people are unwilling or unable to leave Opelousas. Pipeline construction and maintenance, refinery, and offshore rig jobs are periodically in ample supply. During boom periods, oilfield companies such as Baker Hughes, Superior Energy, Schlumberger, and Halliburton offer employment within driving distance of Opelousas.[22] The bust cycles that follow the booms are painful for everyone. Lafayette Parish, which borders St. Landry, lost an estimated 8,300 jobs in the oil and gas sector after commodity prices collapsed in 2014.[23]

Even though whites dominated that workforce, and hence felt the brunt of the recession, some jobs in the oil business were so punishing that they couldn't attract white workers. These were the ones that employed blacks and, on occasion, women. Zadie Joubert, an African American resident of Opelousas, took one of those awful jobs. "I worked offshore, as a tank cleaner," Zadie recalls. "In Morgan City, me and my son was working together offshore. That is the dirtiest job. You scrape the tanks. Then you got all this grime and metal and rust and stuff. You fill these five-gallon buckets up with it. By the time you fill them up, those buckets weigh like sixty–seventy pounds. You lift it . . . over the hole with a rope. We'd tie the bucket to [the rope], pull it up and go empty it." There weren't many "opportunities" like this one, nor were there many people—men or women—willing to do such strenuous, grimy labor.

Aside from the local farms, the general hospital, and the nearby construction and energy industries, many people in Opelousas are employed in the service sector. Chain stores like Family Dollar, Wendy's, McDonald's, and Taco Bell are always looking for employees, since the wages they pay are low and the turnover is high.[24] The Evangeline Downs Racetrack and Casino, which has about 650 workers, is cut from the same cloth. Walmart's distribution center in Opelousas employs 580 workers and Walmart Supercenters in St. Landry puts almost 700 on the payroll.[25] None of these employers are union-friendly, so they have never been pressured to create a pension system or provide much in the way of postretirement health care. Retirees are on their own.

At 15 percent, Louisiana has a higher elder poverty rate than any other state in the country.[26] But Opelousas is in far worse condition still: over 28 percent of the community's elders are poor. The region's economy catches its seniors in a bind, since people who have been poor all their lives are likely to stay that way when they can no longer work.

LIVING IN A MEAN STATE

Social Security and Medicare, two major planks of the US welfare state, have been responsible for enormous improvement in the longevity and quality of life of older Americans.[27] This is especially true for people of color, who lag behind whites when it comes to having pensions and retirement savings.[28] Only a third of black Americans, and only a fifth of Asian Americans and Hispanics, receive income from pensions, IRAs, or 401(k) accounts.[29]

Black elders in Opelousas are a case in point. Like many of their peers in other parts of the country, they rely on Social Security or federal disability payments, and they rarely have private pensions to supplement those federal benefits.[30] Because they live close to the edge of poverty during their active working years, most Opelousas residents also have little to nothing saved for retirement.[31] In this, their struggles are an amplified version of the difficulties that plague millions of Americans: over half of American workers have no private pension coverage whatsoever, and one-third of the nation's retirees have no savings at all.[32]

Opelousas seniors face a particularly hard situation because they live in a mean state. Louisiana is one of the tougher places to access benefits that flow more easily to low-income elders in the North and the Midwest. In the South, the tradition is to crack down on access to federal programs, minimize state contributions of any kind, and plague people with long wait times that discourage them from claiming what is rightfully theirs. In general, the attitude is that poverty—including working poverty—is a disease for which the affected individuals themselves are responsible. "Coddling the poor" is definitely not the Louisiana way.

This attitude makes federal benefits, which are relatively sheltered from local and state variations in enthusiasm, all the more important. Medicare, for instance, is essential to the survival of Opelousas seniors, as it is for many Americans over sixty-five. It is an insurance program administered by the federal government. This puts it in sharp contrast with Medicaid, an assistance program combining federal and state resources to address the needs of low-income people.[33] Because of its state component, Medicaid benefits vary depending on where one lives.

Federal assistance also comes to the fore because a high proportion of Opelousas seniors, particularly those whose jobs were physically strenuous, are disabled. Not surprisingly, they also suffer disproportionately from the chronic diseases and injuries that accompany poverty, especially heart problems, diabetes, and other obesity-related disorders.[34] For those who meet federal qualifications for disability, two important programs provide cash payments, and Opelousas seniors are critically dependent upon both of them. The first one is Social Security Disability Insurance (SSDI), available to any person who has paid into the Social Security system for at least ten years but became disabled before reaching the age of sixty-two (at which point regular Social Security benefits can be accessed). The second is Supplemental Security Income (SSI), which is designed to meet the basic needs of elderly, blind, and disabled individuals who would otherwise have a hard time paying for food and shelter. Elders and the disabled with "limited income" and less than $2,000 worth of cash, stock, cars, land, or any other salable property can receive SSI benefits, subject to a lifetime maximum.[35]

Many elderly Opelousans also rely on the Supplemental Nutrition Assistance Program (SNAP), formerly known as food stamps.[36] A means-test program, SNAP is run by the US Department of Agriculture, which also takes responsibility for surplus food distribution. Louisiana has one of the highest take-up rates of SNAP in the country: almost 19 percent of the state's 4.6 million residents participate in the program. It helps to attack food insufficiency, but for the poorest of the poor hunger is still a problem.[37] Lydia Chevalier, a nonprofit leader and community activist in Opelousas, is incensed by the low benefits the government provides to its neediest. "Who decided the elderly don't need to eat?" she asks. "This is what amazes me, when I start getting their paperwork—sixteen dollars' worth of food stamps for a month?" From her vantage point, the stingy food stamp policy seems calculated to make poor people miserable in their old age.

John Jarvis is among the people whose SNAP allotment seems almost absurdly low. "Them food stamps, they don't give me but thirty dollars. Now, what can I get for that?" he asks. Yet he is afraid to question this meager allowance, lest even that get cut. "So many people get ten, that's all they get, only get ten dollars for food stamps," he says. "What can you get with that? You get a loaf of bread and a gallon of milk, that's all. Ten dollars. I don't want to go down there [to the food stamp office] messing with them, they may take the thirty dollars." Annabel Carter, an eighty-two-year-old cancer survivor, is even worse off than John. "I don't get nothing," she says. "Nothing at all on food stamps." She receives about $750 a month from Social Security and SSI to support herself and her two grown, but disabled, children, and some $200 of that goes for groceries. She usually goes shopping on the first of the month, as soon as her check arrives.

Subsidized housing is another crucial federal benefit for old people in Opelousas, especially if their home is falling apart or they have never owned one. A few apartment buildings in town are part of a federal Housing and Urban Development (HUD) program called "Section 202." It serves very low-income elderly people and enables them to "live independently but in an environment that provides support activities such as cleaning, cooking, transportation, etc."[38] The rent is very modest because the landlord has to be a nonprofit organization that puts up a small amount of money in order to receive a forty-year no-cost mortgage.[39] That mortgage stays in place as long as the landlord is serving low-income elderly tenants.[40] Section 202 has been a godsend to the elderly poor in Opelousas—it is responsible for providing the apartment of Arnold Ledoux, the seventy-eight-year-old retired farmer, for example. However, this is perhaps the last generation to benefit from it. In 2012, Congress discontinued all new construction on Section 202 housing as part of negotiations over the federal budget.[41] The Trump administration has proposed $42 million in cuts to the program.[42]

Federal programs help Opelousas seniors survive, but life still unfolds on the local level. And while we think of the United States as one country, when it comes to being poor, it isn't. States differ sharply in how generous or mean-spirited they are toward those in need. In this they reflect variations in regional history that are at least as old as the Civil War and in many instances stretch back to long before. Northeastern states, especially New York, New Jersey, Massachusetts, and Vermont, tend to be on the liberal side of this equation; they are dominated by Democratic legislatures, influenced by union politics, and progressive on cultural issues ranging from gay marriage to abortion. California and Washington State fit into much the same tradition.

The South is another country. Its history of slavery, the ongoing primacy of property rights, and its avoidance of income and property taxes have created thin support for public schools, hospitals, roads, and public administration. Southern states are notorious for turning down programs designed to help the poor, even when the costs are largely borne by the federal government. Even during the Great Depression, with unemployment at catastrophic levels, southern states typically refused relief payments for their citizens, on the grounds that the federal government would eventually expect contributions from state and local sources.[43]

Bobby Jindal, who served as governor of Louisiana from 2008 to 2016, exacerbated this tendency. The poor of his state have not gotten over the damage caused by his insistence that the state budget be balanced without any tax increases.[44] Devastating cuts to higher education and health care followed, since neither enjoys constitutional or statutory protection.[45]

In parishes like St. Landry, the lack of industry produces a low tax base, so it must rely on other sources to support local government and public services. St. Landry cities and towns depend on very high taxes on food as well as on revenue from fees, fines, and speeding tickets.

Because of this kind of revenue collection, Opelousas is a hard place to be poor. A loaf of bread costs 10 percent more than it would in a state that doesn't tax food; the sales tax exacts a much bigger hit on the income of a poor household than that of a millionaire.

Fees and fines of the sort imposed in Opelousas are all hallmarks of a regressive tax regime, which is known to be punishing to the poor, impacting their health and longevity.[46] The town of Washington, ten minutes north of Opelousas, took in $1.3 million in speeding tickets and other fines and forfeitures in a single year, which provided 84 percent of the town's revenue.[47] Such overreliance on fines produces very strained relations between the police who administer the system and the African American community, whose members are pulled over constantly for minor violations such as broken tail lights or failing to signal a left turn.[48] And it adds a similar burden to the lives of already struggling Opelousas residents.

Professor David Yarbrough is the Dean of Community Service at the University of Louisiana at Lafayette.[49] A middle-aged white man, he has lived in the South for most of his life. His expertise is child and family studies, and he has many years' experience as a social worker in Washington, DC, Alabama, Texas, and Louisiana. Yarbrough is a keen observer of the political climate in Louisiana and its impact on the disadvantaged. "We're caught in [a] kind of political carousel," he notes. "We're challenged to come up with more efficient and effective revenue streams, but the political will to do that is pretty rough . . . The greatest consequence then is on those who are underemployed, who are unemployed, who are old, who are poor, who are in rural areas as opposed to urban areas." People with few resources are not able to move in order to access the services that people who are located in cities can put their hands on more easily. "They're in a place that they've lived maybe fifty, sixty, seventy years," Yarbrough explains. "And their community left them behind."

Louisiana is leaving its residents behind in other ways, too. Climate change sounds like a distant problem, but as Texas and Louisiana discovered during the brutal reign of Hurricane Harvey in 2017, it is producing local damage that elderly retirees cannot easily contend with. Opelousas is a long way from Louisiana's coast, but storms are becoming more powerful and penetrate inland more often than in the past. "We recently suffered from what they call the hundred-year flood," Ginger LeCompte says. "Those homes that were already very fragile—some have been condemned, and some are having to be practically rebuilt from the ground up. They probably weren't suitable for habitat in the first place." But it costs money to rebuild, money that no one in the poor neighborhoods of Opelousas has on tap.

HOW THEY LIVED: OR, WHY THE ELDERLY POOR ARE POOR

While some people enjoy a comfortable standard of living during their working years and descend into financial difficulty only as they grow old, most of the elderly poor in Opelousas came from working poor households and have never been free of hardship. The area's agrarian economy provided few chances to earn enough money even for a technical or vocational education, much less the kind of college degree that would have made a major difference in earning power. Indeed, the biographies of African Americans in this community suggest that for some, the nineteenth century may as well not have ended.

Jocelyn Winters was born in 1955 in Bunkie, Louisiana, forty minutes north of Opelousas. She grew up "in the fields, picking cotton and picking sweet potatoes . . . I mean, we had to eat." Jocelyn was glad to go to school because that meant "I was out of the fields. But I still worked for people in their houses, cleaning the floor, cleaning up. You know, it was hard at that time." She would also babysit on weekends. After finishing high school, in 1974, she went to college for two years. That was a remarkable achievement for someone who had so little in life, and a testimony to Jocelyn's determination to find a way out of agriculture. She attended a business school in Lafayette for those two years but decided, in the end, that her best bet for work was in taking care of people. "I really liked old people," she explains. "I was supposed to go to nursing school, but I worked with older people in a nursing home."

Nursing home aides are at the bottom of the wage structure, and taking up this occupation almost guaranteed that Jocelyn would be working poor. She landed jobs in various convalescent facilities, first in Opelousas and then in Lafayette, where she earned a bit more. She also did private home care for the elderly. All in all, she put in thirty-five years for different employers. The earnings were never good.

Jocelyn's Opelousas neighbors were similarly stuck in occupations that paid poorly, and the prospects for a decent retirement were further diminished for those whose paychecks had to stretch to raise a family. Taking care of children, working long hours with no benefits, and living paycheck to paycheck, they had no chance to save. Since even low-wage jobs were hard to find, no one in Opelousas could afford to be too choosy. Nina Rochefort, a single mom, has worked since her teenage years. She spent most of that time in fast food jobs, and even those opportunities were scarce. She blames that on nepotism: even if you apply for open positions, she says, "you never get hired. They keep hiring their families and stuff. You can't get no jobs like that. Opelousas does that terrible."

Nina's search for employment was hampered by the fact that she was too broke to own a car. In a region with no real public transit options, that is a paralyzing handicap. Sunset, the town where she lived when her children were young, is ten miles from Opelousas—a three-hour walk each way. She moved there because she thought it would be a calmer place to live. "I just wanted a change. It was quiet and peaceful," she says. She found childcare and walked those ten miles every day to get to work. "My first job was Mama Fried Chicken on Landry. That was a good job," she recalls. "I was there for—how many years? Lord. Five or six years?" She then worked at some other fast food jobs, and eventually got a lucky break: a job opened up in the general hospital, serving food to patients. At $12 an hour, this was by far the best Nina had ever done.

But after six years there, when she was just shy of sixty years old, her arthritis flared up and made it very hard to work. She had to leave the hospital and retire. Now Nina lives with her son, who has cerebral palsy. She covers their living expenses on her Social Security check of $756 per month and his disability check of $743. Between her lifetime of low wages and her son's needs, she hasn't been able to save much. There is no margin in her life.

Zadie Joubert couldn't save either, even though she has worked doggedly to provide for her four children. Support from her two ex-husbands has been inconsistent, leaving her struggling to keep her family above the poverty line. With the exception of the years when she was hauling grime out of the oil rigs, the jobs she's had have been low-wage positions, making it impossible to do any more than scrape by. "Most of my jobs was in fast food places and restaurants," Zadie recalls. "My first job was in a motel, cleaning rooms. I did all kind of jobs . . . I worked at Fat Albert [fried chicken restaurant] in Grand Coteau. And back then we was making seventy-five cents an hour, which I didn't think was right at all. That wasn't even minimum wage. The man was very prejudiced. But he hired me and I worked there. Seventy-five cents an hour. We barely made nothing."

Zadie is a hard worker who puts up with a lot of stress and surveillance on the job. "You're always busy," she says. The job comes first; the worker comes last. "At Burger King, it was like we were in the army. We couldn't use the bathroom unless we asked to use the bathroom . . . [We needed permission] to eat or drink just a glass of water. Which I didn't think made any damn sense."

Her working life has largely been made up of a string of jobs like this. Even as a new mother, she has been on the job. Her poverty in old age is not a consequence of a lifetime on easy street. It is a classic story of working poverty, a life made even more difficult by her employers' habit of hiring a large number of people like Zadie to work part-time. The arrangement lets them avoid having to pay benefits, and saves on insurance and overtime pay. "Opelousas, they don't pay much neither," Zadie says. "Most places pay minimum wages anyway, but you don't really get no hours here. Because they always hire so many people."

"We barely made nothing" is pretty much what Zadie has had to live on for most of her adult life.

HOW THEY LIVE NOW

While most people in this book try to plan ahead for retirement, the elderly black folk of Opelousas generally just stop working when they cannot go on any longer. Some are too ill or exhausted to work; some have a disability that makes it impossible to continue; some have to quit working to take care of a family member. They have no savings to cushion them. Social Security and disability payments provide their only safety net.[50]

These conditions would be hard even for people who are old enough to qualify for age-related benefits like Medicare. Unfortunately, the working poor are often so beat by their early sixties that they must stop work a good five years before they can access the health insurance they need.

In 2005, Milton Gerard had an accident while working in a nursing home. Milton was injured trying to break the fall of a patient. He continued going to work after having surgery but couldn't do much physical labor. Instead he could only supervise the people he trained. He was given minuscule compensation for his injury on the job through workman's compensation, then retired at age sixty-two. When he tried to go back to work after retiring, the company refused to take him.

Tapping Social Security at sixty-two exacts a high cost. It is the earliest allowed point for accessing Social Security benefits, so the monthly payments are cut dramatically to make up for what, in theory, will be a longer time that the beneficiary receives them. The monthly payments increase for those who can afford to wait. Anyone who starts at sixty-two might easily come to regret their decision, as John Jarvis knows all too well. "At sixty-two, everybody wanna get what they can get. Might not live to be sixty-five," he explains. "Now I'm seventy-one . . . If I could have [gone] back and said 'Hey wait now, you're gonna make it,' I'd a been getting a thousand dollars."

Annabel Carter, the cancer survivor who gets nothing at all from food stamps, has seen a lot in her eighty-two years. She was born in Opelousas in 1934 and raised by her mother and stepfather. Her home, light gray and cream, sits a few feet off the ground. The windows are framed with wooden shutters, the door is behind a white screen, and the front porch—where she loves to sit—sports some green plastic deck chairs, a small charcoal grill, and a bicycle for her grandkids and great-grandkids to use. Annabel's clothesline is drawn across the porch as well, placed where the drying clothes can catch an occasional breeze.

Inside, the small living room is very dark, with the blinds drawn to keep out the heat that permeates Opelousas even in February. The one-story house has three tiny bedrooms on a common hallway. The floors are linoleum and yellowed with age. The bathroom has seen better days: it has had serious problems with mold caused by flooding. A small living room is stuffed with oversize couches in plaid and artificial leather. The large armchair is Annabel's favorite place to sit. Annabel's adult daughter and son are both disabled and still live with their mother. They watch a lot of TV, as does Annabel. There is one on in every room.

One of the reasons Annabel is so broke in her old age is that unlike most other women in Opelousas, she never worked outside the home. She got married when she was twenty. Her stepfather got sick and stayed in the hospital for a year, so the family needed her help with care-taking.

Annabel's husband worked for a car dealership, doing various jobs for the owner, and retired at the age of eighty after working fifty-one years for the same employer. Just two years after retiring, he died of cancer. That was three years ago. With no Social Security in her own name, and as the widow of a low-income worker, Annabel was left in a very difficult position. She now lives off of a $600 monthly spousal benefit from her late husband's Social Security account, and a $151 monthly SSI check for being low income. She tried to qualify for Social Security disability payments but was denied. "They say that I'm not classified as disabled," she explains. "I had one kidney removed, and I had breast cancer, both breasts removed. Then I had colon cancer. Twice. But they still say I'm not qualified as disabled. So that's all I get: 600 dollars in one and 151 the other."

Nationally, disability rolls have been growing as access to welfare has become more restrictive and the value of it has declined. But getting on disability is not easy in the South, compared to other parts of the country. Here applicants meet skepticism and intentional barriers at every turn. They need to persuade local doctors, disability examiners, administrative judges, and staff from the local Social Security office that they are qualified. They must visit each benefits office several times in the quest for approval, bringing various forms of paperwork which they may know little about and have a hard time gathering. It is not uncommon to find that they have to start over again, explaining themselves to different workers, every time they apply. Louisiana is tough on people who seek assistance and only those with the strength to persevere can succeed. Even after they qualify, they must wait, often for five or six months, before checks appear in the mail.[51]

Zadie Joubert, sixty years old, is on disability now. Her health has been impaired in her later years, but she has stayed on the job as best she could. "I had five strokes," she explains, which left her partially paralyzed on her left side. "The third one was bad." After the second stroke, the doctor told her she couldn't really do any physically strenuous work anymore, but Zadie kept working for years thereafter.

> Because I had four kids to raise. I had to work to pay bills. So it was like, I had no time to rest. It was just stress all the time. Because I'm at work and wondering what my children doing because I had nobody there with them. I had to go back to work. I had to take care of my kids. I had four of them in school. School, school supplies and everything, uniforms, that costs a lot. A whole lot. For four children. And I had to do that because their daddies wouldn't do nothing for them. I took care of them. By myself.

After many discouraging trips to benefits offices, Zadie finally got on SSDI at the age of forty-three. It certainly helps: she could not manage without this lifeline. But it remains erratic, and requires constant vigilance despite her record of health disasters. At times, her benefits would be cut off for no apparent reason, and Zadie had to muster the energy to get them reinstated.

Housing, a big expense for everyone, is nearly always the most substantial cost for low-income retirees. Private homes, especially those that have been in the family for generations, are treasured but are also hard to keep in good repair. More than one Opelousas retiree has gone deeply into debt at an age when they cannot really hope to pay it off, just to repair the roof or eliminate the mold that always follows from flooding. Nina Rochefort, who lives in her family home,

knows the burden that home ownership places on the poor. She had
to take out a second mortgage to fix her house before she could move
in, since it wasn't habitable otherwise. Her monthly mortgage payment is $342, and at the age of sixty-four Nina still has twenty years
left to go on it.

Valerie Miller also has a "house bill," a local phrase for mortgage.
She took out the mortgage because her daughter, Joleen, couldn't keep
up with the loan payments on her car. Joleen couldn't get to work without transportation, and her wages are a mainstay of her parents'
household budget. Refinancing Valerie's house to redeem that car from
the "repo man" is a punishingly expensive way to manage the situation:
Valerie has five years left on the mortgage, and when she is finished, she
will have paid nearly $10,000 for a car that isn't worth more than
$4,000. But no one in the Miller family has $4,000 to spare.

Utility bills also add up quickly for those living in private homes,
pushing them deeper into debt or forcing them to rely on their adult
children for help. Valerie is always scared to open the electricity bill.
"The light bill in the summer be like eighty-nine dollars, you know,"
she says. "When my daughter comes, it goes over a hundred. I'm from
the country, I can deal with the heat a little bit, but not them." Left to
her own devices, she swears she would turn off her air conditioning
altogether to keep the bill affordable. But she worries her kids would
stop visiting her if she did.

When Nina Rochefort's air conditioning began to leak, she saw her
electric bill soar from $300 to $700 a month. She could not afford to
pay up, so for energy assistance, she turned to the St. Landry Parish
Community Action Agency, which depends on the charity of local utility companies. Without this support, Nina would have been in serious
trouble. Lydia Chevalier, the community activist, objects to the pricing
policies of the utility companies and wonders why the first step toward
helping people like Nina isn't changing the cost structure. After all, a
credit for a month or two only goes so far. Why not just lower the rates
for everyone, she says? No deal.

Many poor elders who don't have a charitable solution turn to pred-
atory payday loan companies to make ends meet. Because so many are

"unbanked," they have no other source of credit. But the payday loan interest rates are brutal.

From her perch at United Way, Ginger LeCompte sees a lot of elders trying to manage their lives on completely inadequate budgets. Their lack of access to any kind of banking services compounds their problems. "If you drive down through downtown Opelousas, you'll see on the right and the left these payday loan companies," Ginger says. "They tend to open shop in the poorest of neighborhoods. And the person that's got the low-income wage goes in there and makes these payday loans and it's perpetual. They never pay them off. It's a cycle . . . They don't live from paycheck to paycheck, they're living worse than that."

Arnold Ledoux was the victim of a payday lending debacle. He owes money for a car that he doesn't even have anymore. Five years ago, a friend borrowed the car and crashed it—a total wreck. Arnold still has to pay off the loan. "I still pay that once a month," he notes sadly. "Four hundred something. The finance company, they charge you a lot of interest. I been paying on that going on three years now . . . It'll be five years and it'll be done. Then I [hope] I see my way out after that."

The end of the month is a tight time for most poor elderly people in Opelousas. Food stamps and Social Security checks arrive on the first and the third of the month, and for a time thereafter, everyone eats better: meat, fresh produce, milk and cheese. Toward the end of the month, volunteers at the church "diner"—the soup kitchen—and the food bank see a big increase in traffic, and the quality of the local diet goes down. At that point in the cycle, canned goods, high in fat and salt, become the mainstays. Those who have relatives they can depend on start leaning on them for help.

These budget squeezes are considerably less onerous for those who qualify for federally subsidized Section 202 housing.[52] In a lot across from the Holy Ghost Catholic Church is group of apartments built with 202 funds through the efforts of parishioners. The apartments are modest one-bedrooms with small combination kitchen/living room spaces. The white and tan walls show their age but are still decent.

Elders in Opelousas are not always enthusiastic about moving into them. They know that 202 housing is seen as a form of charity, and that hurts their pride. But Tammy Erwin, the assistant property manager at the apartments, thinks the choice is clear enough when the alternative is private homes that are falling apart, unheated, or unsafe. She is often able to persuade seniors that what she has to offer would be better, and isn't an "old folks home." To live in these apartments, one must be in good health, hence most residents are in their sixties and seventies. They have not yet hit some of the more devastating illnesses that are so common in one's eighties. There are no common meals or medical services; people who need that kind of support end up in a Medicaid-supported nursing home.

The basic plan of 202 housing is bare-bones, though in this apartment complex, church-related volunteers and managers help residents get to the doctor or go shopping. They put on events to entertain the residents and reinforce the sense that they are part of the community. Because the housing complex is unofficially tied to the charitable mission of the Catholic Church, parishioners also lend a hand by fundraising to benefit the apartment residents. It is a testimony to the close ties that permeate the black community in Opelousas that so many people turn out to help. "We did a barbeque dinner," Tammy notes as an example. "Just word of mouth."

The price of the subsidized housing is definitely right for a low-income retiree like Milton Gerard. "I never thought I would want to live in apartments," he says. But "you're not gonna find a decent place to rent for 257 dollars a month. You're just not gonna find it, you know? . . . So I accept it. I said, 'Hey, it's a nice place.'"

RACE AND FAITH

It is no accident that the community with the highest proportion of elderly poor in the nation is 75 percent black. Race has everything to do with why Opelousas retirees often live in dilapidated housing, and why they face such difficulties in accessing supports that would be easier to come by in a more progressive state.

Opelousas residents who came of age after World War II know exactly how racism shaped their parents' lives and their own. They prefer

not to dwell on the discrimination, instead highlighting how they—
and the generations before them—worked around it. But that does not
make them any less aware of injustice than the "Black Lives Matter"
generation, nor does it remove the bitterness that a lifetime inflected
by prejudice and inequality creates. It just means the elders focus on
the values they believe have been responsible for whatever good fortune they have experienced.

Elaine Evans was born in 1943 in Lafayette, Louisiana, and grew
up in Opelousas in a working-class household with a strong moral com-
pass. Her father was always involved in social justice. He was an army
veteran who came back to Opelousas after his tour of duty. "He had
gone only up to third grade and was denied entry to a veteran's program because of his race," Elaine says. Indeed, racial discrimination
built barriers around her father for his whole life, and he responded by
summoning the moral strength to make his way regardless.

As Elaine recalls, "eventually, the decision was made that if there
was a school for colored children, that [my father] should be allowed
to attend school with the children." That he did, going as an adult to the
Opelousas Colored School, also known as the St. Landry Parish Training School.[53] "The principal read all of the documentation and said to
him, 'August, if you're going to be here all day long, would you mind
[also] being the janitor?'"

Elaine's father did become the janitor, as well as the school's lone
bus driver, all the while going to classes to complete his own elementary school education. That took determination and grit, qualities that
Elaine admires and tries to emulate. She understands that she has benefited from the determination of a poor father who did everything he
could to surmount the punishments meted out by Jim Crow racism.

Even though he never achieved a high level of education in the eyes
of many, he was so well educated in life that he made sure his family
was going to be well taken care of. And he was an avid reader. My
mom kept the newspaper until he came home. He started on the front
page and read whatever connecting story. Then that page was passed
on to the next child. And after that to the next one and so on down

the line. And after the entire paper was read, he posed questions to us and we had to have an opinion . . . So then his push was for us to become educated.

That push worked: Elaine and her two siblings all went to college.

After graduating, Elaine went to work as a teacher. She believes that whatever progress she and her siblings have made is due to the values that were imparted to her by example. She learned early on how high her parents' expectations were for her, even though their own working lives never rose above a very modest level. Racial prejudice was in the foreground every step of the way, but it was the fortitude they displayed in the face of it that moved their family forward.

Elaine would be quick to say that the racism of the Jim Crow era was virulent, inescapable, and life-threatening. Today, at least the white progressive souls in her community are embarrassed about this history. Yet the past isn't entirely past. It is reflected in the underlying racism that leads government programs in Louisiana to be so meager. In the shadow of that weak welfare state, it is the church that stepped in to fill the gaps—to help the poor, especially the black poor, survive. Religious institutions are active everywhere, supporting housing rehabilitation, food pantries, a soup kitchen, and a set of visiting programs that provide company and prayer partners for elders who might otherwise be isolated.

Louisiana's history as first a Spanish and then a French territory has meant that Catholicism is the mainstay in the town, albeit one with its own racial history.[54] African American worshippers broke away from St. Landry's Catholic Church to found the Holy Ghost Catholic Church in Opelousas nearly one hundred years ago. Today, it stands as the largest predominantly black Catholic congregation in the United States. With 2,740 families and almost 6,000 parishioners, it is a formidable institution. It inhabits an impressive building, even if St. Landry Church, just a few blocks north, is older and somewhat grander.

Holy Ghost is a solidly built redbrick structure with stained glass windows. Its long, narrow chapel is adjoined by well-kept lawns and a new multipurpose hall, while newly renovated rectory offices are across the street. Inside the church, a stunning series of stained glass windows are inscribed with the seven principles of Kwanzaa: *Umoja* (unity), *Kujichagulia* (self-determination), *Ujima* (collective work and responsibility), *Ujamaa* (cooperative economics), *Nia* (purpose), *Kuumba* (creativity), and *Imani* (faith).

Father Lester Limpele, who ministers to Holy Ghost, is a member of the Society of the Divine Word.[55] The primary mission of the society is to bring the word of God to marginalized people—the poor and the less fortunate. Lester took three vows—poverty, obedience, and chastity—before he was ordained. Assigned for his first fifteen years to parishes in Lafayette, Limpele then moved to Opelousas, and was posted to Holy Ghost Church in 2016. A solid fixture in the black church from his years in Lafayette, he captures the values of Opelousas very clearly when he describes its members as "old-school." African Americans in Opelousas "perceive family as the center of everything," he says. "They treat the church or any other public function as the center of their social life . . . People here believe that when they go to church, they have to go as a family. And whatever that they learn from their parents, that's what they going to pass on to their children. People here are very respectful. Family here is very strong."

Tammy Erwin, the assistant manager for Holy Ghost's Section 202 apartments, agrees, saying that in Opelousas it still takes a community to raise a kid. The same old-school values incline parishioners to turn to the church when they are in need. Because Opelousas is a poor community, the level of need is both high and constant. "Here, in this parish, every week, we have probably five, six, seven people come to ask for assistance," Father Limpele explains. "For everything. Light bill, buy food for their children, gas, phone bill, rental . . . I just helped somebody with a funeral . . . We keep a record of whom we help this year. So each person can get help only once a year. By doing that, we give opportunity also to other people to come in, to get help."

Holy Ghost parishioners are mainly elderly, but they do what they can for the poorest of their number. Elaine Evans explains that "we pass the hat [among] at least four organizations I am involved with. We use [the collection] to buy things for the elderly or just buy a gift card and they can do what they want with it." Father Limpele adds that most of the parish's financial support comes from older people. "Even people who have very little will sometimes give."

Money is not all that people provide for the elderly. Elaine visits people from Holy Ghost who are either too old or sick to get out of their homes, to pray with them and also just check up on them.[56] And the Holy Ghost soup kitchen serves hot lunch three times a week to anyone in need. Church volunteers serve people of all ages, but Opelousas seniors are their most constant customers. John Jarvis eats meals at the Holy Ghost "diner" whenever he is able to get there. "If I get a ride, I'll go . . . Sometimes they have pretty good food over there. Yesterday they had some pretty good baked chicken and greens. They give you something healthy to eat. Snap beans."

An interfaith network of churches and volunteers staffs the local food bank.[57] It was the brainchild of Deborah Ryan, the pastoral secretary of her church. In 2000, her priest asked Deborah to go to a diocesan council on poverty and take some notes for him. "So I went and I saw the numbers just in my parish alone, much less how bad the state truly was—figures don't lie, you know?" She came back and told her priest. The following summer, he asked her to go observe a food bank and then to start one that she would take charge of under the auspices of the Opelousas Area Ministerial Alliance. Food drives began and volunteers started popping up. The organization has been virtually all-volunteer since 2002. Most of the volunteers could be receiving food from the food bank themselves, but choose to give their time to helping others. The elderly look out for one another.

Lydia Chevalier's small nonprofit rehabilitates the homes of low-income seniors, most of whom are in their seventies and eighties. Her crew is entirely made up of volunteers, most of them recruited via the church. Lydia considers the endeavor her personal contribution to a community of elders who sacrificed to have what little they own. Every spring, the board of her organization chooses homes in need of rehabilitation and works with volunteers to transform them. Her mission is both pragmatic and symbolic: she aims to keep people in their homes, but also to protect their dignity.

When you look at that little home, and you say, "Oh my God, I think
we need to tear it down and get her in a project, or get her in an
assisted living or something," you're talking about what they worked
for all their lives. The little land that they own.

So you're talking about who they actually are, that identifies that person. That's why they're healthier in their own home . . . They learn how
to do without, but they're proud. So they don't [tell anyone] that they
have been without water for five years in the bathtub. They just make
do. They don't share the little things, or they don't complain. If they
don't have anybody to do it, they just kind of improvised, you know?

In 2016, Lydia's organization fixed up eighteen houses in Opelousas, eight of which were sufficiently dilapidated to qualify for funding
support from the "Section 504" home repair program of the US Department of Agriculture Rural Development Office. This federal funding
stream provides loans and grants to address the problems of homes
belonging to the low-income elderly.[58] The local bank in Opelousas
partners with Lydia as the fiscal agent, receiving and disbursing the
funds while Lydia handles the paperwork. The bank also oversees the
list of repairs that Lydia guarantees her organization will complete.

Annabel Carter's housing situation haunted Lydia because her house
was basically unfit for habitation. "I dream about her at night," Lydia
says. "She was the reason that God sent this USDA program. I know it
had to be. She had mold in her house because they couldn't turn their
water off because of a broken pipe in the tub. So they had a drip. The
mold had been spreading . . ."

Annabel's husband died of cancer, a condition that Lydia is sure was
affected by the mold. By the time he passed away, the house was tip-
ping over. "The pillars was sinking in," Lydia recalls. "If we didn't get
it fixed soon, it was going to [create] a foundation problem and [under-
mine] the floor. But that was all from that leak in the bathroom where
the floor was going, and over that was putting water in that area, you
know? One little leak was just doing the whole thing."

Conservatives might wonder why it takes a federal program to take
care of leaky plumbing. Some people in Opelousas would say that Lydia

is coddling people who should learn to take care of themselves. She bristles at the notion. "They make so small of the person or the situation. You know, 'Why you didn't get a plumber?' Well, there's a lot of [situations] where you couldn't. They don't understand."

What the state and the church cannot provide, family members are often called upon to deliver. Most elderly Americans, even if they are middle-class, have to rely on kin. The long arc of reciprocity matters even more for the low-income seniors. Tammy Erwin has often seen this ethic at work. "We have a lot of people that their kids take care of everything for them," she notes. "They come in and help clean for them. Pay their bills." Sons and daughters who are economically stable or live nearby are in the best position to assist their aging relatives, even if their parents avoid depending on them unless they absolutely have to.

Adult children who are not as vulnerable as their parents can be very helpful. Annabel can turn to one of her thirty grandchildren when the need arises. She is fortunate to have them nearby to do chores and check up on her regularly. But adult children who are doing well do not always extend support—in time or money—to a retired parent. Lorna Rideau's daughter, for example, lives in Lafayette, is married, and has three daughters of her own. She rarely comes around to visit Lorna, because she is busy working as a lawyer in Baton Rouge. Her husband also commutes for his work, as a doctor at a prison. Lorna is proud of their success and delights in her granddaughters. But she doesn't benefit from her daughter's good fortune.

On the other hand, the problems that beset the elderly poor are often a long time in the making, and have impacted the generations before and after them. When adult children are themselves poor and work hard at low-wage jobs, they are not as available. Zadie Joubert's daughters work at Walmart and a local restaurant chain; one of them is studying to be a registered nurse. They can't give so freely to their mother.

When poverty becomes an intergenerational condition, retired people—even those who are poor—may in fact experience pressure to send assistance in the other direction, to help their adult children. Valerie Miller's daughter is married to a violent man, and on more than one occasion has had to lean on her mother for comfort and support.

Valerie came back from church one Sunday and caught her son-in-law choking her daughter. "I'm just praying for her," she says, shaking her head. The two of them still live together, leaving Valerie to worry about her daughter's safety. Valerie tries to ease the pressure by giving them some money, which is why she took out a mortgage to cover her daughter's car payments.

Zadie's neighbor, who is elderly and reliant on SSI as well, has grown kids who always drop by early in the month. They know her checks arrive in that first week and are looking for a share. "Every time she gets her check, her grown children want money," Zadie observes. "They always come to her wanting money."

MODEST EXPECTATIONS

"Managing" is a fine art that poor retirees in Opelousas have learned out of necessity. Yet it is also a state of mind. People like Valerie and Annabel are determined to take care of themselves and, at the same time, have no illusions about what standard of living they can reasonably expect. Unlike many of the more fortunate white-collar and blue-collar workers in this book who are bitter and vocal over their pension losses, Opelousans of this generation have come to the conclusion that nothing is going to change, since they never had much economic security to begin with.

They make do in a determined fashion because they see no other possible course of action. "I'm going to make it, because you see me," says Valerie. She has experienced privation nearly all of her life. Hardened by years in poverty, she knows she is prepared for what she faces now.[59] It doesn't daunt her. "A lot of people sometimes wonder how you're making it, but you manage to know—you're going to survive." John Jarvis has a similar outlook: just do the best you can. "My 'niece' cooks, you know," he says, referring to a young friend. "Whatever it is to eat, we eat. But we try to manage it to live."

And there is always the possibility that life will improve. This is more than a pipe dream. Even Opelousas elders who have been working poor most of their lives have experienced some moments of upward mobility along the way. When there happens to be more than one income in the household, or a job materializes at the general hospital, things do genuinely look up. The elderly poor are not destined from the beginning to stay where they are now. For most, the periods of good fortune do not last long enough to create a permanent cushion, and rough patches turn into more permanent problems. But at times, even some of the poorest people in Opelousas have done well for themselves.

Valerie Miller is a case in point. She grew up in extreme hardship and in the early years of her marriage, her family was struggling.

> I had to clean houses . . . for five dollars a day. Five dollars a day . . . I can, you know, always manage. Like I told my kids when they went through school. My husband wasn't making but twenty-five dollars a week [as a carpenter] . . . I had the first two kids eleven months apart. I was seventeen [when I got married]. And then my husband worked and we managed.
>
> We managed very good because [I wouldn't say] "I want to go to the store and get something." I wasn't that type of person . . . He would do carpenter work . . . I did house [cleaning] work. We didn't have no babysitter. It's like, one day he go to work, the next day he stay home with the kids and I go to work. That's how we did it until he started working [more] and making a little bit more money.

Their fortunes improved over time, but they still had to be very careful with their money and school their children in the art of managing on a tight budget.

> Then my husband started making like seventy-five dollars [a week] . . . I'm not a person to waste that money . . . They used to laugh after my kids when they go to school because they didn't have no name-brand tennis shoes . . . I told my kids, "When you finish school and you go work, you'll get your name-brand tennis shoes." And they did it too . . . They wasn't perfect. But I ain't never had no problem with my kids.

Eventually Valerie and her husband did well enough that they were able to boost their kids up out of poverty and into middle-class occupations. "We have one daughter and three sons," she explains.

We did good, me and my husband. [The kids] went to school like I said. They [all] finished. My daughter went to college. My baby son went to college. My oldest son, he graduated in Waco, TX, to be a truck driver . . . That's why he can drive anywhere. In snow, anything. The one living [in] Lafayette, he finished high school but he didn't want to go to college. As long as he didn't get into trouble, it's okay.

They all finished school at Opelousas Senior High . . . The baby son's name is Mitchell and he lives in Houston. He's a band director. He writes and teaches music. My son Mark, he works for Moss Motors in Lafayette. My oldest son lives in Maryland. He's a truck driver. My daughter's a teacher in Baton Rouge.

Lorna Rideau is an example of both inter- and intragenerational upward mobility. She was born in the late 1940s in Houston and grew up in Opelousas. With her smooth, lightly freckled skin, brown eyes, and white hair braided behind her back, she looks youthful for her age, although she uses a walker and moves slowly. Growing up, Lorna lived with her grandparents, who were among the first African Americans to receive Social Security. "I kept hearing them talking about old age pension," Lorna remembers. At its inception in the 1930s, the Social Security program specifically excluded agricultural and domestic workers, occupations that were almost entirely African American. It took several decades before a succession of amendments to the original legislation incorporated those workers.[60]

Lorna ended her education at fifteen and married her high school sweetheart. She was a housewife for many years, a period of financial stress since her husband was never able to get better than minimum-wage jobs. When they divorced, she went to college for a degree in fine arts, then went to technical school and became a licensed practical nurse. She worked in hospitals and nursing homes for nineteen years thereafter, and did pretty well for herself. "My first nursing job when I got out of school—I mean, I couldn't believe—at the time for me that was a lot, a lot, a lot of money."

Lorna came up in poverty and remained poor in her early married years, but she pulled herself up through her own determination. Once she had the nursing degree she needed, she was able to manage well, until her own poor health took her out of the labor market.

FOR MILLIONS OF Americans who have come into retirement with imploding pensions and disappearing health care plans, betrayal is their most palpable emotion. The Teamsters, Verizon workers, United Airlines engineers, and Detroit's civil servants all experienced the anger that comes with losing a future on which they had depended because they had earned it. For the elderly poor of Opelousas, the atmosphere surrounding retirement is different. Many grew up in conditions that differed only by degree from the sharecropping deprivation common throughout the southern states in the aftermath of the Civil War. They were born to farmers; they worked in the fields; they had no shoes. Only by dint of hard work have they managed to stabilize their families, and for many, comfort was never truly possible.

As adults they worked in jobs that taxed their bodies, provided only modest incomes, and rarely offered pensions or any margin to save. They may have been part of the gray labor force for a while, but they experienced such debilitating health problems that they couldn't work any longer. They "retired" when they simply could not go on. Their paychecks stopped arriving because they couldn't stand, hold anything, or even breathe properly. And for many, that spelled a deeper experience of poverty, especially in Louisiana, where public benefits are meager and the punishing toll of sales taxes and fees make life more expensive.

Betrayal is not the emotion they feel, even if, in a larger sense, the country has abandoned them from the get-go. They have struggled to stabilize themselves and are proud if they have accomplished that goal. Self-sufficiency, pride in independence, and "making do" are the themes they dwell on in talking about their life histories. For those who are deeply religious, there is comfort in the embrace and fellowship of the church, and in the support it offers through its nonprofit extensions. It is the leaders of such organizations who more often express outrage at the diminished circumstances of older Opelousans. They recognize that in a country as wealthy as this one, the elderly poor deserve better.

Historic Twenty-Fifth Street in Ogden, Utah, which has the lowest inequality and the largest proportion of middle-class residents of any city in the United States. Although it has had its economic ups and downs, Ogden has recovered from many of its losses and capitalized on its attractive location at the foot of the Wasatch Mountain Range.

7

KEEPING THE PROMISE

by Rebecca Hayes Jacobs

While the American middle class is under economic assault in many parts of the country, Ogden, Utah, is bucking that tide.[1] Indeed, Utah is the number-one state in the country for income *equality*. The Ogden-Clearfield metropolitan area is the most egalitarian region in the state and in the United States as a whole.[2] With 60 percent of its population in the middle class, Ogden and its neighboring communities have the narrowest income gap among all of America's metropolitan statistical areas with 500,000 people or more.[3] As a result, Ogden is a community where people are more likely to live a good life in their working years and be able to retire comfortably.

Utah's good fortune is partly due to the ongoing contributions of the federal government, particularly from the second half of the twentieth century through the present. In states like Louisiana, New York, or Massachusetts, extremes of wealth and poverty are far greater and more ubiquitous than in Utah, where the bedrock of employment—especially in the Ogden area—is strengthened by the relatively stable presence of the Air Force and the Internal Revenue Service.

In addition, life in Ogden is heavily influenced by the moral codes of the Church of Jesus Christ of Latter-Day Saints (the LDS Church), also known as the Mormon faith. It is a place where conservative beliefs in self-reliance coincide in very concrete ways with an ethos of care for others. The notion that people should take care of themselves is integrated into a religious sentiment that all the world's people deserve care. Everyone is your neighbor, your brother, your sister. Retirees who are members of the LDS Church have strong family ties and insist on remaining productive members of their community. Support for the aged of all faiths is largely organized through private means and based on strong family social bonds, a powerful culture of volunteerism and service, and a Christian desire to help the poor.[4]

In some respects, Ogden is similar to Opelousas. Both cities have religious underpinnings that foster active religious and secular volunteer groups, which seek to serve their members and the broader community. But in Opelousas, there is a limit to the effectiveness of the faith-based "charity" model. In spite of the valiant efforts of people like Lydia Chevalier, the hard economic realities of life in Opelousas make it difficult to build on volunteers' efforts and create systemic change, through either local churches or federal support.

In Ogden, the combined economic power of the LDS Church and the federal government has made volunteer organizations much more elaborate and effective. Although Ogdenites rarely speak of the government's role in their good fortune, they have significantly benefited from mid- to late-twentieth-century policies that sent wealth, jobs, and government contracts to the Sun Belt and the West, spurring a diversified, strong economy in northern Utah.[5]

Utah's relative economic equality makes a difference for retirees like Louise and Randy Nathanson, who are living a meaningful and stable retirement in Ogden. Members of the LDS Church, the Nathansons live in a midsize western-style ranch house with a tidy yard and freshly cut front lawn. It lies off a busy thoroughfare, where a Smith's grocery store and chain restaurants give way to the hilly, winding streets of North Ogden. The majestic Wasatch Mountains lie off to the east, providing dramatic scenery for the Nathansons' daily walk through their neighborhood. Louise and Randy know most of their neighbors well and wave to them as they stroll around the area. Many are members of the same church "ward," an LDS name for a congregation. Sundays find them all together just up the hill from where the Nathansons live.[6]

Randy and Louise both came from families of modest means, and they were able to do better for themselves thanks to work opportunities they found through both church contacts and the federal government. Randy is seventy-two years old, wiry, with thick glasses that make his eyes look large and thinning white hair that still shows traces of his life as a blond. Natives of Ogden, Louise and Randy met on a blind date in 1966, when they were students at a local college, and were married eighteen months later. By the time Randy graduated in 1970, he was drafted by the military and sent to Montana to train for the Air Force. Louise relocated as well, and their first two kids were born a stone's throw from the base runways.

At the end of Randy's service, they pulled up stakes and moved back to Utah to live with Louise's widowed mom. Randy had picked up a lot of skills in the Air Force, and without much trouble he landed a job as a clerk with the railroad. Eventually they moved into their own home, which they could easily afford with Randy's good union job. They started settling into their roles, with Randy as breadwinner and Louise at home with the kids.

They soon discovered that Randy's union wage came with a lot of inconvenient night shifts. "Sometimes he'd have a day job and then have to return only eight hours later to start a night shift at midnight," Louise recalls. Eventually, though, Randy became a crew dispatcher, which stabilized his schedule, and he rose through the ranks of the union leadership. Louise thought they were set for life. The job came with a pension, and they could look forward to a secure retirement.

It was not to be. After thirteen good years, the Great Salt Lake causeway that the railroad crossed over washed out due to repeated heavy rains, and the railroad had to be moved away from Ogden. The Nathansons' kids were still small. "They closed the [repair] shops," Louise remembers. "They closed everything . . . We decided to take a buyout from the railroad. It was a lot of money, but when you have five children, that money doesn't last very long."

This was the first real setback in their lives, and they lost their bearings. They bought a big car to carry their children without knowing exactly how they would pay for it. "Bad choice!" Randy says ruefully. They wound up spending part of the money from the buyout on it. But they had faith that everything would work out. "I think the Lord had a good hand in . . . I just know that He was there," Randy says.

Indeed, after a rough patch, Randy landed on his feet—because unlike unemployed workers in the rust belt or in Opelousas, Ogden residents had options. The federal government rarely experiences the kind of boom/bust employment cycles that impact industries like auto manufacturing, trucking, or oil. It is significantly more stable than the municipal government in Detroit, which is subject to the ups and downs of a local tax base. To boot, Randy had a strong support network through the LDS Church, which stepped up to help as he sought a new job. After Randy was laid off by the railroad in January 1988, a temporary position with the local branch of the Internal Revenue Service materialized almost immediately. He stayed at the IRS for only five or six months; by August he had secured a job at Hill Air Force Base, just south of Ogden, working hard on the midnight shift putting big disks in a computer. A permanent position in accounting followed. He hardly missed a beat.

The wages were high and the benefits were good. Randy would have preferred a defined benefit pension, but in a place like Ogden, unlike other parts of the country, a 401(k) plan with government matching was enough to shore up his retirement. Given the affordability of the area and the Nathansons' modest mortgage, the family didn't need to dip into that 401(k) until they retired.

Most families in Ogden can still live well on one breadwinner's salary. Like many LDS women, Louise was a stay-at-home mom, raising their five children for several decades. Only when the children were grown did she decide to become a schoolteacher. In the late 1980s, she sought recertification at a local college and went to Ogden city schools to apply for a teaching job. She knew people through her church who worked at a neighborhood school, and they helped her get started as a fill-in while a permanent teacher was on maternity leave. Louise taught fourth grade for ten years, then switched to kindergarten. Most of her students were from Catholic Latino immigrant families. She retired after twenty-five years of teaching, but she stays in touch with the Latino families in the neighborhood whose children attended the school where she worked for so many years.

The Nathansons' experience is a mirror image of what happens to people who are unemployed in Opelousas. Tight social networks in Louisiana cannot overcome the challenge of living in a region with few job opportunities apart from low-wage positions at the casino or in fast food, coupled with historically racist hiring practices in the best industries. Ogden, too, is a tight-knit community, but this predominantly white community also has relatively low unemployment and an abundance of good job opportunities in federal government, health care, and manufacturing.[7] Personal networks there are rich with leads on employment, especially for members of the LDS Church.

For the Nathansons, government employment has bequeathed stability in retirement that residents of Opelousas would be overjoyed to have but can rarely attain. "We weren't rich before," Louise remarks, "and we're not rich now," but they are comfortable and secure. In addition to Randy's 401(k), Louise gets a teacher's pension and has a small 401(k) of her own. They have health problems, but their health care is taken care of. Because Randy had worked for the railroad for thirteen years, Louise explains,

> when we reached retirement age, and we went to apply for Medicare, he had enough time to qualify for railroad retirement. It's really been a blessing for us . . . This one medicine that I'm supposed to take is ten thousand dollars a month. And we [only] have to pay an eighty-dollar copay . . . My husband's had heart surgery, right now has a low[-grade] form of leukemia. We haven't had to pay for anything. It's all been covered.

Most of the Nathansons' children still live close by. Randy and Louise have thirteen grandchildren and are able to spend a great deal of time surrounded by family. Louise putters around the kitchen cutting up watermelons in anticipation of their next visit. She is proud of her homemaking skills, like sewing and canning fruits and vegetables. "The last couple of days, I've canned sixty pints of apricot jam!" she exclaims.

Family is very important in both Opelousas and Ogden, but the divergent economic makeup of these two cities means that people in them have vastly different experiences of the role of kin in supporting people in retirement. In Opelousas, extended families are close and adult children often try to take care of their elders. But quite often the children of the elderly poor are also poor and struggling themselves; many are dependent on their parents' resources to survive, and hence are at least sometimes more of a burden than a support. This is a persistent cost of inequality. In contrast, Ogden is a place where for most families, intergenerational support unfolds without the burden of poverty.

LDS Church members, like the members of Holy Ghost Church in Opelousas, also very much value their religious community. As observant Mormons, the Nathansons attend church services every Sunday through their ward.[8] When services end, the meetings begin. The LDS Church is under the direction of male leadership known as the priesthood authority.[9] But at the local level, the LDS Church is also a lay church, which means it is run by volunteers in rotating positions, a different setup than the Catholic Church's hierarchical structure.

More than most religious organizations in the United States, LDS Church members are given ample opportunities to get involved through structured volunteer work that requires a significant weekly time commitment. At one point, Randy was his ward's "bishop"—a volunteer leadership role open to adult male members to oversee a ward. Louise, like other Mormon women, has helped to run the ward's Relief Society, an organization within the church for women to provide each other with mutual support.[10] She has also taught LDS "primary school"—religious instruction for young children provided by women.[11]

Randy and Louise have an active social life involving members of their ward. Empty nesters like the Nathansons regularly gather with other Mormon couples for a potluck dinner with chips and pasta salad piled high on plastic tables. These enjoyable social rituals quickly convert to essential support in times of crisis. Louise and Randy lost a son to cancer in the 1990s, and they received an outpouring of concern and affection throughout that difficult time.

Louise loves the way that the church connects her to other members of her ward through acts of giving. "Through the church, we have what we call a visiting teacher," she explains. The program assigns women to teach LDS doctrine to other women of various ages once a month, one on one. The volunteers dwell on the meaning of scripture during their visits, but also extend a helping hand.[12] Retirees get to both mentor someone younger and have someone looking out for them as they age, especially if they are infirm or living alone. Louise herself has several people whom she visits every month.

> If they're sick, I will help them. I will take them a meal, or I'll get someone else to take them a meal . . . We are taught to be charitable. We're not forced to be, but I have had many acts of service given to me, and especially through the death and sickness of our son. And you know, once you've had that, you never forget that feeling. You'll never miss an opportunity to help somebody else.

Louise and Randy are proud that their church is concerned not only with matters of the spirit but also with material welfare.[13] Members are instructed to follow the example of Christ, to assist the "poor and needy" and "help the people to help themselves."[14] When they retired, the Nathansons started volunteering with various organizations in their neighborhood as part of their church "calling"—a responsibility to help based on what each member as an individual uniquely has to offer the community. In their case, this involved tutoring Latino children from the area in reading. More recently, Louise and Randy have been working on a two-year voluntary senior "mission" in Ogden. Alongside several young missionaries, they try to convert people outside the faith, but also help church members in financial trouble.[15] "Sometimes we helped people move," they explain. "We took people places. Sometimes we'd end up helping with kids . . . We've helped people clean their house. We kind of taught people self-sufficiency."

The support the Nathansons provide extends well beyond the Mormon community. This way of operating in the world spreads social protection and funnels resources to all kinds of people in need, including those who are not LDS Church members, while enabling retired church members like Louise to serve in roles that matter. At one point, for instance, Louise tutored a boy whose family had recently emigrated from Mexico. The family was undocumented, with three children, including an infant. One day the father was apprehended by Immigration and Customs Enforcement (ICE), who kept him in a detention facility for two years. For that whole stretch, Louise left the mother diapers on her doorstep.

The Nathansons do not see themselves as particularly lucky for being able to maintain a middle-class life as they age—they are just living it. But the presence of federal employment, coupled with strong social networks in a prosperous church that preaches mutual aid, have made it much easier for them to get by in retirement than it would be if they lived in Opelousas, where there are no such opportunities.

In concert with the LDS Church goal to proselytize and convert all people to the Mormon faith is a belief that no one should be left out of its bounty in this life, or in the afterlife. The belief that wealth should be shared is not unique to the Mormons: it is indicative of a broader "moral language" in American life, which Robert Bellah and his coauthors described in their celebrated 1985 book *Habits of the Heart*.[16] However, as inequality soars, Ogden is better at implementing this communitarian moral code than are many other places across the United States today. In other American communities, the values of commitment and mutual aid are present, but not dominant.

Among other effects of the mutual aid philosophy is the fact that in Ogden, and northern Utah more broadly, there is a strong community commitment to helping individuals create a secure, satisfying retirement. Those values, coupled with the wealth brought by the prominent role of federal government in the region, have made Ogden a place where retirees can thrive.

THE PLACE AND ITS POSSIBILITIES

Like most western cities, Ogden spreads out in a gridiron pattern, with straight streets and avenues set perpendicular to one another, forming large square blocks. With the snow-capped Wasatch Mountains rising on the east side of town and rail yards slashing along the west, Ogden unfurls on a north-south axis. Located forty miles from Salt Lake City, it is the northernmost stop on the commuter rail line, making this city of 86,000 people a bookend for the urban development that has sprung up east of the Great Salt Lake.[17] (The overall Ogden-Clearfield metropolitan area has a population of 665,000.)[18] Past the eastern edge of town, the rugged beauty of the Ogden Valley is known not only to locals but also to tourists, who come from near and far.

Washington Boulevard, one of the city's main thoroughfares, is a commercial strip lined with fast-food outlets and car repair shops. Near the center of town, it morphs into a civic axis, with landmarks such as Ogden City Hall and the Ogden Temple—an imposing house of prayer for members of the LDS Church—anchoring a mix of offices, hotels, restaurants, theaters, and shops. The newer and larger of these businesses, equipped with parking facilities and catering to an upper-middle-class clientele, create an entirely different character from the older, smaller, more eclectic storefronts that still predominate on some blocks. Intersecting Washington Boulevard is Twenty-Fifth Street, the town's revitalized historic "Main Street," with yoga studios, cafés, and vintage boutiques next to an older generation of bars and a diner. Past these businesses, the street terminates at the defunct but physically preserved Union Station, now a museum.

Some parts of Ogden are more prosperous than others, but the differences between rich and poor neighborhoods are less stark here than in states like Louisiana. The nicest residential neighborhoods nestle up against the mountains to the east, with easy access to hiking paths and other outdoor recreation activities. Here the homes, while not palatial, are well kept, with flowering plants and trees in the yard.

Moving west and down the hill, to the flatter areas in the heart of downtown, one finds houses in need of repair. Paint is flaking and

porches visibly sag. A modest middle-class exodus from the center of
the city occurred several decades ago, but the blocks remain mostly
intact. Working people have hunkered down and preserved the neighborhoods as best they could. Twenty-first-century residential development is filling in the areas that were once demolished. A lot of retired
people living on fixed incomes find homes in these neighborhoods.
Those low-income residents, many of whom are not LDS, benefit from
northern Utah's broad social safety net, maintained through an informal public-private network of religious and nonprofit institutions.

Ogden certainly feels the presence of the LDS Church, but it is not
a homogeneous city. Diversity is rooted in its history, which makes it
unique in the state. Utah historically has had a large, predominant LDS
population. But Ogden, a railroad town, has long attracted trade and
non-Mormons.

Utah is known as the "Beehive State" because of the apiary's symbolic meaning for LDS pioneers.[19] Beginning in 1847, after decades of
violent persecution in the Northeast and Midwest, Mormon pioneers
made their way by the thousands to the Great Salt Lake Basin. Out of
necessity, they lived an austere lifestyle.[20] The nineteenth-century leaders of the LDS Church drew on references to the honeybee in Mormon
scripture to encourage industriousness in the pioneers as they weathered challenging conditions.[21] This is the backdrop to the church's continued emphasis on self-reliance and collective survival.[22]

Of course, it makes a difference that Utah Mormons are largely
white, Republican, and well educated. They marry young and have
larger than average families. Their incomes are higher than the national
average, and LDS women are less likely to work outside the home than
other American women.[23] These features contrast sharply with Opelousas, where a history of racial discrimination, weak education, low-wage
employment, and less-conventional family structures—common consequences of economic inequality—create greater burdens.

Ogden's history as a railroad town goes back a century and a half:
the Union Pacific and Central Pacific railroads met at Promontory
Summit near Ogden in 1869. Because of this history, Ogden's LDS population has been particularly integrated with other communities. The

city has long had a significant working-class population, including the descendants of Chinese and Japanese laborers brought in to build the railroad. Defense Depot Ogden, which operated in the town for decades, and the large Air Force base just south of town have also brought people of all races and religions into the Ogden orbit. In 2014, 63 percent of Utahns identified as LDS members, but Weber County (which contains Ogden) was only 58 percent Mormon and the city itself even less so.[24]

Although Ogden is more prosperous than Opelousas, it has had its own challenges. The center of the city went through a serious economic decline in the 1970s–90s after the railroad left town. Only in recent years has it experienced economic growth and new development along the downtown shopping streets. Even with the new development, many stores along Washington Boulevard are either struggling or shuttered. Ogden still has its share of urban ills, which affect seniors living in the city. It has a high rate of homelessness for Utah, a high proportion of the state's struggling veterans, and a higher crime rate than many other places in the state.[25]

In the last few decades, Ogden has seen an influx of Catholic Latino families, some of whom are undocumented. They are attracted by work opportunities in construction, agriculture, and the service industries.[26] LDS Church doctrine has encouraged its members to take a more accepting stance toward these newcomers than what they might encounter in states like Arizona.[27] Unlike some of her more conservative neighbors, Louise Nathanson welcomes these families, a sentiment honed over the years she devoted to teaching the children of first-generation immigrants at her elementary school.[28] She appreciates the ways in which her immigrant neighbors, like LDS pioneers of previous generations, came to Utah in search of a better life. But Louise's perspective is not universal. The newcomers have been targeted by the police, and other longtime residents have had a mixed response to them.[29]

DAY-TO-DAY ECONOMICS

Ogden's mix of industries and employers has made it a good place to live. Jack Lachlan and his wife Margaret, who live up the road from the Nathansons, were raised in the city in the 1960s. "It was a great place to grow up," Jack recalls.

> We could ride our bikes everywhere, lots of kids to play with, everybody watched out for everybody else. I have really great memories. The schools were good. Good home life . . . You've got a river running right through town . . . Our parents were able to work . . . Hill Air Force Base; the IRS was in town. They were solid employers. The railroad was a big employer for a lot of the kids growing up, too. And there was a lot of medical care in the town. It was a good mix. And you had a college town too, because you had Weber State.

The Lachlans recognize that they have benefited from the good life that northern Utah's economic stability made possible for much of the twentieth century. The contrast with Opelousas is stark. Southern Louisiana has depended on low-wage agriculture, derived few advantages from the oil industry (which is too far away to be a source of employment for many Opelousans), and has struggled to find an economic "play" that could enhance the job base. There's no sign of the federal government there. The best that Opelousas town leaders have been able to do is to attract low-wage service industries such as gambling and warehouse distribution, and even this has created only a paltry number of jobs compared to the number of people who need work. None of those jobs carry retirement benefits on par with the kind that are typical in Ogden.

If anything, Ogden's advantages are multiplying. Over the last half-century, jobs have moved from the rust belt to "right to work" states like Utah, and companies have been attracted by "business friendly" corporate tax policies in the West.[30] Defense contracts also have been funneled to western states, particularly Utah. The Air Force base and the IRS office provide jobs that pay well and offer great health care, pensions, and generous 401(k)s. Subcontractors and ancillary industries that support the federal jobs create a positive ripple effect.

To be sure, Ogden is not immune to hard times, and federal employment is not as plentiful as it once was. But the city's organizational resources enable a more effective response to downturns, too. When Defense Depot Ogden closed in 1997, for example, the city created Business Depot Ogden in the same space, and encouraged employment in tech and advanced manufacturing to replace some of those lost government jobs. Tom Christopulos, director of community and economic development for the city of Ogden, describes the process.[31]

> The Defense Depot was one of the first base conversions in the United States. So we took that roughly fifteen thousand acres and converted it. Now there's sixty-some-odd companies, a little over six thousand employees, that are out there. And that's all happened since 2004. [It's] been one of the major [sources of] job creation . . . Call centers, manufacturing work, and technology work. And it's very specialized. We have small bicycle manufacturing companies, all the way to Hershey's. You can come in and work part-time, because we're running, right now, about 3.5 to 3.7 percent unemployment, so they've had to come in with flex shifts, and attract a lot of people so that they can get more people into the work force. So that helps a little bit with some of the retirees that want to go back to work or need to supplement incomes.

Manufacturing is now a strong part of Ogden's economy. In 2014, manufacturing accounted for more than 20 percent of the gross domestic product of Ogden-Clearfield, significantly higher than the national figure of 12 percent.[32]

Another positive feature of life in Ogden is that Utah's population is in excellent health. It ranks right up there with Massachusetts, one of the healthiest states in the country, but for just over half the annual cost per person—$5,013 versus $9,278.[33] This good fortune reflects the fact that Utah residents are relatively young, well educated, and healthy, since Mormon custom dictates abstention from alcohol and tobacco. In addition, strong social networks and large families provide support when people get sick. Typically, Utahns are discharged from hospitals sooner and receive home health care more rapidly than in other parts of the country. For example, Medicare hospital patients in Utah spent an average of 0.83 inpatient days in the hospital, compared to 1.42 days nationally.[34] Because the population is generally healthy, the hospital and health care system in Utah is one of the best in the country for all demographic groups, including seniors and those with a low income.

Alongside good health, the region boasts a flourishing health care industry, whose jobs compare favorably to those at the Opelousas general hospital. For example, Intermountain Healthcare, the largest hospital system and insurer in Utah, has a major hospital in downtown Ogden that still offers its employees modest defined benefit pension plans in addition to a 401(k) with employer matching, a decision that its management explains is both value-driven and economically sound.[35] Elsewhere in the United States, defined benefit pensions in the highly competitive health care sector have all but disappeared.

Ogden's low consumer costs also make retirement easier. Housing and food are less expensive than in many other parts of the United States with good job opportunities. As a result, home ownership and upkeep is more affordable, even for those residents whose companies are cutting back on pensions. Not only is household income relatively high in Ogden, but it stretches further, too. "The average wage right now is around thirteen dollars an hour entry-level," Tom Christopulos points out. "So with the cost of living and cost of earnings at the entry level, it's still possible for people to buy homes in the area."

Northern Utah is both affordable and well supplied with job opportunities, in contrast to Opelousas, which has inexpensive housing but few jobs. In Ogden, the median household income is $41,036, and the median property value is $129,800.[36] Opelousas has a median household income of $20,434, and the median property value is $88,300.[37] The ratio of income to property values in Ogden is thus more favorable for homebuyers than in Opelousas. In other words, relative to income, homes in Ogden are in fact more affordable. And that advantages retirees both in their working years and in their retirement lives, exacting less financial stress across the lifespan.

RETIREMENT AND CULTURAL VALUES WITHIN THE LDS CHURCH

> [I have so] many opportunities to just serve others . . . Looking around
> you and seeing needs that people have, food that needs to be brought in,
> helping out with a young child that needs to read, or is sick and needs
> the parents to have a night out. That's how I want to spend a lot of my
> retirement—just reaching out to others.
>
> —Christine Ericson, retired early education professor
> and LDS Church member

Between family obligations, church activities, and volunteer hours with
local organizations, there are many ways that middle-class LDS retirees occupy themselves in retirement.

Mormons are expected to rely first on themselves, and compared to
Opelousas—where poverty has often left people disabled and without
any retirement savings—in the LDS community self-reliance is more
economically feasible. But if LDS members do need help, there is a specific order in which they are expected to ask for support. Todd Wilson,
an LDS doctor from Ogden in his fifties, describes the ranking:

> The church's philosophy is, when you have need, you lean on your
> family first, the church second, and the government is your last resort.
> And so the church prepares itself, and its members, to be able to be
> self-sufficient, to help one another, and to help when needed from
> church resources. So low-income members of the church can, I think,
> be relatively assured that when they're able to contribute, and they
> have a need that's legitimate—not a want, but a need—that that need
> will be met.

The support comes with expectations, however. It is neither open-
ended nor free of reciprocal obligation, including for those members in
their sixties and seventies. The Mormon ethos is conceived as a counter-
model to a "welfare mentality" or a one-way charity, as Todd explains:

> If somebody's just given something, it tends to devalue them. And their
> self-worth lessens. And they start to become dependent. The goal is

to have people be independent and to feel valued and to feel capable. So, the church adapts opportunities to an individual's capacity . . . There's going to be an opportunity for you to give and to serve and an expectation that you're going to do that, to have your own needs met.

So there's less reliance on social programs, and a greater reliance on local community members. Because of that there's more connection and there's more opportunity. And so people feel more elevated and more capable and less dependent in a community like this.

The Mormon philosophy can regard government support as a very last resort because the LDS Church has an abundance of wealth that supports people throughout their lives. In Opelousas, even the most generous church donations and heroic volunteer efforts can only go so far to support people in need. In Ogden, LDS Church members who are struggling can reliably access food and other basic supplies from a food bank called the "bishop's storehouse."[38] The private welfare system is well organized and suited to the individual in need.

This help is not simply as an act of charity. True to a very American definition of virtue, those in need must perform work in return and demonstrate that they are seeking gainful employment. Jay Phillips, a doctor and the president of his "stake" (an agglomeration of local Mormon wards), captures this mix of moral virtues well:

> The system is meant to get people back on their feet. It's not meant for long-term assistance, although there are some cases where employment is not going to happen just because of physical limitations or disabilities. Anyone who receives welfare assistance from the church can also do something to help . . . It may be just a couple of hours a week, but most of the time this is meant to be short-term, to get them back being productive.
>
> Each ward has an employment specialist. We also have a stake employment specialist, and I get a report every month: how many members are out of work, and what the status is of their job search.

Usually it's a very small number, less than ten. And most of them have jobs, they're just looking for new jobs to upgrade.

Anywhere else in the United States, this kind of service would be professionalized and supported by tax dollars. In Utah, it is provided for free on the back of volunteer labor.

The Mormon perspective differs from that in Opelousas, where seniors see the value of government intervention for helping those in need, but are routinely frustrated with how little help they actually receive. African American members of the Opelousas Catholic and Protestant churches subscribe to the value of self-reliance—after all, many of them were raised in an agricultural community, where growing one's own food would help families get by when cash was scarce. But they were never able to build up savings, due to the meager wages they made in industries with no retirement benefits whatsoever. When their bodies break down, often at a much younger age than those of the white LDS residents of Ogden, African Americans in Opelousas see the value in federal programs like Medicaid and SNAP. It is much easier for white LDS members—who are connected to one of the nation's wealthiest private religious organizations, and for whom abundant job opportunities with benefits are the norm—to believe that self-reliance will be sufficient.

This is not to say that white LDS retirees have it easy. They still face the challenges of aging while taking care of both younger and older generations. The ethical obligations of both self-reliance and mutual support generate significant demands on their time. They must balance the obligation to care for others in their broader community with the need to care at the same time for their own grandkids and other family members.

Colin and Karla Yates are among those facing this double burden. They were both born in Ogden and met in high school. Their fathers both worked for the federal government while their mothers stayed at home. They started college in Ogden, but Karla dropped out after two years. Then they moved to a small city an hour north, where Colin finished college and stocked shelves at a local grocery store while Karla did the payroll for a small cheese company. Eventually he got a master's degree in business and marketing from Utah State and took up a teaching position at a local college. But after three years the teaching dried up, so he started working at another grocery store on the night shift, stocking shelves again. Karla recalls, "The thing I appreciated as a wife was the fact that he'd be willing to go and throw groceries again just to give us something."

Money was tight for a few years. Their home, which they still own today, cost $21,000 in the mid-1970s, the equivalent of approximately $110,000 today. That seemed like a lot of money, but they had a huge garden in the backyard and could save money by growing their own vegetables. (Having a lot of kids is expensive, Karla notes, but "very useful when picking beans.") Eventually, Colin got a call from a former professor who connected him with a position at a community college in Salt Lake City. For the next thirty-seven years, he commuted back and forth between the Ogden area and Salt Lake City, leaving Karla to look after their growing family. Colin didn't have a large salary or a pension, but Salt Lake Community College offered a 401(k) with a generous employer matching program, and their mortgage was reasonable.

Both before and during retirement, Karla and Colin have taken on a lot of responsibilities connected to their church and their family. They have five children and sixteen grandchildren, and since retiring they've done a lot to help them out. "We've got a great family," Colin says, but there have been some financial problems. Karla elaborates:

> We had a son that was out of work. And he's got six children . . . The house payment was like eight hundred dollars, and an apartment would've been twelve or fourteen, so we just decided we'd pull together as a family, and some of our kids that were able to helped [pay the mortgage] . . . We covered a few house payments for them till he was able to find work.

Meanwhile, one of Karla and Colin's daughters and two of their grandchildren lived with them for ten years because her husband did not step up for his family:

Two little granddaughters have been in our home, the mother and them, for the last ten years . . . She pretty much had to stay with us. Her husband hasn't been the best supporter . . . She had a stroke when she was giving birth to the second child. And because of insurance purposes, preexisting conditions, it would be hard for her to get insurance because of the stroke. So she stayed with us so that she could work with the company here . . . then [Karla] took care of the kids.

More recently, Karla and Colin moved out of their home just south of Ogden and in with Karla's father and stepmother, who are in their nineties and live in Ogden itself, to help them in their old age. Karla does the cleaning and the cooking for them, and Colin shuttles them around to doctors' appointments, grocery shopping, and an occasional lunch at their favorite Chinese restaurant. Unlike people in their sixties and seventies in Opelousas—who will do anything to help out their grown kids, grandkids, and aging parents, but who have to sacrifice their own next meal, home repair, or car payment in order to do so—Karla and Colin can support their family and still have resources for their own comfortable retirement.

On top of devoting many hours to their own families, retirees put in long hours as volunteers in their roles within the church. "We have a lay ministry," Jay Phillips notes. "Very few people are paid." In addition to the ministry positions, there are intergenerational volunteer groups that make sure people are taken care of in times of need. Young men learn from older men, and young women and children learn from older women. These connections across generations are deliberate, says Jay. "You're sharing some of your experience, but you're also receiving back some of that energy and vitality and enthusiasm from the younger generations."

Jill Lambert is the current Relief Society president for her ward in South Ogden. She works for the phone company, but her large volunteer role in the church is really what gives her life meaning. Jill grew up in the South, but her parents were from Utah, and she knew she would eventually live there.

Jill started out as an operator for the phone company as a summer job when she was in high school, and following college she took a position as a service representative in Provo, Utah. Eventually she moved to Ogden to be near her parents. "My dad was stationed at Hill Air Force Base for his last year of his career, and he retired there," she explains. "I thought, 'I'm gonna move up by them.' So my dad acted as the general contractor, and we built a house up here in Ogden." It was a large, comfortable dwelling in the hills above Harrison Boulevard.

At the phone company, Jill worked her way up to a manager position. Eventually, as happened to the Verizon workers described in chapter 2, she found her pension frozen, her retirement health care coverage gone, and her 401(k) matching diminished. She is not thrilled about any of that as she thinks about retiring in seven years, when she hits sixty-five. Yet unlike many of the Verizon workers in Massachusetts or New Jersey, Jill lives a pleasant, happy life, largely due to the affordability of Ogden and her involvement with the LDS Church. "I like my lifestyle the way it is," she says with a laugh. "I'm single. I've never been married. No kids." Her volunteer work fills up much of her free time and gives her great pleasure.

In Opelousas, members of Holy Ghost Church can likewise expect home visits that provide religious instruction for the infirm. And there are also regular cookouts, large church gatherings where people share food on the lawn outside of Holy Ghost. The creole food festival organized by Lydia Chevalier is a major fund-raiser. But in Ogden, the LDS Church can provide such support on a much larger scale, delivering meals and coordinating services through a methodical, well-funded organization. All LDS Church members who can do so give a portion of their income as tithings to the church headquarters via their local leaders. These donations are used to maintain church facilities, support local congregations, and fund education programs and church history research.[39] LDS members also partake in a monthly "fast offering," a Sunday fast after which people donate the money they would have spent on food that day to the church.[40] Wealthy LDS families give even more through church-related charity.

With its resources, the LDS Church can meet all kinds of needs that the Holy Ghost Church in Opelousas cannot, given its parishioners' limited financial means. But money is only one factor. It also matters that people with secure retirements are able to devote themselves to full-time work organizing these kinds of privatized social safety net programs.

Christine Ericson is an LDS woman in her early seventies who not only has benefited from the visiting teaching program, but has played a leadership role in providing such services. She gazes out of the floor-to-ceiling windows of her large, newly renovated kitchen onto the brush and wildflowers at the foothills of the Wasatch Mountains.

Christine's husband, Garry, recently died of cancer, and she has received much support from her visiting teachers since her husband's death. She reciprocates by giving support to others. "Since I was in college, I've been a visiting teacher," she says.

> You just give a brief lesson [in scripture], and mostly it's checking up. "What are your needs? How can I help you?" And jumping in if there's a death in the family, if there's a new baby. You're the first one that gets called to help out and to support in times of need. Visiting teaching to me is just such a blessing. Both [as a teacher and] as someone who was visited and cared for.

Since her husband passed away, Christine has been staying busy through her church commitments. She is currently the Relief Society president for her stake, an uncompensated volunteer position that requires a tremendous amount of coordination and time. It is effectively a second job, minus the salary.

Besides formal leadership positions, there are many other ways that LDS seniors can be of service to their community. Retirees are expected to stay active as part of their responsibilities to the church, and perhaps even to do more than they were called on to contribute during their working years. As Jay Phillips puts it:

> In the church there really is no such thing as retirement. Even though you're retired from your employment, you're not retired from the church. So you're still expected to fulfill a church "calling" . . . We

hope that you'll take on even more than what you've done in the past because now you have more time, so to speak. But there are numerous volunteer assignments that we [also] ask our members to fill . . . We have what's called church welfare missions . . . And they can involve anything from food production to family history, genealogy work, to working at Temple Square doing tours in Salt Lake . . . A secondhand store and employment training center for members. The list goes on and on.[41]

When Jay retires from his medical practice at sixty-five, he and his wife plan to go on a mission wherever he is needed, either locally or abroad. The mission will make use of his medical skills, which is good for him and good for others. "Sometimes you take these people that have had this vast richness of experience throughout their whole lives and they retire and they just lose that," he says. "But in the church, we recognize that they do have those experiences, that wisdom, that knowledge that younger people don't. It'd be really foolish of us not to tap into that, and not to utilize that. And they're willing. It gives them more purpose, gives them more meaning."

Louise and Randy Nathanson, with their tutoring of children and their work at the senior mission in Ogden, provide an example of this kind of extensive volunteer work after retirement. Ron and Sally Maurer, another retired couple, also showcase the appeal of meaningful volunteerism. Ron worked for twenty years in head and neck surgery, while Sally stayed at home to raise their five children. After practicing medicine for more than forty years, Ron retired in 2013. The Maurers had been active with the church their whole lives, but they became even more involved after that point.

"I retired *to* something," Ron emphasizes. After retiring, he went back as a volunteer for two days a week, attending to missionaries who were coming home sick. "I loved working with their diseases and trying to help them in whatever way I could," he says. "And I'm certainly not the only one doing it. But the church is wonderful in that: if you ask, and if you do reasonable work, a lot of times they'll let you do things in your own field, which you did [before retirement]. And I think that's been a wonderful help."

Ron also volunteers once a week in Salt Lake City, seeing ear, nose, and throat patients there. "It's been a great experience and extension of what I was doing."

Ron feels validated by his volunteer work because it matches the skill set he built up during his career. Unlike the gray labor workers profiled in chapter 4, who spent decades developing a skill set only to have it declared irrelevant when they sought work at an older age, Ron has found volunteer work through the church that affirms his identity as a doctor even in retirement.

His wife Sally also does volunteer work that matches her own interests and skill set. She is working on a project digitizing LDS Church archives as a volunteer with the church headquarters in Salt Lake City. This kind of work reminds Sally of her work in research, writing, and reading that she did as an administrative assistant for her federal employers in Washington, DC. She also fulfills her "calling" to the church by playing the piano in LDS primary school, the religion classes for children.

Because LDS members find so much personal meaning in their work for the church, they aren't as disappointed if they don't get satisfaction from their day jobs. Their identity isn't exclusively drawn from the work that they do for income.

Jack Lachlan is sixty-two and nearing retirement from the gas company where he works. A larger company recently purchased his employer, and Jack is frustrated by the impact of the buyout. "I think we're gonna find out we worked for a great company, and a good company just bought us," he says with a laugh. "Bigger isn't better." Under the new management, the retirement plan is no longer what it used to be, and neither is the personal connection. "When I hired on it was family," Jack says. "I think it was fourteen, fifteen hundred employees or something in all. I've sat at company parties with the president. I have socialized with him, talked with him. I know who they are. They're approachable. They know me. That's not gonna happen now."

However, Jack's most important commitments in life do not come from his day job, but from his volunteer work as a lay bishop running the bishop's storehouse.

If [people are] coming to us, they're probably against a pretty hard wall . . . And you look at that skill set, no matter what they have and say, "Okay, what are your assets? What are your negatives? You tell me a plan to get from where you're at now to where you need to be, and then we'll see what we need to do to help you."

So you buy their groceries for six months; they do what they need to do, and then you don't see them again. They just had that one little bump in their life and they're good . . . The thing you realize is how many people are living check to check. That's just a reality in America. And you have one little bump in that and it dominoes. And that's what happens to a lot of these people. Either they lose their job or something major—car repair or something. So those are the things we try to balance out.

From his firsthand experience with his employer, Jack knows that companies do not always deliver on their pension promises. Perhaps because he has felt the impact of corporate changes that have been out of his control, Jack—maybe more than other people in his position within the church—realizes that self-reliance isn't necessarily possible or fair to expect of people. He knows that it can be hard to save money, even for LDS members in a place of relative wealth like northern Utah. He sees how the LDS Church plays an essential role in filling the financial gaps and making retirement work for its members.

BEYOND THE LDS CHURCH

The social work of the Church reaches out beyond the community of the faithful. People who are non-LDS can receive some help from the LDS bishop's storehouse supplies, for example, although less support than LDS members would receive, and with some strings attached—such as visits from missionaries encouraging them to join. "We would not see people go hungry, but we don't have an obligation to them," Jack Lachlan explains. "We do help nonmembers, as long as they're willing to keep some of the rules we have."

Civic life in Ogden is strong, and informal social bonds are important to the support that people provide.[42] Christine Ericson enjoys helping out her neighbors who are not LDS. "Mormons tend to reach out," she says. "When there's a health issue, a death, or anything. And [others have] reached out to me. These people, they were at [my husband's] funeral. Every one of my neighbors around are non-LDS, but every one of them went to Garry's funeral."

The tradition of responsibility for others that Mormons began in the nineteenth century laid the moral groundwork for a more generalized culture of care today. Utah has the highest rate of volunteerism in the United States.[43] Not only Mormons, but people of various denominations outside of the LDS Church as well, are involved with volunteering in both formal and informal ways. The most common form it takes in Utah is tutoring, followed by mentoring youth, collecting and preparing or distributing food, engaging in general labor, and providing management or office services.[44]

One popular program to engage with people outside the LDS community is known as JustServe. Church members and others in the community identify opportunities for service, like painting a house, clearing a path, cleaning up a park, or preparing hot meals. JustServe is open to the general public, so all families, congregations, and other organizations can look up volunteer opportunities there.[45]

That general culture of volunteerism saves the Ogden local government a substantial amount of money, which keeps taxes down. Tom Christopulos, the director of community and economic development, has seen how it helps the city:

> When we call for volunteers, people show up. In Ogden we run a marathon that's completely volunteer-oriented. It has about fifteen hundred people that are volunteers that show up . . . And they're not LDS . . . We run a concert series on a budget of fifteen thousand dollars. And everybody shows up that takes the money and serves the beer, and all the other stuff. They're all volunteers . . . When we had a bad wind storm three months ago, it took down hundreds and hundreds of trees . . . The city crews didn't even go out and get them. They were all packed and gone, just from community [volunteers] . . .

That's one of the reasons you can run a community like ours on fifty million dollars.

The money saved allows the local government to use its funding more strategically to improve the lives of low-income Ogdenites. For example, Weber Human Services is a local government agency that serves Weber and Morgan counties, providing services that range from mental health and substance abuse programs to a wellness clinic.[46] It is supported by state, federal, and local funding, but it also partners with many area nonprofits. The robust volunteer base helps it save money by keeping personnel costs down. The agency oversees a variety of volunteer programs available to seniors, including a general volunteer program, a program for seniors who want to tutor children in schools, and a senior companion program for people who are homebound. It also offers an array of services to support retirees, including thirteen senior centers with inexpensive meals, a free rides program, help doing errands, and a service that educates people on how to use the new regional transport system so they can get to Salt Lake City and other places by train. These kinds of practices are fairly routine for the LDS community, and they spill out into the larger civil society through these countywide volunteer efforts.

THE LIMITS OF SUPPORT FOR OUTSIDERS

In spite of all this support for others, there are boundaries, both geographical and cultural, that set limits to the generosity. The experience of retirement in Ogden can be decidedly more mixed for those who are not part of the LDS Church. It can be even more difficult for those who are not straight, or not white, or not US citizens. Accessing resources within the community is not as simple for them as it is for the LDS insiders.

The church rarely extends itself to retirees who are not in obvious need and express no interest in joining LDS. Fred and Paige Cantrell are a white couple in their midsixties who live in nearby Ogden Valley. Fred was a lawyer and Paige a legal secretary. They were able to afford to retire young, and moved from the Midwest to Utah eighteen years ago because they love to ski. But they haven't really felt comfortable with their LDS neighbors; none of their close friends are members of the church. This is not the community they had hoped for in retirement.

Fred is constantly reminded of the LDS presence in the area. "There's always the element of religion pervading pretty much everything," he says. "You go to a restaurant, and there will be a Zion curtain there"—a partition at the bar to separate bartenders from the patrons who order drinks, so that children can not see the drinks being made.[47]

> It's a reminder that there's a heavy, heavy religious influence in this area and you can't get away from it, and it rears its head all the time. And that annoys me. The liquor laws. The decisions of the legislature. The judiciary. Virtually every judge on the bench in this state is LDS. I don't want to say that there's pro-LDS influence in court, but I suspect that there may be.

Paige thinks she would have a hard time getting a job in the area if she needed one.

> If our financials went the wrong way and we needed to work, say back ten years ago—as marketable as we are, it would've been difficult for us to find good jobs . . . I would hate to be in the job market. There's a lot of retirees who want to come out and work part-time, and unless you've established yourself in some field, say as a teacher or something, it would be very difficult to compete.

Paige has experienced rejection by some LDS members who are particularly conservative, including the mother of a good friend, who refuses to meet her. "Some older Mormons . . . don't even associate with anyone who's not LDS. Period." Paige has cancer, and she has not had much support from her neighbors thus far, even though the chemotherapy treatment has made her hair fall out, a sign visible to everyone. She does not think her LDS neighbors would rally for her if things got worse. Although Paige's LDS neighbors may have reached out had they known she wanted support, she has accumulated enough experiences of exclusion over her years in the Ogden Valley to feel strongly that they would not spend the kind of time with her that they would with another Mormon.

LGBT residents also find Utah a difficult place to live, since Mormon doctrine is antagonistic toward their orientation. Janice Harper, a retired flight attendant, has experienced this kind of subtle discrimination in Ogden. Janice moved to Utah because it was affordable, but she came to realize that culturally it would be difficult for her. The area has its advantages: "I can buy a house here. I can't buy a house in California," she explains.

> Once you buy a house . . . then you're here. And then you start appreciating what is good about Utah. The outdoors, the nice people. You just have to get yourself away from the first shock of, "Who are these crazy Mormons? I don't want to be around them. They don't like me." You feel like you're a minority . . . People are nice to your face, [but] the religion and the culture really weren't accepting of someone like me.

Despite this feeling of cultural distance, Janice remained in Ogden because she fell in love with a woman who was tied to the community through her work as a public school administrator. They had a daughter, got settled into the place, and it became hard to leave. Janice retired a bit young, in her fifties, to be a full-time mom for her daughter, but she does not have the best retirement package from her company. "I guess you could say I lucked out because I got a pension . . . They froze pensions but I retired before they froze them," she explains. "But it's low. It's not even a thousand dollars a month. While the CEOs are making millions . . . It's frustrating when you see how much companies like [my airline] are making and how little they are giving for pensions." Adding to her frustration, her airline's retirement plan does not cover her health care.

Janice and her wife considered moving with their daughter to Portland, but they couldn't afford it. Janice gets along fine with her LDS neighbors but doesn't feel embraced by them. "I've lived next to LDS people everywhere I've lived. And they've always been nice to me," she says. "I lived up on a very nice street in Ogden Valley, and I'd say half of the people on that street were LDS. And they were nice and the kids played together. But it's always a little bit of a distance." At least now she feels much more comfortable than she used to walking around downtown Ogden while holding her wife's hand. She hopes things will continue to improve for LGBT people in the city.

People of color in Ogden in their sixties and seventies, particularly those who are black or Latino, speak about facing systemic racism, xenophobia, and anti-immigration policies that made life more difficult. There is a long history of racial exclusion built into LDS Church doctrine: black men were not allowed into the priesthood until 1978, nor were black people permitted to partake in important temple rituals.[48] This exclusion from the symbolic rituals of the church was matched by discrimination in daily life. The best jobs went to white men, and to this day they still do, leaving many of Utah's people of color in precarious financial positions when they retire.[49]

Carmen Lee is a Catholic Latina and a member of the gray labor force. Born in the early 1940s in Colorado, she is part Native American and part South American. Her family left Colorado to come to Utah when she was ten, and she has been in Ogden ever since. She remembers the old rough-and-tumble Twenty-Fifth Street from her childhood, with its bars and restaurants next to the train station, and how the military used to unload freight there. The area was known as "Porters and Waiters," she says—"'Cause all the porters and waiters from the train would rent their rooms there and then they would eat there." Carmen's mother stayed at home and her father had a job with the Ogden City sanitation department, but he passed away before he could draw any kind of pension.

Carmen dropped out of high school because she got married at seventeen. Her first husband was abusive, and she divorced him after she had two children with him. Eventually, she had six children, four boys and two girls, and raised them all by herself. She did appreciate the LDS influence when she was dealing with the kids on her own in the

1960s. "It was so easy to raise children here in Utah," she says. "The biggest thing that they could think to do was drink beer sometimes on the sneaks. So it was real easy for me."

She has had a series of low-wage jobs in manufacturing, government, the service industry, and the nonprofit sector to support her family. "I have struggled, but it's made me a better person," she confesses. As a young woman, she worked for a cosmetics manufacturer, inspecting the perfume bottles as they came down the assembly line. She waited tables at several restaurants for a while, and she worked in shipping and receiving for a time at the Air Force base. Eventually, Carmen got involved in Head Start, a nonprofit reading program, as a staff assistant and a bilingual teacher. She then took over the program's kitchen for nine years, and ended up getting a commercial driver's license and driving the Head Start bus. She enjoyed working at such a great nonprofit organization, but it didn't provide good benefits. When she retired from Head Start in 2009, she had no retirement savings at all.

Social Security provides Carmen with a modest $500 per month, and she gets a small widow's benefit from the account of her late third husband. But at age seventy-five, she is now working thirty hours a week, cleaning office buildings to make extra money because she needs to support her family. Carmen raised her granddaughter, Elvira, and now she is raising Elvira's children, her great-grandchildren. Their father, who is Mexican, was deported for being undocumented. As much as she loves her city, Carmen has had to work hard to get by as she ages, unlike her LDS neighbors who live up in the foothills.

Carmen's third husband was African American. Although he grew up in Ogden, he experienced discrimination in the city's housing market, and she has too. "I was trying to find a home for my children," she recalls. "And there was a house about a block down from my mother's house. It had a beautiful fireplace. They said that they had just rented it out." Day after day, though, as she kept going by that house to go to the grocery store, she kept seeing it empty. "I went and bought a blonde wig . . . and I rented that house. Because they thought I was white."

To this day, residents of color in northern Utah disproportionately hold jobs in the low-paying blue-collar and service industries, and are underrepresented in white-collar employment. Like them, Aaron Dean, an African American resident, didn't get the best-paying jobs in the city, even though he has lived in Ogden all his life.[50] His family had fewer resources, so he had to rely on sports scholarships in college and then go into the military. His experience in the service scarred him, affecting his retirement decades later.

"Most African Americans live pretty well here," Aaron explains. "Because of the railroad, and the Air Force base, and the IRS, most people had nice jobs." Aaron's father was a bartender and waiter on the railroads for Union Pacific. Aaron went to public school from elementary to junior high, and he sang in the choir at his black Baptist church. He also participated in the Boy Scouts and in NAACP activities, and played sports. His life was very well structured. Even so, he had fewer opportunities than his white LDS classmates. "Most of the blacks' children and me, and Spanish students, we had to work in the summer months, help our parents to get our school clothes and get stuff together. And when everyone took a vacation, you're stuck right there."

Aaron particularly remembers the high school football coach who, he felt, purposefully denied students of color—who were almost always working-class kids—leadership roles on the team. They had to work summers to earn money for clothing, rather than go to the expensive sports training programs the coach organized during the summer months. Aaron believes the coach knew that students of color would never be able to attend, yet did nothing to accommodate them. He resents that to this day.

Aaron's family couldn't afford college when he graduated from high school, so he enlisted in the military. After a tour of two and a half years in Vietnam, a football scholarship to college, and an unsuccessful attempt at professional football, he became a house painter, running his own business for twelve years. Eventually, though, the experience in Vietnam caught up with him. "Starting in my late forties, I started having these problems," he recalls. "And I didn't know what was happening. By the time I was fifty-four, fifty-five—they tell me I have symptoms of PTSD." He was preoccupied and stressed out by crowds, worried about mass shootings. He couldn't handle the pressure of managing his own business, so he got a job working on the Air Force base. He painted tanks and billboards. He continued to struggle with anxiety due to the PTSD, and he ended up using most of his retirement savings during a low point. He is fortunate to own his home, obviating the need to pay rent or a mortgage.

Aaron now works part-time as a tour guide in a local museum in Ogden through the Easterseals–Goodwill SCSEP (Senior Community Service Employment Program) of Ogden.[51] This national program provides federal support for low-income seniors to work part-time jobs for nonprofits for up to four years.[52] "I've learned a lot of history and stuff, and I walk around and you get to meet people," Aaron says. Sometimes he takes people around the museum, and some days he is in an assigned area to discuss that particular room with visitors as they enter. Although he enjoys the work, and Aaron and his family get by, it's clear that he has not experienced the kinds of job opportunities and community support available to white LDS men.

Donna Lane similarly experienced the difficulties of being black in Utah.[53] She was born in 1944 in a small town in Texas, in a family of fourteen kids. She and her family moved to Ogden when she was ten because they had an aunt there whose husband had a job with the railroad. When Donna's father arrived in Ogden, he got a job on the Union Pacific railroad cleaning trains, and also did other odd jobs to make ends meet. Hers was a big family, so Donna's mother and all the older kids worked to survive. Donna was fourth oldest and had to stay at home to care for all her little siblings. Her mom worked cleaning houses on Saturdays, and Donna would go and help her.

Donna got married at nineteen, and didn't finish high school but got a GED. She divorced her husband after having two kids with him, then had another child with another man. She was in her twenties and looking for work to support her three children, because her ex-husband didn't provide much financial support. Although it was difficult to find jobs that paid well, she wanted to ensure that her children had better opportunities. "I wanted that because I know the ways of the world would be hard if they didn't have it. So all three of them have a degree," she says. She struggled to raise the kids on her own for several years.

We went through some hard times. And mostly, do you know what it was? Utility bills. The gas was off, then the water—it was like they took turns going off. It was just devastating. I remember I came home one Christmas in particular. Everything was on. I went to work. We had set up the tree . . . The kids had the presents. Then I come home from work. When I walked in the house, I thought, "Oh no, they've cut the gas out." Because I felt the cold. My heart just broke.

Living in Ogden didn't spare Donna from the fate of African American women in Opelousas, who also struggled to pay utility bills because they had to raise children on minimum-wage jobs. It was only when Donna remarried that she was able to become more financially secure.

Donna had some jobs that were rewarding because they provided a chance for her to help others, but they didn't pay very well. And because she was unmarried, she could not afford to work for low wages or volunteer while relying on a spouse's income, so Donna and her kids had to manage on her own meager salary. She ran a senior citizen care center out of her home for a while, taking care of "senior citizens and people that had problems that couldn't really help themselves . . . I had fourteen people." She also "did a little bit of everything" for nonprofits in the area, including helping people with disabilities, addictions, and homelessness. Today, she is low-income and has a mortgage, but she shares a home with her daughter, and they split the household bills. Her second husband's pension from the railroad helps a bit too. She works for a nonprofit as a receptionist part-time through SCSEP.

In spite of some of the good experiences Donna has had with nonprofits in Ogden, as a black woman she has never felt included by Ogden's LDS community. "Some LDS people are very prejudiced. Some are not," she says. "Maybe that's just the way they feel. Maybe they were just raised that way. If you're raised a certain way, it's hard to get out of that." The result is a constant wariness, a sense of having to keeping track of everyone's level of racism. "I would tell my kids, "You've got to know who is and who isn't.'" In Ogden, although the wealth and resources of the LDS Church create conditions for a strong middle class—and in some ways the wealth is shared by all—for those who are not LDS there is an implicit limit to the generosity, and Donna Lane has known that limit throughout her life.

It is no accident that Carmen, Aaron, and Donna all work at least part-time. There is a gray labor force in Ogden too, even if at lower rates than elsewhere.[54] Many single women and people of color, even if they are LDS members, generally earn lower wages than white men in Ogden, and therefore often struggle to pay the bills, let alone save for retirement. Ogden also has a significant degree of elder poverty— much lower than Opelousas, but higher than the US average, at 14.5 percent for residents over age sixty-five.[55]

Hazel Lidell is a white woman in her midseventies who has worked her whole life but still couldn't save up enough money to live comfortably in retirement.[56] Like Carmen, Aaron, and Donna, she is a member of Ogden's low-income gray labor force. She spent most of her life working in various low-wage jobs, and only recently became a member of the LDS Church. At one point she was out picking fruit in California only six weeks after having a C-section for her third child. She moved to Ogden in 1993 to be near her daughter and has stayed there ever since. Initially she got a job in Ogden as a bank teller, but in her sixties she started delivering newspapers, which came with no vacations or time off. She cleaned offices on the side, working the midnight to 6 a.m. shift.

Living at poverty level, Hazel struggles to get by. Getting into government housing, for instance, meant that she lost her SNAP benefits, due to restrictions on the total amount of federal government aid one can receive. Like her impoverished counterparts in Opelousas, she knows how difficult it can be to save when you are living paycheck to paycheck, and therefore she is critical of the government's stingy calculations. She is angry—at the federal government, at the state government, at big businesses, at the wealthy.

> They say they want to help [senior citizens]. You're not helping. If someone is making less than six hundred dollars a month, or less than a thousand, you're still in the poverty . . . We're not asking for a handout, because we paid taxes to the state of Utah for years. So it's actually our money. But they want to use it for the roads. They want to

use it for other things. CEOs want to take the money and give it to themselves . . . So what's fair about this? . . . The greed is unreal in this world. Really, it is very bad. And how much money is it going to take to make you happy?

Hazel's perspective differs from that of many other white LDS Ogden-ites because, unlike them, she is not middle class. Still, living in Ogden, with its relative affordability and its strong nonprofit network, has eased Hazel's burden somewhat. She is now working part-time as an administrative assistant at a nonprofit business development organization, through a placement with SCSEP, the same program that employs Aaron and Donna. It is a fulfilling job, perhaps the most satisfying one she has ever had.

THE AMERICAN DREAM still resonates for Ogdenites like Randy and Louise Nathanson. Ogden residents who are LDS, white, and middle-class tend to benefit from affordable education, work in stable jobs in strong industries, and own reasonably priced homes.

Though it does not figure much in their personal narratives, they owe much of their economic stability—and thus their ability to retire comfortably in Ogden—to the outsize presence of the federal government in the local economy. The community has experienced economic downturns, but it has a strong base derived from military spending, the large IRS office, and businesses that serve people employed by these federal installations. Nothing remotely approaching this kind of government investment has ever been made in Opelousas.

Retirees from the LDS Church find meaning in Ogden's abundant support networks and volunteer opportunities, which let them both receive and give in their retirement years. Outsiders to the LDS community often benefit as well, but their advantages are in many ways more limited. At a time when retirement is eroding across the country, in this city a confluence of social, economic, and geographic factors has coincided with cultural values about family and community, setting up a secure, meaningful retirement for many—though not all—of its residents.

CONCLUSION

The financial impact of pension erosion is clear enough: retired workers are at risk of losing their homes, access to health care, and the standard of living for which they worked over many decades. The disappointment is particularly sharp among the millions of workers who sacrificed wages and conceded benefits in order to keep the firms they worked for solvent. When Butch Lewis gave up 15 percent of his earnings to help his trucking company avoid bankruptcy, he was told he would see the reward in retirement. No one ever told him this was a "maybe" deal or a fair-weather promise. Now his widow faces the consequences, in the form of pension losses she will never be able to recover.

Some workers cope with their losses by staying on the job past the usual retirement age or coming back into the work world after retirement, even if the jobs they can secure after the age of sixty-five are neither as well paid nor as satisfying as the careers they once had. But for most people, this is not a very realistic option, or at least it isn't feasible for very long. Employers discriminate against older job applicants; wages for these "encore jobs" are often low; and many elderly workers are no longer in good enough physical shape to spend hours on their feet or to lift heavy objects. The ability to work with new technologies is often a prerequisite for good jobs, and members of the gray labor force may have trouble accessing or mastering the skills necessary for those positions.

Pension losses fall heavily on retirees, but also spread well beyond their households. Younger generations feel the pinch too, as they are asked or pressured to come to the rescue when their elders are in need. In low-income families, the reverse flow of help is not unusual either. Many retired Teamsters and Detroit civil servants were the steady earners in their extended families and, even in retirement, have been helping to support their adult children and grandchildren. They cannot continue to play that role when their own survival is threatened.

Such problems are familiar to anyone who lived through or has studied the Great Depression. In the 1930s, with unemployment skyrocketing to 25 percent and beyond, working parents found it very difficult to support their elders and their dependent children at the same time. This squeeze on the "sandwich generation" was one of the factors that led President Franklin D. Roosevelt to create the New Deal's Social Security safety net, which was enriched by President Lyndon Johnson's addition of Medicare and Medicaid during the War on Poverty.[1]

If Social Security could keep up with the needs of America's retirees, we might not be seeing this squeeze recur. Unfortunately, the declining "replacement rate" of these benefits means that the complementary value of private pensions is increasingly central to retirement security. So too is the availability of retiree (and spousal) health care coverage, especially for anyone who is out of the labor force but not yet old enough to qualify for Medicare. The addition of prescription drug benefits under President George W. Bush and the increase in insurance coverage created by the Affordable Care Act under President Barack Obama have been vital for all Americans, but especially for retirees: paying for health care has become a persistent worry for them, as employers increasingly back out of their promises to continue insurance policies for retired workers and their dependents.

As defined benefit pensions disappear and 401(k) plans fail to make up for the gap, the problem that should have been solved by the New Deal is surfacing again. To be sure, it is not as severe as it was in the 1930s. But that is hardly a salutary benchmark for the twenty-first century. Retirees have made choices based on the expectation that their pensions would enable them to take care of themselves for the rest of their lives. Having to depend on grown children is humiliating enough when the fault is that of the pensioner; it is infuriating when it results from the bad judgment of Wall Street investors or from corporations shirking their responsibilities.

Fixing this situation will not be easy, especially given the toll of rising inequality. Even without the failures of trucking firms or the poor state of city finances, the United States is facing serious problems that burden some groups more than others. Changes in retirement policies, combined with the impact of the Great Recession, have disadvantaged particular groups of Americans. Monique Morrissey, a researcher at the Economic Policy Institute, points out that the shift from traditional defined benefit pension plans to individual savings of the 401(k) variety has widened the gaps between high-income, college-educated, married, and largely white workers on the one hand, and lower-income Americans—including African Americans, Hispanics, those without a college degree, and unmarried people—on the other.[2] These less affluent Americans typically have *no savings whatsoever* in their retirement accounts. Among the few in this group who do have some money squirreled away, the amounts are very modest. The median black or Hispanic family with retirement accounts is holding only $22,000, enough to last perhaps one year at the poverty line. For whites, the number is $73,000, over three times as much but still far from sufficient.

This generally troubling situation, Morrissey points out, has become far, far worse as a result of economic downturns such as the Great Recession. Savings rates had already dropped before that meltdown, but the staggering loss of wealth in the recessions of 2000–2001 and especially 2007–2009 has exerted a powerful downward drag. "In 2013, most families still had not recovered their losses from the financial crisis and Great Recession, let alone accumulated additional savings for retirement," Morrissey notes. The impact of the crash has been highly unequal. The top 10 percent of American households lost 5 percent of their wealth. But the median family—those at the 50th percentile mark—lost more than half of their retirement savings. Full recovery from a blow of this magnitude is almost impossible.

The issues the United States faces in managing its retiree health care and pension systems, both public and private, are not unique. Virtually all of the world's advanced economies have had to confront the impact of increasing longevity; few have planned adequately for the financial consequences of longer lives. Many countries, including the much-admired Nordic nations, are contending with lower levels of labor force participation, which depresses retirement savings. Nonetheless, there are better and worse countries in which to retire, because national commitments to reducing inequality—during childhood, the working years, and retirement—vary so dramatically.

The Melbourne Mercer Global Pension Index scores thirty countries according to three very sensible factors that capture the basic elements of postretirement well-being:

- **Adequacy:** measures how much a country's pension system benefits poor and median-income earners, as well as the country's household savings rate and its level of home ownership (to account for nonpension sources of financial security).
- **Sustainability:** accounts for the level of coverage, pension assets, and projected demographics that the pension system is expected to cover.
- **Integrity:** measures how well pensions are governed and protected, and the extent to which private-sector benefits contribute to retirement security to avoid placing all burdens on the public purse.

The three countries that come out on top of this index are Denmark, the Netherlands, and Australia.[3] Our northern neighbor, Canada, ranks eleventh. The United States trails most countries evaluated, coming in at number seventeen out of thirty. We are the wealthiest nation in the world, but our pension score places us in the bottom half in terms of adequacy, sustainability, and integrity, behind much poorer countries such as Colombia and Chile.

How do the three top countries in the list manage to do so much better than the United States?

DENMARK

All Danish citizens receive guaranteed pensions from the government when they reach a specified "state pension age." In addition, everyone receives a supplementary income-related pension, through a program to which Danes and their employers must contribute by law. Beyond this, at age sixty-five (gradually rising to sixty-seven by 2022), every Dane receives a means-tested pension supplement and qualifies for rent allowances and fuel subsidies.[4] The Danish pension system is the best in the world, both because it provides so much security to retirees and because it's so well funded into the future. Denmark has set aside approximately 168 percent of its annual GDP to fund future pensions.[5] While Danes grumble about the high taxes they pay to sustain this system and the rest of the country's generous welfare state, they also appreciate what they get in return. Denmark comes out on top of international comparisons for the highest levels of life satisfaction and overall well-being.

Much separates the United States and Denmark besides their obvious differences in size. Historically, Denmark has been a very homogenous country, with an immigrant population composed mainly of people from other Nordic nations. Only in recent years has Denmark become more diverse, as newer waves of immigrants and refugees have arrived from Turkey, Albania, Iraq, Afghanistan, and Somalia.[6] Higher unemployment rates among immigrant groups have strained the pension system.[7] Other entirely indigenous demographic changes also have had to be assimilated into the Danish retirement policy, including rising divorce rates, a rapidly aging population, more frequent movements of workers between firms, and rising unemployment among the younger generation.[8]

Denmark's policy adjustments are worth considering as a model for the United States. Changes are being made to the Danish pension system to encourage people to delay their retirement and to assist them in saving extra money on their own in the years leading up to retirement.

In 2023, people will be able to place up to 50,000 kroner (about $8,000) annually into a tax-free savings scheme up to five years before their retirement age, without reducing their state pension. In addition, if they don't take early retirement, they can withdraw from that account tax-free.[9] In summer 2017, the age qualification for the pension system was also restructured. From 2025 onward, Denmark's retirement age will be indexed to life expectancy, and will likely continue to rise as a result.[10]

These are not earth-shattering reforms. They are well within reason, as long as Danish voters accept the continued tax burdens that it takes to support their country's generous system. Yet when we look at the system's benefits, they are profound: Danes do not worry about poverty or health care in retirement. They do not experience a massive gap between haves and have-nots. While the wealthy in Denmark can afford more luxuries in retirement because of their additional private savings, no one sinks beneath a "floor" that provides for a very comfortable life for everyone.

THE NETHERLANDS

The Dutch pension system, like the Danish one, also enables workers to count on a secure retirement. Unlike in the United States, where funds set aside for Social Security can be (and have been) raided to support other parts of the federal budget, in the Netherlands there is a legally unbreachable wall between pension funds and all other expenditures.

The state pension system covers virtually anyone who lives in the Netherlands, regardless of nationality. Every year of living in the country gives rights to 2 percent of the state pension; an immigrant who has lived in the Netherlands for fifty years would receive the full pension amount.[11] By 2015, Dutch immigrants had pensions that were, on average, 77 percent of the state pension norm. As a Dutch news site points out, this time-based scheme means that "there are wide differences in the pension rights earned by different immigrant groups. People from Surinam"—who most often arrived decades ago—"are likely to qualify for 91% of the Dutch state pension, but more recent arrivals from Africa and the Middle East are only likely to get 65%."[12] However, anyone who does not receive the full pension and does not reach a minimum income level from other sources can qualify for an income supplement once they have reached pension age.[13]

In addition to the state pension, Dutch workers contribute nearly 18 percent of their pay to professionally run pension funds, which are usually managed by nonprofits. Dutch companies contribute a capped amount to the pensions as well, keeping employer contributions stable through both bull markets and recessions. Pension funds must also undergo strict actuarial assessments to be sure there are never unfunded liabilities. That is one of the key responsibilities of the Dutch central bank, which maintains a surplus for future payments. Moreover, the bank is required to keep a close watch on actuarial tables to be sure that unrealistically optimistic forecasts do not blind it to problems that might be building in its accounts. In 2014, approximately 90 percent of Dutch workers earned defined benefit pensions at their jobs, and those pensions amounted to around 70 percent of their lifetime average pay—which is what most financial planners recommend as a replacement rate for a secure retirement.[14]

These private pensions include almost all industries, from hairdressers to butchers and retail workers. They are all participants in pension pools made up of tens of thousands of people. "Pensioners have never had it as good as they do now and poverty among this group is at a historic low," noted the chief economist of the central Dutch statistics agency. "Just 4% of pensioners have a 'very low income.'"[15]

Of course, some adjustments are needed periodically. They were particularly crucial in the aftermath of the worldwide Great Recession. As Mary Williams Walsh of the *New York Times* notes, "After the financial collapse of 2008, workers and retirees in the Netherlands took the bitter medicine needed to rebuild their collective nest eggs quickly, with higher contributions from workers and benefit cuts for pensioners." The benefits were cut by only 2 percent, but some people were still angry about that.[16] In addition, the retirement age has been increased to sixty-seven as the population gets older and lives longer, and may be increased further.[17] Such small cuts and age-limit increases are made in the present to ensure the fund is intact for future generations.

AUSTRALIA

Australia's state pension system is unique in that workers do not contribute to it. Accordingly, the system is not linked to a citizen's income during his or her work life. Instead, it is a "flat rate" system with an income test. To qualify for an age-based pension, a person must be at least sixty-five and a half years old, have income and assets under a defined level, and must have lived in the country for ten years or more (legal refugees are exempt from the ten-year rule). People who exceed the income or asset limits receive a reduced pension or no pension at all.[18]

Australians have a mandatory retirement savings program, in which employers must contribute 9.5 percent of every worker's salary to a long-term savings account. Workers can contribute even more if they want to. This is a relatively new system, created to address the kind of retirement inequality the United States is experiencing. Prior to 1992, less than half of Australian workers had retirement pensions. Low-wage workers were even more disadvantaged: only 23 percent were covered. Today, all Australian workers are covered by a retirement plan and its holdings are 2.3 trillion Australian dollars (AUD), which is roughly equivalent to the country's annual gross domestic product.[19]

As of 2014, a single person with a pension can earn up to 312 AUD (246 in US dollars, USD) extra per month before their pension begins to be reduced, and up to 3,880 AUD (3,066 USD) per month before they are disqualified for a pension entirely. Single people who own their homes can have up to 196,750 AUD (155,448 USD) in assets before their pensions begin to be reduced, and up to 672,750 AUD (531,526 USD) before they lose their pensions. As a result, many retired Australians are homeowners but still collect pensions.[20] The pensions are the largest single item of social security spending in Australia today, and there are some concerns about the long-term health of the pension system going forward, so these formulas could change in the coming decades.[21]

In addition to the age-based pension funded by taxpayers, Australian employers make contributions to another fund called a superannuation or "super," which people can access only when they retire or turn sixty-five. There are laws requiring super payments by employers, even for people who work part-time or are temporary residents.

IF WE MUST look to other countries as exemplars, a reasonable objection might be raised that they are simply too different from the United States to serve as models for reform. Yet even within the country, there are significant variations in how well we take care of the retirement needs of workers who have spent decades saving for a well-deserved rest. As the account of Opelousas suggests, it is particularly bad to be low-income, elderly, and African American in a southern state like Louisiana, which has taken a dim view of government programs of all kinds for much of its history. It's also bad to be in a place with high levels of income inequality. Aside from Opelousas, the true "underbelly" of American retirement can be seen in places like Gallup, New Mexico; Laredo, Texas; the Miami-Miami Beach-Kendall metropolitan area in Florida; the Brownsville-Harlingen metropolitan area in Texas; and Forest City, North Carolina, all of which are located in states that have seen income inequality grow over the last thirty years. Over 20 percent of the elderly in these cities live in poverty.[22]

Northeastern states are typically more generous than states like Louisiana from cradle to grave, and especially so for retirees. And in places like Ogden, the government is not especially helpful, but private nonprofit institutions step in to make an effective difference. This is true not only for the majority population of white Mormons there; the ethic of care also extends to the increasingly diverse Latino community that is now growing in Utah.

For another model the rest of the country can emulate, we might look to the city of Las Vegas, where benefit programs are driven largely by the heavily unionized and politically influential entertainment industry. The 57,000 members of the Culinary Workers Union have seen to it that even the lowest-paid workers have solid pensions, on top of other benefits that make the glittering gambling city a beacon of retirement security.

Bartenders, waitresses, and hotel workers in Vegas enjoy much better wages during their working lives, and better health care and pensions in retirement, than their counterparts elsewhere in the country. Women and people of color fare particularly well.[23] In a 2004 profile of the Culinary Workers Union, for example, the *New York Times* noted that it was 65 percent nonwhite and 70 percent female. It includes "immigrants from Central America, refugees from the Balkan wars and blacks from the Deep South."[24] Its members don't pay a monthly premium for health care for their families, have reduced copays for prescription drugs, and have access to a special employee health center.[25] They have a defined benefit pension, plus an optional 401(k) on top of that. Employers pay into the pension plan by the hour so that part-time workers can also qualify for benefits.[26] This is similar to the way that unions like UNITE HERE and the United Automobile Workers have been able to secure better wages, health care, and retirement plans, setting people up for a middle-class lifestyle, homeownership, and a secure retirement.

The state of Nevada is not known for being a paradise of social benefits.[27] It struggles with poor health care rankings because its population has grown faster than its capacity to handle their medical needs.[28] Yet a retired Teamster living in Nevada is in much better shape than one in the Central States pension fund. In 2016, when the multiemployer Western Conference of Teamsters pension fund turned sixty, its union chairman announced: "The Trust's financial position is strong, and we have every reason to believe it will be for the next sixty years."[29]

The Las Vegas unionized labor force didn't land in their enviable position by accident. They arrived there by dint of organizing and some special natural features that make an almost German-style form of labor/industry relations possible. The skills required for the gambling industry require significant training, so the investment that businesses make in maintaining a well-honed workforce is considerable.[30] Las Vegas is also surrounded by desert, so there is no large population center nearby to push wages down. Retirees from the same gambling industry in Atlantic City or Opelousas are not as fortunate; they are more easily replaced by the unemployed who are standing right outside the door waiting for their turn. Nonetheless, the relatively strong retirement system in the Las Vegas service sector tells us something important: it is entirely possible to fare better in the United States than many seem to be doing now.

It tells us something else as well: it would be a mistake to isolate the retirement system and devote attention to fixing it separately from the inequalities that beset our labor markets. As countless economists and progressive politicians have noted, the benefits of wage growth have accrued almost entirely to the top 1 percent of American workers. Retirement systems would be far more secure and beneficial if the wages that people receive, the hours they work, and the benefits they accrue across the entire arc of their working careers were more equal, steady, and generous. What makes the Las Vegas workers more secure is not just that they have negotiated good pensions; it is that they have been able to guarantee better jobs and wages throughout their working lives, which means they are building pension benefits based on more robust earnings from the beginning.

Aside from good pensions, the most important retirement benefit is the provision of health care coverage. This has become particularly important with the arrival of Donald Trump in the White House, which signaled the onset of a divisive fight over the future of health care in the United States. No one was listening more closely than the nation's retirees and the workers soon to join their ranks. Seniors were already mindful that expenditures on doctors, home health aides, medications for chronic conditions, and nursing homes can upend carefully planned retirement. Hence, the announcement in February 2018 that President Trump's budget proposal contained dramatic cuts to Medicare was unwelcome news.

Younger retirees also need to worry about their health care coverage until they reach the Medicare eligibility age of sixty-five. This gap period can be ruinously expensive to insure, especially if the workers have to find coverage as individuals rather than as part of larger group plans. Detroit's retirees found out just how punishing that can be, and they are still paying the price.

The Affordable Care Act, popularly known as Obamacare, went

some distance toward addressing these concerns through expanding Medicare prescription drug benefits, increasing Medicaid coverage for older adults, and keeping down the cost of health care premiums for people in their fifties and sixties who are not yet eligible for Medicare.[31] Republicans have promised to "repeal and replace" the ACA, but those plans are at an impasse for the moment. Meanwhile, the idea of single-payer coverage is gaining popularity, at least among Democrats. In January 2017, Rep. John Conyers (Democrat of Michigan) proposed an "Expanded & Improved Medicare for All Act," which would radically remake the US health care system, implementing a nonprofit single-payer system for all Americans in just two years.[32] Vermont senator and 2016 presidential contender Bernie Sanders has suggested phasing in a more gradual expansion of Medicare, starting with all those over fifty-five years old and eventually adding other age groups. This would greatly improve the situation of older adults as they approach retirement and would serve to fill the gap between retirement and Medicare eligibility for people who retire in their early sixties.[33] An innovation of this kind would have been a salvation for many of the people in this book.

PENSION REFORM

Policy makers and think tank scholars are hard at work on solutions that will provide better coverage and more dependable retirement benefits. Some (though not many) retiree organizations, such as the Association of BellTel Retirees, have made headway in advocating for a better retirement through legal challenges and publicity efforts.[34] At the same time, banks are thinking harder about programs that will attract small savers. Those who have watched the deficiencies of 401(k) programs are advancing ideas about mandatory savings plans that would be matched at varying levels by employers or state governments. One promising proposal is to let people partake in savings programs on an "opt-out" rather than "opt-in" basis.[35]

One of the most respected forums on this topic takes place under the auspices of the Aspen Institute's Financial Security Program.[36] The program encourages making 401(k) plans more like the Thrift Saving Plan (TSP), a retirement plan for federal workers. The TSP is markedly more efficient than traditional 401(k) plans: TSP participants "earn market returns while paying less than 0.03% of assets each year in plan administration and investment expenses."[37] The Aspen program also advocates the expansion of state-sponsored payroll deduction IRAs (sometimes known as auto-IRAs or Secure Choice) for people who are employed by small businesses that do not offer 401(k) options.[38] California, Connecticut, Maryland, Illinois, and Oregon are already taking steps to create these Secure Choice plans, which would automatically enroll people working for small businesses unless they opt out.

Another proposal from the Aspen Institute involves creating "side-car" savings accounts, which would link a short-term savings account to a traditional retirement account. "The idea is simple," the institute explains. "Workers would fund a short-term savings account that could be used for emergencies, and once a sufficient savings buffer was built up, additional contributions would automatically be diverted to a traditional, less liquid retirement account."[39]

Since most social insurance programs include forms of employee contributions, such ideas are well within the traditions embraced in the United States and most advanced countries. Ensuring that coverage extends to citizens who work for employers that do not currently contribute (especially to low-wage workers) would, in theory, make a positive difference in coverage. In a world where people switch jobs frequently, enabling those accounts to be portable and attached to individuals rather than employers would also be helpful.

All of this is to the good. But it is not sufficient. Americans in the bottom quarter of the wage distribution simply do not have enough of a margin to permit saving at any meaningful level. They need all of their resources just to put a roof over their heads and food on the table. The poor and the near-poor, in particular, often go without, failing to meet basic needs even when they spend all that they earn. For these people—and there are millions of them—setting aside *any* amount to be socked away in a retirement account would be very difficult. One look at the national data on the retirement savings these workers do have tells us that relying on personal savings is not a realistic solution, absent significant restructuring of the labor markets in which they participate and the wages they earn.[40]

Even people in the middle class, which includes most workers mentioned in this book—except for those in Opelousas, who have been poor most of their lives—find it difficult to create financial space for savings. Massive downturns like the Great Recession have knocked them sideways because their cash savings are almost always modest; their real cushion is in the increasing value of the homes they own, which would normally provide a financial backstop when they downsize in retirement.[41] That is what disappeared as an option in 2008 for millions of American homeowners. As Monique Morrissey's research tells us, they have not yet recovered and may never be able to do so.

THE MORAL DILEMMA

Pension erosion and the retraction of health care coverage are not simply a financial disaster for the nation's retirees. They are symptomatic of a broader and deeper social question. When we make promises, how responsible are we as a society for keeping them? How sacred are they? Should they be swept aside if economic conditions make them more difficult to fulfill? Or are we obligated to preserve these commitments even if it means changing the way we fund or insure retirement?

And who, exactly, is the "we" here? Employers? Government? The most affluent among us? Generations still in the labor force? All of us? If demography changes the economic landscape, wild gyrations upend the stock market, or the defense budget eats up more of our tax revenue in one decade than another, then should pension and health insurance promises based on one reasonable set of forecasts remain forever in place even after those best guesses turn out to be wrong?

Answers to these questions are as much matters of politics or moral principles as they are issues of finance or policy design. They have to do with the most fundamental issue before any democracy: ensuring faith in the institutions that serve its citizens. When employers or the government create a social contract and require that workers devote forty or fifty years of their working lives to fulfill it, defaulting on that bargain has serious consequences for the confidence people have in political institutions, in the market, in the firms where they work, and in leaders across the board. Because the losses fall especially heavily on the least advantaged among us, retirement insecurity ignites divisive skepticism about the ties that are supposed to bind the rich and the poor, the well educated and the least educated, the old and the young.

Members of the broad middle class may not be at risk for poverty, but they are experiencing a significant downward slide in the standard of living they expected and worked for. Rita Lewis is sure she will lose the house that she and Butch had worked all their lives to afford. This experience has left her bitter, angry enough to mount any stage she can stand on to denounce the institutions that put her and thousands of other Teamster families in this soup. There are thousands of people lining up behind her, not to mention those pumping their fists in the crowds in front.

Anxious Teamsters, disappointed veterans of the Verizon Yellow Pages, demoralized public servants of Detroit, the working poor in the "gray labor force," and millions of others are looking up from their bank statements and utility bills to question whether they can trust any institution or leader any more. They are simply stunned that powerful people made these promises and then walked away. Even more disturbing is the fact that fine print buried in an omnibus budget bill took away pension protections that had been in place for more than forty years and permitted fund managers to slash benefits. How could congressional representatives have let something that important happen without debate? Without any public hearings?

Managers at Verizon wonder what it means when the company spins off a subsidiary that is basically bankrupt in order to shed its retirement obligations. Verizon is one of the most profitable corporations in the country, but it has abandoned its people as if it were on its last legs. United Airlines went through a very bad patch and arguably did have to trim its costs. But it has recovered handsomely. Why has it forgotten the skilled engineers whose hard work made it the airline behemoth it is now? This is not the kind of behavior that instills confidence in private enterprise. It creates the opposite: bitterness, skepticism, and yes, class conflict.

It is for this reason, as much as for financial justice, that the country must come to grips with the retirement crisis. There are several broad problems to be solved. First, future generations must be secure in the benefits they have earned; firms should not be able to walk away from their promises. Gen Xers should not bear the brunt of pension erosion, nor should the cohorts coming up behind them. Their confidence in the institutions that undergird the United States needs to be restored.

Second, pensions must be walled off from the rest of the financial structure of companies, and Social Security from the reach of the rest of the government. They are holders of sacred money, and should be treated as such, not as piggy banks that can be raided when they reach a swollen state. Finally, we must shore up the finances of the Pension Benefit Guaranty Corporation, so that it is not endangered and can provide retirees whose firms have gone bankrupt a larger percentage of the pension benefits they had been promised.

Many of these ideas are enshrined in a piece of legislation fittingly entitled the "Butch Lewis Act," which was proposed by Senator Sherrod Brown (Democrat of Ohio) to the Senate Committee on Banking, Housing, and Urban Affairs in November 2017. The bill would create a new office in the Treasury Department, the Pension Rehabilitation Administration (PRA), which would enable pension plans to borrow the funds they need "to remain solvent and continue providing retirement security for retirees and workers for decades to come."[42] If Brown's law passes, the PRA would be able to sell Treasury bonds to support its costs, lend pension plans money for thirty years at low interest rates, and help the plans to invest it wisely, leading to increased resources to pay current retirees. "The bill would not allow any plan to borrow more than it can pay back to taxpayers," Brown notes. "It would also prohibit any borrowed funds from being used to make risky investments. And it requires plans that borrow money to submit reports every three years to demonstrate that the plans are on track to getting back on solid footing."[43]

Reforms that accomplish the goal of ensuring the retirement well-being of American workers of all generations do not come cheap. They tend to produce howls of protest from those who oppose tax increases, and admonitions that we must learn to live within our means. But when "our means" puts the pensions and health care of hardworking people at risk, it is time for us to make good on the promises they have depended on. That must be treated as a national commitment at least as important as those we make to our troops—or our investment banks.

The retirement crisis is not the only area of financial policy where the United States currently falls short. The poverty rates of American kids, for example, are a national scandal, and the children deserve an equally profound pledge of support. But these interests should not be pitted against each other. The country can, and should, address childhood poverty and elder poverty at the same time.

Encouraging personal savings and matching contributions, as proposed by the Aspen Institute and some other leading think tanks, is worthwhile. But any system that relies on individual savings is bound to run up against the limits of what workers can really afford and the fundamental inequalities that surround the labor market. Instead of focusing on individual savings alone, therefore, we also need to shore up Social Security, which is one of the most important vehicles we have for addressing the needs of the nation's retirees. We should follow the lead of countries like Denmark and Australia, whose citizens enjoy good coverage and adequate replacement rates from their respective state pension plans.

Social Security is a progressive institution that returns to low-income retirees more than what they contribute, but it reaches everyone and must continue to do so. Getting to that goal over the next century, and in the face of declining birth rates (which yield fewer workers to contribute to the program), means we will have to make some changes to its funding structure. Many proposals have been put forward to see us to that end point, the most sensible of which involves lifting the cap that presently shields all income over $127,200 from any Social Security contributions whatsoever.[44] We know that this cap is neither wise nor necessary. If it were eliminated, wealthy Americans would hardly feel the bite.

As Nobel laureate economist Paul Krugman has pointed out, this one simple step would stabilize the Social Security system indefinitely.[45] Americans could then have the same peace of mind about retirement that their Nordic or Australian counterparts routinely experience. That is what American workers have planned on, and it is what they deserve.

NOTES

INTRODUCTION

1. "Retirement Benefits: Access, Participation, and Take-up Rates, March 2018," US Department of Labor, Bureau of Labor Statistics, National Compensation Survey, Table 2, Private Industry Workers, https://www.bls.gov/ncs/ebs/benefits /2018/ownership/private/table02a.htm.
2. Joelle Saad-Lessler, Teresa Ghilarducci, and Kate Bahn, "Are U.S. Workers Ready for Retirement? Trends in Plan Sponsorship, Participation, and Pre- paredness," Schwartz Center for Economic Policy Analysis, The New School, http://www.economicpolicyresearch.org/images/docs/research/retirement _security/Are_US_Workers_Ready_for_Retirement.pdf.
3. Except for public figures, all the names in this book are pseudonyms.
4. Dan Walters, "77 California Cities on 'Economically Challenged' List," *Sacra- mento Bee*, November 18, 2015, http://www.sacbee.com/news/politics-govern ment/capitol-alert/article45376695.html.
5. Sarah Anderson and Scott Klinger, "A Tale of Two Retirements," Institute for Policy Studies, October 28, 2015, http://www.ips-dc.org/tale-of-two-retire ments/.
6. Patricia Cohen, "We All Have a Stake in the Stock Market, Right? Guess Again," *New York Times*, February 8, 2018, https://www.nytimes.com/2018 /02/08/business/economy/stocks-economy.html.
7. This book builds upon important work by economists on how we got into this mess. See Teresa Ghilarducci and Tony James, *Rescuing Retirement: A*

Plan to Guarantee Retirement Security for All Americans, foreword by Timothy Geithner (New York: Columbia University Press, 2018).

8. Charles D. Ellis, Alicia H. Munnell, and Andrew D. Eschtruth. *Falling Short: The Coming Retirement Crisis and What to Do About It* (New York: Oxford University Press, 2014).

9. Teresa Ghilarducci, *When I'm Sixty-Four: The Plot Against Pensions and the Plan to Save Them* (Princeton: Princeton University Press, 2008), 9.

10. Catherine Rampell, "Pensions, 1980 vs. Today," *New York Times*, September 3, 2009, https://economix.blogs.nytimes.com/2009/09/03/pensions-1980-vs -today/.

11. "Union Members Summary," US Department of Labor, Bureau of Labor Statistics, economic news release, January 19, 2018, https://www.bls.gov/news .release/union2.nr0.htm.

12. Alicia H. Munnell, "401(k)/IRA Holdings in 2013: An Update from the SCF," Trustees of Boston College, Center for Retirement Research, Number 14–15 (September 2014), http://crr.bc.edu/wp-content/uploads/2014/09/IB_14-151 .pdf.

13. Of course, there are many possible solutions to this problem, from lifting the cap that currently leaves incomes over $127,000 untapped for Social Security tax to increasing the age at which we retire. These are among a host of policy remedies that would fairly painlessly alleviate the financial difficulties projected for Social Security.

14. Nari Rhee, *Race and Retirement Insecurity in the United States*, National Institute on Retirement Security, December 2013, https://www.nirsonline.org /reports/race-and-retirement-insecurity-in-the-united-states/.

15. Emily Badger, "The Dramatic Racial Bias of Subprime Lending During the Housing Boom," CityLab, August 16, 2013, https://www.citylab.com/equity /2013/08/blacks-really-were-targeted-bogus-loans-during-housing-boom/6559/.

16. Evelyn Nakano Glenn, Professor of Women's Studies and Ethnic Studies at the University of California, Berkeley, has written about how caregiving is often more kin-dependent in families of low-income people of color than whites. See Evelyn Nakano Glenn, *Forced to Care: Coercion and Caregiving in America* (Cambridge, MA: Harvard University Press, 2010).

17. Katherine S. Newman, *A Different Shade of Gray: Mid-Life and Beyond in the Inner City* (New York: The New Press, 2003).

18. "IBM and Verizon Replace Pension Plans with 401K," *PBS NewsHour*, https:// web.archive.org/web/20150320020500/http://www.pbs.org/newshour/bb /business-jan-june06-pensions_1-09/; "PBGC Pension Insurance: We've Got You Covered," Pension Benefit Guaranty Corporation, https://www.pbgc .gov/wr/find-an-insured-pension-plan/pbgc-protects-pensions.

19. "Spotlight on Statistics: Older Workers," US Department of Labor, Bureau of Labor Statistics, July 2008, https://www.bls.gov/spotlight/2008/older_workers/.

20. Laurence J. Kotlikoff and Scott Burns, *The Coming Generational Storm: What You Need to Know About America's Economic Future* (Cambridge, MA: MIT

Press, 2005); Sylvester J. Schieber, *The Predictable Surprise: The Unraveling of the U.S. Retirement System* (New York: Oxford University Press, 2012).

21. Alicia H. Munnell and Dina Bleckman, "Is Pension Coverage a Problem in the Private Sector?," Trustees of Boston College, Center for Retirement Research, Number 14-7 (April 2014), http://crr.bc.edu/wp-content/uploads /2014/04/IB_14-7-508.pdf.

22. Richard Eisenberg, "Gen X: Sleeping Through the Retirement Wake-up Call," *Next Avenue*, August 27, 2015, http://www.nextavenue.org/gen-x-sleeping -through-their-retirement-wake-up-call/.

23. In analyzing the recent Census Bureau report on poverty, researchers at the National Women's Law Center found that from 2011 to 2012, the rate of extreme poverty rose by a statistically significant amount among those sixty-five and older, meaning that a growing number of America's elderly were living at or below 50 percent of the poverty line. In 2012, this was $11,011 a year for an older person living alone. Kathleen Geier, "The New York Times on the Scary Growth in Extreme Poverty among the Elderly: A for Effort, F for Policy Prescription," *Washington Monthly*, October 6, 2013, http://wash ingtonmonthly.com/2013/10/06/the-new-york-times-on-the-scary-growth-in -extreme-poverty-among-the-elderly-a-for-effort-f-for-policy-prescription/.

24. Leah McGrath Goodman, "As Wealth Inequality Soars, One City Shows the Way," *Newsweek,* September 24, 2015, http://www.newsweek.com/2015/10 /02/inequality-wealth-gap-ogden-utah-375820.html.

1. TEAMSTERS IN TROUBLE

1. While most names in this book are pseudonyms, Rita Lewis, her husband, Butch, and their parents are presented under their real names because they are public figures well known to Teamsters throughout the country. Rita has been a consistent and very public advocate for the cause of protecting union retirees from Central States Pension Fund cuts.

2. Young people in Teamster families relied on those connections to find work, making it much harder for outsiders to break into Teamster jobs, even the "pink-collar" ones. Mercer L. Sullivan, *Getting Paid: Youth Crime and Work in the Inner City*, Anthropology of Contemporary Issues (Ithaca, NY: Cornell University Press, 1989); Jan O. Jonsson, David B. Grusky, Matthew Di Carlo, and Reinhard Pollak, "It's a Decent Bet That Our Children Will Be Professors Too," in *The Inequality Reader: Contemporary and Foundational Readings in Race, Class, and Gender*, 2nd ed., ed. David B. Grusky and Szonja Szelényi (Boulder, CO: Westview Press, 2011), 499–516.

3. For an account of strikes by midwestern Teamsters in the 1930s, see Farrell Dobbs, *Teamster Rebellion*, 2nd ed. (New York: Pathfinder, 2004).

4. Paul Stephen Dempsey, "The Rise and Fall of the Interstate Commerce Commission: The Tortuous Path from Regulation to Deregulation of America's Infrastructure," *Marquette Law Review* 95, no. 4 (Summer 2012): article 7,

1151–89, http://scholarship.law.marquette.edu/cgi/viewcontent.cgi?article
=5129&context=mulr.

5. Deregulation also brought down the nation's air traffic controllers during the
same period. Airlines were flying planes half-full as a bevy of new carriers
entered the industry. With rising fuel prices, the behemoths like Pan Am could
not compete with low-cost airlines like People Express, to name just two companies that no longer exist. When the air traffic controllers went on strike for
higher wages and better working conditions in 1981, Reagan took the opportunity to teach organized labor a lesson. He fired 11,000 air traffic controllers in a single day, banning them from all future federal employment. The
airlines responded by grounding much of their fleets. Since they were all in
the same situation, no airline suffered relative to its competitors. They returned
to the air only when they could fly full planes. See Katherine S. Newman, *Falling from Grace: The Experience of Downward Mobility in the American
Middle Class* (New York: Free Press, 1988).

6. Shane Hamilton, *Trucking Country: The Road to America's Wal-Mart Economy*, Politics and Society in Modern America (Princeton, NJ: Princeton University Press, 2008), 230–31.

7. "Interstate Commerce Commission," *Federal Register: The Daily Journal of
the United States Government*, https://www.federalregister.gov/agencies/inter
state-commerce-commission; Dempsey, "The Rise and Fall of the Interstate
Commerce Commission," http://scholarship.law.marquette.edu/cgi/viewcontent
.cgi?article=5129&context=mulr.

8. Kassel, Director of Transportation, et al. v. Consolidated Freightways Corporation of Delaware, 450 U.S. 662 (1980). See also Raymond Motor Transportation, Inc., et al. v. Rice, Secretary, Department of Transportation of
Wisconsin, et al., 434 U.S. 429 (1977).

9. William R. Leach, *Country of Exiles: The Destruction of Place in American
Life* (New York: Vintage Books, 2000), 40.

10. John Brinckerhoff Jackson, *Landscape in Sight: Looking at America* (New
Haven, CT: Yale University Press, 1997), 262.

11. Tom Lewis, *Divided Highways: Building the Interstate Highways, Transform-
ing American Life* (New York: Penguin, 1999), 286–7.

12. Michael H. Belzer, *Sweatshops on Wheels: Winners and Losers in Trucking
Deregulation* (Oxford, UK: Oxford University Press, 2000).

13. Dale L. Belman and Kristen A. Monaco, "The Effects of Deregulation,
De-Unionization, Technology, and Human Capital on the Work and Work
Lives of Truck Drivers," *Industrial and Labor Relations Review* 54, no. 2A,
Extra Issue: *Industry Studies of Wage Inequality* (March, 2001): 506–7, http://
www.jstor.org/stable/2696106.

14. Shane Hamilton argues that the deregulation of trucking contributed to the
low-wage, low-price "Wal-Mart economy" of the final two decades of the
twentieth century and the early twenty-first century (Hamilton, *Trucking Country*, 8, 231).

15. Belman and Monaco, "Effects of Deregulation," 508.

16. In this, multiemployer pension plans are not unlike TIAA, the financial company that counts many university professors among its clients. TIAA enables them to move from one university to another while keeping constant their access to pensions to which their many employers contribute.

17. Alicia H. Munnell and Jean-Pierre Aubry, "Private Sector Multiemployer Pension Plans—A Primer," Trustees of Boston College, Center for Retirement Research, Brief IB#14-13 (August 2014).

18. Steve Viscelli, a sociologist and authority on truckers, has described the long history of efforts to protect these workers in their old age. It is a story bound up with the long road toward collective bargaining, a victory for blue-collar employees that stood strong until deregulation introduced punishing competition that vastly reduced union density.

> The history of trucking can be divided into three periods according to the way the state regulated the industry over time. The first, the preregulatory period, extended from the advent of motorized trucks in the early 1900s to 1935. The second, the regulatory period, began with the Motor Carrier Act of 1935, which authorized federal economic regulation of the industry under the auspices of the Interstate Commerce Commission (ICC). The third period began after a series of executive and legislative efforts, most notably the Motor Carrier Act of 1980, removed federal economic regulation . . .
>
> Throughout the pre-regulatory period, truckers struggled collectively to improve their pay and working conditions, and often enjoyed significant success in major cities. Under regulation, unionized truckers gained control throughout the US in every sector but the hauling of agricultural goods, which was always exempt from regulation. In the process they built the largest and most powerful union in American history, the International Brotherhood of Teamsters (IBT). By the 1950s, the IBT had achieved better working conditions and pay for most truckers across much of the US. And by the 1970s IBT members were among the best paid blue-collar workers in the country, earning as much as 20 percent more than even unionized auto and steel workers.

Steve Viscelli, *The Big Rig: Trucking and the Decline of the American Dream* (Oakland, CA: University of California Press, 2016), 12.

19. "Facts About Multiemployer Pension Plan Funding," Pension Rights Center, May 29, 2014, http://www.pensionrights.org/publications/fact-sheet/facts-about -multiemployer-pension-plan-funding#WhatAreMEPs.

20. Olivia Mitchell and David Blitzstein, "Multiemployer Pension Plans in Crisis: Troubled Plans Need Public Resources to Survive," *Investing* (blog), *Forbes*, January 11, 2017, https://www.forbes.com/sites/pensionresearchcouncil/2017 /01/11/multiemployer-pension-plans-in-crisis-troubled-plans-need-public -resources-to-survive/.

21. Viscelli, *Big Rig*, 1–27.

22. In 2015, a five-year "phaseout" of federal control began, which will return the Teamsters to self-governance. Benjamin Weiser, "Under New Agreement, U.S. Will End Oversight of the Teamsters in Five Years," *New York Times,*

January 14, 2015, http://www.nytimes.com/2015/01/15/nyregion/under-new
-agreement-us-will-end-oversight-of-the-teamsters-in-five-years.html.

23. The maximum pension benefit guaranteed by the PBGC is set by law and adjusted yearly. For plans that end in 2016, the maximum guarantee for workers who retire at age sixty-five is $60,136 yearly ($5,011.36 monthly). "Who We Are," Pension Benefit Guaranty Corporation, https://www.pbgc.gov/about /who-we-are.

24. Patrick Purcell, "Summary of ERISA," National Coordinating Committee for Multiemployer Plans, CRS Report for Congress, April 10, 2008, https://web .archive.org/web/20160605034847/http://www.nccmp.org/resources/pdfs /other/Summary%20of%20ERISA.pdf.

25. "Health Plans & Benefits: ERISA," US Department of Labor, https://www.dol .gov/general/topic/health-plans/erisa.

26. "About," The Partnership for Multiemployer Retirement Security: A Business Labor Initiative, http://www.solutionsnotbailouts.com/About; Randy G. Defrehn and Joshua Shapiro, "Solutions not Bailouts: A Comprehensive Plan from Business and Labor to Safeguard Multiemployer Retirement Security, Protect Taxpayers and Spur Economic Growth, A Report on the Proceedings, Findings and Recommendations of the Retirement Security Review Commission of the National Coordinating Committee for Multiemployer Plans," February 2013, http://webiva-downton.s3.amazonaws.com/71/59/b/39/1 /Solutions_Not_Bailouts.pdf.

27. "Resources for Participants in Multiemployer Pension Plans in 'Critical and Declining' Status," Pension Rights Center, June 4, 2016, http://www.pension rights.org/publications/fact-sheet/resources-participants-multiemployer -pension-plans-%E2%80%9Ccritical-and-declining%E2%80%9D-.

28. "Summary of the Pension Cutback Provisions in the Multiemployer Pension Reform Act of 2014," Pension Rights Center, http://www.pensionrights.org /issues/legislation/summary-pension-cutback-provisions-multiemployer -pension-reform-act-2014.

29. Hazel Bradford, "Treasury Rejects Central States Benefit Reductions," *Pensions&Investments*, May 6, 2016, http://www.pionline.com/article/20160506 /ONLINE/160509909/treasury-rejects-central-states-benefit-reductions.

30. When large pension funds default to the PBGC, the pension insurance system supporting multiemployer plans becomes vulnerable. The Central States fund's problems therefore pose an outsized threat to the viability of the PBGC itself. Inadequate reserves will be left to cover payouts to other pension plans that might need support in the future.

31. As Hazel Bradford reports,

> As many as 114 multiemployer pension plans expect to become insolvent within the next 20 years, according to an analysis released Tuesday by actuarial consulting firm Cheiron.
>
> The 114 plans have declared themselves to be in 'critical and declining' status, a category created by the Multiemployer Pension Reform Act of 2014 to alert regulators to plans in worsening financial condition that expect to fail

within 20 years. The 114 plans have total assets of $43.5 billion and liabilities of $79.9 billion, and represent 1.3 million participants.

Of the $36.4 billion in underfunding for all 114 plans, 62.6% comes from three plans: Teamsters Central States, Southeast & Southwest Areas Pension Fund, the Bakery & Confectionery Union and Industry International Pension Fund, and the United Mine Workers of America 1974 Pension Plan. The three plans together have $22.8 billion in unfunded liability and cover 603,000 participants.

Hazel Bradford, "Cheiron Finds 114 Multiemployer Plans Heading to Insolvency," *Pensions&Investments*, August 22, 2017, http://www.pionline.com /article/20170822/ONLINE/170829954/cheiron-finds-114-multiemployer -plans-heading-to-insolvency.

32. Josh Gotbaum, personal communication, January 14, 2018.

33. "How partitioning would work under the Keep Our Pension Promises Act

    1. Trustees of a financially-troubled multiemployer plan that is likely to run out of money within 10 to 20 years will be able to apply to the PBGC for a partition order.

    2. If the partition order is issued, the plan will not have to pay the full benefits of its "orphaned" pensioners who are retired as of the date of the partition order. (Orphaned retirees are those whose former employers went bankrupt or withdrew from the plan without fully paying what they owed.)

    3. The PBGC will transfer money to the plan each year in an amount equal to the "guaranteed benefits" the PBGC would have had to pay to these orphaned retirees if the plan were "insolvent" without enough money to pay promised benefits in that year.

    4. A new Legacy Fund will be created at the PBGC supported by general revenue from the U.S. Treasury. The revenue cost will be offset by money raised from closing two tax loopholes that primarily benefit high-income individuals and their estates, the "like-kind exchange" and "minority valuation discount" provisions of the Internal Revenue Code.

    5. The money that the PBGC transfers to the partitioned plan will come from both its current multiemployer pension insurance fund and the new Legacy Fund.

    6. The plan that has been partitioned will pay the difference between the guaranteed benefit amounts funded by the PBGC and the retirees' full benefits, up to specified limits.

Plans will continue to pay full benefits for non-orphaned retirees."

"Keep Our Pension Promises Act of 2015," Pension Rights Center, June 29, 2015, http://www.pensionrights.org/issues/legislation/keep-our-pension-pro mises-act-2015.

34. Richard Teitelbaum, "PBGC Raises Possibility of Program Insolvency," *CFO Journal* (blog), *Wall Street Journal*, March 31, 2016, https://blogs.wsj.com/cfo /2016/03/31/pbgc-raises-possibility-of-program-insolvency/.

35. "Pension Benefit Guaranty Corporation Insurance Programs," *US Government Accountability Office,* 2017 High Risk Report, http://www.gao.gov/highrisk /pension_benefit/why_did_study.
36. In this feeling, he was not unlike the working-class people interviewed in Richard Sennett and Jonathan Cobb, *The Hidden Injuries of Class* (New York: W. W. Norton and Co., 1972).
37. Katie Lobosco, "Treasury Rejects Pension Cuts for 273,000 Workers and Retirees," CNN Money, May 6, 2016 http://money.cnn.com/2016/05/06/retirement /central-states-pension-fund-treasury/.

2. WHITE-COLLAR DAMAGE

1. "Origins," AT&T, http://www.corp.att.com/history/history1.html.
2. "Origins," AT&T, http://www.corp.att.com/history/history1.html. The NYNEX operating area did not include the Rochester, New York, region.
3. "Telecommunications Act of 1996," Federal Communications Commission, June 20, 2013, https://www.fcc.gov/general/telecommunications-act-1996.
4. Mark Landler, "Bell Atlantic's Board Approves Nynex Merger to Create Colossus," *New York Times*, April 21, 1996, http://www.nytimes.com/1996 /04/21/us/bell-atlantic-s-board-approves-nynex-merger-to-create-colossus .html; Leslie Cauley, Gautum Naik, and Bryan Gruley, "Bell Atlantic, Nynex Make Merger Agreement Official," *Wall Street Journal*, April 22, 1996, http:// www.wsj.com/articles/SB83019858082509000.
5. "Bell, GTE Merger Approved," *CNN Money*, June 16, 2000, http://money.cnn .com/2000/06/16/deals/gte/.
6. In addition to the Yellow Pages, Verizon also spun off the former White Pages, business directories and magazines, an online directory and search services, website design and hosting services, and a directory for wireless subscribers.
7. David McLaughlin, "Verizon Sued by Idearc Creditors over 2006 Spinoff," *Bloomberg,* September 16, 2010, http://www.bloomberg.com/news/articles /2010-09-16/verizon-sued-by-idearc-creditors-claiming-2006-spinoff-led-to -bankruptcy; David McLaughlin and Tom Korosec, "Verizon Wins Ruling in $9.5 Billion Lawsuit," *Bloomberg,* January 13, 2013, http://www.bloomberg .com/news/articles/2013-01-23/verizon-wins-ruling-in-9-5-billion-lawsuit -over-spinoff-1-.
8. Steven Davidoff Solomon, "In Spinoffs, a Chance to Jettison Liabilities," *New York Times*, March 12, 2013, http://dealbook.nytimes.com/2013/03/12/in -spinoffs-a-chance-to-jettison-undesirable-liabilities/?_r=0.
9. McLaughlin and Korosec, "Verizon Wins Ruling," http://www.bloomberg .com/news/articles/2013-01-23/verizon-wins-ruling-in-9-5-billion-lawsuit -over-spinoff-1-.
10. Ibid.
11. Solomon, "Spinoffs," http://dealbook.nytimes.com/2013/03/12/in-spinoffs-a -chance-to-jettison-undesirable-liabilities/?_r=0.

12. Employers are not legally required to establish retirement plans. The law merely establishes minimum standards that employers who do offer plans must meet. Under ERISA, the law:

- Requires plans to provide participants with information about the plan including important information about plan features and funding. The plan must furnish some information regularly and automatically. Some is available free of charge, some is not.
- Sets minimum standards for participation, vesting, benefit accrual and funding. The law defines how long a person may be required to work before becoming eligible to participate in a plan, to accumulate benefits, and to have a non-forfeitable right to those benefits. The law also establishes detailed funding rules that require plan sponsors to provide adequate funding for a plan.
- Requires accountability of plan fiduciaries. ERISA generally defines a fiduciary as anyone who exercises discretionary authority or control over a plan's management or assets, including anyone who provides investment advice to the plan. Fiduciaries who do not follow the principles of conduct may be held responsible for restoring losses to the plan.
- Gives participants the right to sue for benefits and breaches of fiduciary duty.
- Guarantees payment of certain benefits if a defined plan is terminated, through . . . the Pension Benefit Guaranty Corporation.

"What is ERISA?," US Department of Labor, Employee Benefits Security Administration, https://www.dol.gov/agencies/ebsa/about-ebsa/our-activities/resource-center/faqs/retirement-plans-and-erisa-consumer.

13. "HR 1322: Shaping Up to Be a Battle of Retirees Versus Corporations," *BellTell Retiree: The Official Newsletter of NYNEX and Bell Atlantic Retirees* 19, Fall 2001, http://belltelretirees.org/content/news/Fall%202001.pdf.

14. McLaughlin, "Verizon Sued," http://www.bloomberg.com/news/articles/2010-09-16/verizon-sued-by-idearc-creditors-claiming-2006-spinoff-led-to-bankruptcy; McLaughlin and Korosec, "Verizon Wins Ruling," http://www.bloomberg.com/news/articles/2013-01-23/verizon-wins-ruling-in-9-5-billion-lawsuit-over-spinoff-1-; "Idearc Exits Bankruptcy, Renames Itself SuperMedia," *Reuters*, January 4, 2010, http://www.reuters.com/article/supermedia-idearc-idUSN0419957620100104; "[Verizon Spinoff] Time Line" Association of BellTel Retirees, http://belltelretirees.org/wp-content/uploads/2010/11/verizon_spin-off_time_line.pdf.

15. Ellen E. Schultz, Charles Forelle, and Theo Francis, "IBM to Freeze Pension Program in '08," *Wall Street Journal,* January 6, 2006, www.wsj.com/articles/SB113649758562938958; Mary Williams Walsh, "I.B.M. to Freeze Pension Plans to Trim Costs," *New York Times*, January 6, 2006, https://www.nytimes.com/2006/01/06/business/ibm-to-freeze-pension-plans-to-trim-costs.html.

16. Ellen E. Schultz, *Retirement Heist: How Companies Plunder and Profit from the Nest Eggs of American Workers* (New York: Portfolio, 2011).

17. Ellen Schultz, "How Business Elites Looted Private-Sector Pensions," Professional Staff Congress, CUNY, May 2012, http://psc-cuny.org/clarion/march-2012/how-business-elites-looted-private-sector-pensions.

18. "Companies That Are Offering Lump-Sum Pension Buyouts," Pension Rights Center, October 15, 2012, http://www.pensionrights.org/publications/fact-sheet/companies-are-offering-lump-sum-pension-buyouts.

19. "Lump Sum Payment to Certain Retirees," *BellTel Retiree: The Official Newsletter of Bell Atlantic Retirees* 14, Spring 2000, http://belltelretirees.org/content/news/vol14news.htm; Ida Bitetti and Renee Lefex, "Bell Atlantic 'Orphans' Speak Out," *BellTell Retiree: The Official Newsletter of NYNEX and Bell Atlantic Retirees* 20, Winter 2001–2, http://belltelretirees.org/wp-content/uploads/2008/10/content_news_Winter%202001.pdf.

20. Julie Segal, "Verizon Retirees Score Victory in Fight for Their Pensions," *Institutional Investor*, June 9, 2016, http://www.institutionalinvestor.com/article/3561311/investors-pensions/verizon-retirees-score-victory-in-fight-for-their-pensions.html.

21. Russ Banham, "The Great Pension Derisking," *CFO Magazine*, April 15, 2013, http://ww2.cfo.com/retirement-plans/2013/04/the-great-pension-derisking/.

22. Jerry Geisel, "Supreme Court Kicks Verizon Pension Derisking Back to Lower Court," *Business Insurance*, May 23, 2016, http://www.businessinsurance.com/article/20160523/NEWS03/160529944/supreme-court-kicks-verizon-pension-derisking-back-to-lower-court.

23. "Companies That Have Transferred Pensions to Insurance Companies," Pension Rights Center, http://www.pensionrights.org/publications/fact-sheet/companies-have-transferred-pensions-insurance-companies.

24. "United Airlines Timeline," *Chicago Tribune*, http://www.chicagotribune.com/news/chi-021205ual-timeline-story.html.

25. David Morris, "Airline Deregulation: A Triumph of Ideology over Evidence," *Huffington Post*, December 13, 2013, http://www.huffingtonpost.com/david-morris/airline-deregulation-ideology-over-evidence_b_4399150.html.

26. See Newman, *Falling from Grace*.

27. "Pilots at United End 29 Day Strike," *New York Times*, June 15, 1985, http://www.nytimes.com/1985/06/15/us/pilots-at-united-end-29-day-strike.html.

28. In 2002, United reported a $510 million first-quarter loss and an $889 million third-quarter loss.

29. "United Airlines Timeline," http://www.chicagotribune.com/news/chi-021205ual-timeline-story.html.

30. Drake Bennett, "United's Quest to Be Less Awful," *Bloomberg*, January 14, 2016, https://www.bloomberg.com/features/2016-united-airlines-struggles/.

31. "United Airlines Finally Flies out of Bankruptcy," Associated Press, NBC News, February 2, 2006, http://www.nbcnews.com/id/11126203/ns/business-us_business/t/united-airlines-finally-flies-out-bankruptcy/.

32. Micheline Maynard, "United Air Wins Right to Default on Its Employee Pension Plans," *New York Times*, May 11, 2005, https://www.nytimes.com/2005/05/11/business/united-air-wins-right-to-default-on-its-employee-pension-plans.html.

33. Mary Williams Walsh, "How Wall Street Wrecked United's Pension," *New York Times*, July 31, 2005, https://www.nytimes.com/2005/07/31/business/yourmoney/how-wall-street-wrecked-uniteds-pension.html.

34. Dale Russakoff, "Human Toll of a Pension Default," *Washington Post*, June 13, 2005, http://www.washingtonpost.com/wp-dyn/content/article/2005/06/12/AR2005061201367.html.

35. The first employee stock ownership plan (ESOP) was introduced in 1956 by banker Louis Kelso for employees of Peninsula Newspapers, Inc., in Palo Alto, California, so that they could buy the newspaper chain. Mr. Kelso was an advocate for business models in which worker-capitalists could gain access to capital credit. (See Alfonso A. Narvaez, "Louis O. Kelso, Who Advocated Worker-Capitalism, Is Dead at 77," *New York Times,* February 21, 1991, https://www.nytimes.com/1991/02/21/obituaries/louis-o-kelso-who-advocated-worker-capitalism-is-dead-at-77.html.) In 1974, these plans were recognized under the Employee Retirement Income Security Act (ERISA). According to the Urban Institute, by 1995 "there were a reported 9,232 ESOPs, excluding one-participant ESOPs, covering 7 million active participants and including $262 billion in assets." (Pamela Perun, "Employee Stock Ownership Plans: A Status Report," The Retirement Series, Urban Institute, Brief Series no. 10, June 2000, http://www.urban.org/sites/default/files/publication/62196/309563-Employee-Stock-Ownership-Plans.PDF.)

36. Farhad Manjoo, "United's ESOP Fable," *Salon*, December 12, 2002, http://www.salon.com/2002/12/12/esop/.

37. Ibid.

38. Kathleen Pender, "United ESOP Tragically Flawed," *SFGate*, December 8, 2002, http://www.sfgate.com/business/networth/article/United-ESOP-tragically-flawed-2747210.php.

39. Andrew Ross Sorkin and Jeff Bailey, "United and Continental Discussing Possible Merger," *New York Times,* December 12, 2006, http://www.nytimes.com/2006/12/12/business/12cnd-air.html.

40. Mary Jane Credeur and Mary Schlangenstein, "United, Continental to Merge Operations in 2011," *Bloomberg News* via *SFGate*, September 20, 2010, http://www.sfgate.com/business/article/United-Continental-to-merge-operations-in-2011-3252328.php.

41. "PBGC Reaches Pension Settlement with United Airlines," April 22, 2005, http://www.pbgc.gov/news/press/releases/pr05-36.html.

42. Schultz, "How Business Elites Looted Private-Sector Pensions," http://psc-cuny.org/clarion/march-2012/how-business-elites-looted-private-sector-pensions.

3. MUNICIPAL BLUES

1. Although Detroit is the biggest Chapter 9 municipal bankruptcy, it should be noted that Puerto Rico (which is a US territory rather than a municipality) now ranks as the largest government bankruptcy in US history. Mary Williams Walsh, "Puerto Rico Declares a Form of Bankruptcy," *New York Times*,

May 3, 2017, https://www.nytimes.com/2017/05/03/business/dealbook/puerto -rico-debt.html; Heather Long, "Puerto Rico Files for Biggest US Municipal Bankruptcy," CNN Money, May 3, 2017, http://money.cnn.com/2017/05/03 /news/economy/puerto-rico-wants-to-file-for-bankruptcy/index.html.

2. Peter K. Eisinger, "Black Employment in Municipal Jobs: The Impact of Black Political Power," *American Political Science Review* 76, no. 2 (1982): 380– 92, doi:10.2307/1961117; Eisinger, "Local Civil Service Employment and Black Socioeconomic Mobility," *Social Science Quarterly* 67, no. 1 (1986): 169–75, http://www.jstor.org/stable/42862037.

3. Isabel Wilkerson, *The Warmth of Other Suns: The Epic Story of America's Great Migration* (repr., New York: Vintage, 2011).

4. Moving North helped African Americans increase their income in the years during and following the Great Migration, but earnings for black Americans living in the North did not increase after the Great Migration had ended:

> Migration from the South can account for approximately 20 percent of the national black-white earnings convergence between 1940 and 1980 . . . I estimate that southern blacks increased their earnings by about 130 percent, on average, by moving to the North by 1940, an increase of about $5,400 annually per migrant . . . Relative black earnings in the North did not increase after black migration from the South tapered off in the 1970s. In fact, from 1975 to 1990, blacks fell further behind whites in the North, erasing whatever small relative gains they had achieved since 1940 . . . Southern in-migration doubled the size of the black workforce in the North from 1940 to 1970. Competition with southern blacks generated larger wage losses for existing black workers in the North than for similarly skilled whites . . . Overall, the Great Black Migration benefited southern migrants, while black workers in the North lost ground.

Leah Platt Boustan, "The Great Black Migration: Opportunity and Competition in Northern Labor Markets," *Focus* 32, no. 1 (Spring/Summer 2015): 24–27, https://www.irp.wisc.edu/publications/focus/pdfs/foc321e.pdf.

5. See Robert H. Zieger, "Affirmative Action and Labor Action," chap. 6 in *For Jobs and Freedom: Race and Labor in America since 1865* (Lexington, KY: University Press of Kentucky, 2007), 200.

6. See Joe T. Darden, Richard Child Hill, June Thomas, and Richard Thomas, "Patterns of Race and Class Disparity," in their *Detroit: Race and Uneven Development* (Temple University Press, 1987).

7. Philip I. Moss, "Employment Gains by Minorities, Women in Large City Government, 1976–83," *Monthly Labor Review* 111, no. 11 (1988): 18–24, http://www.jstor.org/stable/41843675.

8. B. J. Widick, *Detroit: City of Race and Class Violence*, 2nd ed. (Detroit: Wayne State University Press, 1989), 3.

9. Thomas Sugrue, *The Origins of the Urban Crisis: Race and Inequality in Postwar Detroit,* updated edition, Princeton Classics (Princeton, NJ: Princeton University Press, 2014), 183–89.

10. Kurt Metzger and Jason Booza, "African Americans in the United States, Michigan and Metropolitan Detroit," Center for Urban Studies, Wayne State University College of Urban Labor and Metropolitan Affairs, Working Paper Series, no. 8, February 2002, http://www.cus.wayne.edu/media/1356/aawork8 .pdf.

11. Sugrue, *Origins of the Urban Crisis*, 233.

12. Sugrue, *Origins of the Urban Crisis*, 125–30, 261–62.

13. Kevin Boyle, "The Fire Last Time," *Washington Post,* July 29, 2007, http:// www.washingtonpost.com/wp-dyn/content/article/2007/07/27 /AR2007072701672.html.

14. In 1967, Detroit's police force was only 5 percent African American. Sidney Fine, *Violence in the Model City: The Cavanagh Administration, Race Relations, and the Detroit Riot of 1967* (Ann Arbor: University of Michigan Press, 1989), 109.

15. Fine, *Violence in the Model City*, 95–99.

16. Robyn Meredith, "5 Days in 1967 Still Shake Detroit," *New York Times,* July 23, 1997, http://www.nytimes.com/1997/07/23/us/5-days-in-1967-still -shake-detroit.html.

17. Sugrue, *Origins of the Urban Crisis*, 259.

18. Widick, *Detroit*, 168.

19. Boyle, "The Fire Last Time," http://www.washingtonpost.com/wp-dyn/content /article/2007/07/27/AR2007072701672.html.

20. Widick, *Detroit*, 238.

21. Nathan Bomey, *Detroit Resurrected: To Bankruptcy and Back* (New York: Norton, 2016), 18.

22. Brad Plumer, "Detroit Just Filed for Bankruptcy. Here's How It Got There," *Washington Post,* July 18, 2013, https://www.washingtonpost.com/news /wonk/wp/2013/07/18/detroit-just-filed-for-bankruptcy-heres-how-it-got -there/.

23. Frank H. Shafroth, "What Michigan and Suburbanites Owe Detroit," *Bloomberg*, December 4, 2013, https://www.bloomberg.com/view/articles/2013-12 -04/what-michigan-and-suburbanites-owe-detroit.

24. "75% of Detroit workers live outside of the city and 63% of those who work in the city but live outside the city earn more than $3,333 per month (the highest salary range reported)." Their city taxes aren't collected by the state or the corporations they work for. Professor Bruce Pietrykowski, personal communication, October 26, 2017.

25. Shafroth, "What Michigan and Suburbanites Owe Detroit," https://www .bloomberg.com/view/articles/2013-12-04/what-michigan-and-suburbanites -owe-detroit.

26. "Until Snyder's changes took effect, Michigan had exempted most pension payments from the income tax, now at 4.25 percent. He created a three-tier system for retirees born before 1946, after 1952 and those in between. Chris Christoff, "Pension Tax Bites Michigan's Snyder in Re-Election Bid," *Bloomberg*,

September 3, 2014, https://www.bloomberg.com/news/articles/2014-09-03/pension-tax-bites-michigan-s-snyder-in-re-election-bid.

27. Christoff, "Pension Tax," https://www.bloomberg.com/news/articles/2014-09-03/pension-tax-bites-michigan-s-snyder-in-re-election-bid.

28. Steven Malanga, "The Public Pension Problem: It's Much Worse Than It Appears," *Investor's Business Daily*, Manhattan Institute, July 22, 2016, https://www.manhattan-institute.org/html/public-pension-problem-its-much-worse-it-appears-9095.html.

29. Curt Guyette, "Swaps, COPs, Lingering Questions in Detroit Bankruptcy," American Civil Liberties Union of Michigan, February 5, 2014, http://www.aclumich.org/article/swaps-cops-lingering-questions-detroit-bankruptcy.

30. Guyette, "Detroit Bankruptcy," http://www.aclumich.org/article/swaps-cops-lingering-questions-detroit-bankruptcy; Susie Cagle, "Is Wall Street Making a Killing Off Cities' Debt?," *NextCity*, October 6, 2014, https://nextcity.org/features/view/pension-obligation-bonds-is-wall-street-making-a-killing-on-cities-debt.

31. Nathan Bomey and Brent Snavely, "Detroit Proposes $85 Million Settlement to Pay Off a Controversial Debt Deal," *Governing*, March 4, 2014, http://www.governing.com/news/headlines/detroit-proposes-85-million-settlement-to-pay-off-a-controversial-cebt-deal-.html.

32. Mary Williams Walsh, "Detroit Wins Judge's Nod for Contract Settlement," *New York Times*, April 11, 2014, https://dealbook.nytimes.com/2014/04/11/judge-approves-pact-to-end-detroit-swap-deal/.

33. Alica H. Munnell, Jean-Pierre Aubry, Anek Belbase, and Joshua Hurwitz, "State and Local Pension Costs: Pre-Crisis, Post-Crisis and Post Reform," Trustees of Boston College, Center for Retirement Research, Number 30 (February 2013), http://crr.bc.edu/wp-content/uploads/2013/03/slp_30_508rev.pdf.

34. Saqib Bhatti, "Why Chicago Won't Go Bankrupt—And Detroit Didn't Have To," *In These Times*, June 22, 2015, http://inthesetimes.com/article/18096/a_scam_in_two_cities.

35. Ibid.

36. Mark Brush, "Detroit Is "the Olympics of Restructuring" Says City's New Emergency Manager," Michigan Radio, March 14, 2013, http://michiganradio.org/post/detroit-olympics-restructuring-says-citys-new-emergency-manager#stream/0.

37. Monica Davey, "Bankruptcy Lawyer Is Named to Manage an Ailing Detroit," *New York Times*, March 14, 2013, http://www.nytimes.com/2013/03/15/us/gov-rick-snyder-kevyn-orr-emergency-manager-detroit.html.

38. Monica Davey and Mary Williams Walsh, "Billions in Debt, Detroit Stumbles into Insolvency," *New York Times*, July 18, 2013, http://www.nytimes.com/2013/07/19/us/detroit-files-for-bankruptcy.html.

39. Wallace Turbeville, "The Detroit Bankruptcy," *Demos*, November 20, 2013, http://www.demos.org/publication/detroit-bankruptcy.

40. Zachary A. Goldfarb, "After Detroit Bankruptcy Filing, City Retirees on Edge as They Face Pension Cuts," *Washington Post*, July 21, 2013, https://www .washingtonpost.com/business/economy/after-detroit-bankruptcy-filing-city -retirees-go-to-court-to-protect-their-pensions/2013/07/21/66e89934-f22a -11e2-ae43-b31dc363c3bf_story.html.

41. Nathan Bomey, "Detroit Bankruptcy: A Master Timeline," *Detroit Free Press*, November 8, 2014, http://www.freep.com/story/news/local/detroit-bankruptcy /2014/11/08/detroit-bankruptcy-timeline/18680129/.

42. Monica Davey, "Finding $816 Million, and Fast, to Save Detroit," *New York Times*, November 7, 2014, https://www.nytimes.com/2014/11/08/us/finding -816-million-and-fast-to-save-detroit.html.

43. Randy Kennedy, "'Grand Bargain' Saves the Detroit Institute of Arts," *New York Times*, November 7, 2014, https://www.nytimes.com/2014/11/08/arts /design/grand-bargain-saves-the-detroit-institute-of-arts.html.

44. Davey, "Finding $816 Million," https://www.nytimes.com/2014/11/08/us/find ing-816-million-and-fast-to-save-detroit.html.

45. Nathan Bomey, Matt Helms, and Joe Guillen, "Judge OKs Bankruptcy Plan; a 'Miraculous' Outcome," *Detroit Free Press,* November 7, 2014, http://www .freep.com/story/news/local/detroit-bankruptcy/2014/11/07/rhodes -bankruptcy-decision/18648093/.

46. Nathan Bomey, "Detroit Timeline," http://www.freep.com/story/news/local /detroit-bankruptcy/2014/11/08/detroit-bankruptcy-timeline/18680129/.

47. Emergency managers have a lot of power but don't necessarily fix debt repay- ment problems. Some states have emergency control boards, but in Detroit it's a single emergency manager, appointed by the governor. Matthew Dolan, "Fitch: Emergency Managers No Panacea Despite Power," *Detroit Free Press*, April 26, 2016, http://www.freep.com/story/news/local/michigan/flint-water -crisis/2016/04/26/fitch-emergency-managers-michigan/83559242/. For how emergency management has become common across Michigan, see Julie Bosman and Monica Davey, "Anger in Michigan over Appointing Emergency Managers," *New York Times,* January 22, 2016, http://www.nytimes.com /2016/01/23/us/anger-in-michigan-over-appointing-emergency-managers .html.

48. Nathan Bomey, "Q&A: Detroit's Chapter 9 Bankruptcy," *Detroit Free Press*, July 18, 2013, http://www.usatoday.com/story/news/nation/2013/07/18/ques tions-and-answers-detroits-chapter-9-bankruptcy/2567131/.

49. Monica Davey, "Detroit's Retirees Vote to Lower Pensions, in Support of Bankruptcy Plan," *New York Times,* July 22, 2014, http://www.nytimes.com /2014/07/22/us/detroits-retirees-vote-to-lower-pensions-in-support-of -bankruptcy-plan.html.

50. Sandra Svoboda, "Annuity Lump Sum Re-Payment: Will Be an Option If Pensioners Approve City's Plan," *Next Chapter Detroit*, June 30, 2014, http:// www.nextchapterdetroit.com/063014-detroit-bankruptcy-annuity-settle ment/.

51. Susan Tompor, "Detroit Retirees Who Owe up to $96,000 to City Face Dead-line," *Detroit Free Press*, February 13, 2015, http://www.freep.com/story/money /personal-finance/susan-tompor/2015/02/13/detroit-bankruptcy-clawback -retirees-susan-tompor/23354157/.

52. In 2006 and 2007, the pension paid the savings plan a total of $176.1 mil-lion by adding 13.5 percent and 15 percent interest respectively on top of the base rate. That raised the total return in those years to 21.4 percent and 22.9 percent. No extra interest was paid from 2000 to 2004, or from 2008 to 2013. Chris Christoff, "Detroit Retirees Got Extra Interest After Their Guaranteed 7.9%," *Bloomberg*, December 2, 2013, https://www.bloomberg .com/news/articles/2013-12-02/detroit-retirees-strike-pay-dirt-with-city -guaranteed-savings.

53. Municipal workers who retired before 2003 (or who didn't or couldn't have been overpaid) did not owe any interest on annuities. People who couldn't afford to pay in or didn't opt in to the annuity account also weren't affected.

54. Some of those people were approved for new income stabilization payments. Susan Tompor, "Detroit Retirees: No Easy Answers on Clawback," *Detroit Free Press*, January 16, 2015, http://www.freep.com/story/money/personal -finance/susan-tompor/2015/01/16/detroit-pensioners-lump-sum-clawback -susan-tompor/21829671/; Chris Christoff, "Detroit Pension Cuts from Bank-ruptcy Prompt Cries of Betrayal," *Bloomberg*, February 5, 2015, https://www .bloomberg.com/news/articles/2015-02-05/detroit-pension-cuts-from -bankruptcy-prompt-cries-of-betrayal; "Detroit Mayor Eyes Legal Action over Pension Shortfall," *Reuters*, February 24, 2016, https://www.reuters .com/article/us-detroit-pensions/detroit-mayor-eyes-legal-action-over -pension-shortfall-idUSKCN0VX2SH; Christine Ferretti, "For Detroit Retirees, Pension Cuts Become Reality," *Detroit News*, February 27, 2015, http://www.detroitnews.com/story/news/local/wayne-county/2015/02/27 /detroit-retirees-pension-cuts-become-reality/24156301/; Lester Graham, "Detroit Bankruptcy Lesson: Underfunded Pension Funds Could Trip Up Other Municipalities," Michigan Radio, December 1, 2015, http://michi ganradio.org/post/detroit-bankruptcy-lesson-underfunded-pension-funds -could-trip-other-municipalities#stream/0; Anna Sysling, "For Detroit Retir-ees, Bankruptcy Still Part of Daily Life," WDET, November 16, 2015, https:// wdet.org/posts/2015/11/15/81926-for-detroit-retirees-bankruptcy-still-part -of-daily-life/.

55. Tompor, "Detroit Retirees Face Deadline," http://www.freep.com/story/money /personal-finance/susan-tompor/2015/02/13/detroit-bankruptcy-clawback -retirees-susan-tompor/23354157/.

56. Robert C. Pozen, "The Retirement Surprise in Detroit's Bankruptcy," Brook-ings, July 25, 2013, https://www.brookings.edu/opinions/the-retirement -surprise-in-detroits-bankruptcy/.

57. Christine Ferretti, "Detroit Health Plan to Drop Some Retirees," *Detroit News*, January 29, 2015, http://www.detroitnews.com/story/news/local/wayne -county/2015/01/29/detroit-city-worker-spouses-health-care/22566071/.

58. "Retiree Health Reimbursement Account (HRA) Information City of Detroit General Retiree Health Care Trust," General Retirement System, City of Detroit, http://www.rscd.org/grsd/Health-Care/General-Plan-Information.

59. It gave the city a reprieve on pension payments until 2024, when it will owe $195 million in the first year. Matt Helms and Matthew Dolan, "Detroit Picks Firm to Help Fix $195M Pension Shortfall," *Detroit Free Press*, May 22, 2016, https://www.freep.com/story/news/local/michigan/detroit/2016/05/22 /detroit-picks-firm-help-fix-195m-pension-shortfall/84337476/.

60. Mary Williams Walsh, "Detroit Emerges from Bankruptcy, Yet Pension Risks Still Linger," *New York Times*, November 11, 2014, http://dealbook.nytimes .com/2014/11/11/detroit-emerges-from-bankruptcy-pension-risk-still-intact/.

61. Yvonne Wenger and Luke Broadwater, "Baltimore Officials See Detroit As a Cautionary Tale," *Baltimore Sun,* July 19, 2013, http://www.baltimoresun .com/news/maryland/baltimore-city/bs-md-ci-detroit-baltimore-20130719 -story.html.

62. However, Puerto Rico couldn't file under Chapter 9, but Title III of the Promesa law, "which contains certain Chapter 9 bankruptcy provisions but also rec- ognizes that, unlike the cities and counties that use Chapter 9, Puerto Rico is not part of any state and must in some ways be treated as a sovereign." Walsh, "Puerto Rico Declares Bankruptcy," https://www.nytimes.com/2017/05/03 /business/dealbook/puerto-rico-debt.html.

63. Wenger and Broadwater, "Baltimore Officials," http://www.baltimoresun.com /news/maryland/baltimore-city/bs-md-ci-detroit-baltimore-20130719-story .html.

64. Mark Reutter, "Release of City Fiscal Forecast Sparks False Reports of Bank- ruptcy," *Baltimore Brew,* February 6, 2013, https://baltimorebrew.com/2013 /02/06/mayors-comments-on-city-finances-spark-false-reports-of-bank ruptcy/.

65. Mary Williams Walsh, "Dallas Stares Down a Texas-Size Threat of Bank- ruptcy," *New York Times*, November 20, 2016, https://www.nytimes.com /2016/11/21/business/dealbook/dallas-pension-debt-threat-of-bankruptcy .html.

66. Tristan Hallman, "S&P Once Again Downgrades Dallas' Bond Rating over Pension Fears," *Dallas News*, January 11, 2017, https://www.dallasnews.com /news/dallas-city-hall/2017/01/11/sp-downgrades-dallas-bond-rating -pension-fears.

67. "Dallas Mayor Says Pension Mismanagement Could Be 'Criminal,'" NBC DFW, December 30, 2016, http://www.nbcdfw.com/news/local/Dallas-Mayor -Says-Pension-Mismanagement-Could-Be-Criminal-408821455.html; Tristan Hallman, "Potential Dallas Police and Fire Pension Fix Emerging in Texas Legislature," *Dallas News,* February 20, 2017, https://www.dallasnews.com /news/dallas-city-hall/2017/02/20/potential-dallas-police-fire-pension-fix -emerging-texas-legislature.

68. Marc Joffe, "New York and Chicago's Finances Are Among the Worst in the US," *Business Insider*, originally published in *Fiscal Times*, January 10, 2017,

http://www.businessinsider.com/new-york-and-chicagos-finances-are-among
-the-worst-in-the-us-2017-1.

69. "At the end of its 2015 fiscal year, the city's general fund reserves amounted
to just 0.67 percent of expenditures—well below the Government Finance
Officers Association recommendation of 16.67 percent (equivalent to two
months of spending) . . . According to a report issued by City Comptroller
Scott Stringer, New York's per capita debt greatly exceeds that of all other
large U.S. cities, and is even 50 percent higher than that of Chicago." Joffe,
"New York and Chicago's Finances," http://www.businessinsider.com/new
-york-and-chicagos-finances-are-among-the-worst-in-the-us-2017-1.

70. Ibid.

71. "These taxable municipal bonds are issued by state or local governments for
payment of obligation to their employee pension fund. Issuing such bonds
allow the state or local government that cannot make its payments to the pension fund to borrow the money, then invest it in the stock, bond, private
equity or real estate markets. A gamble if there ever was one." Marilyn Cohen,
"Beware of Pension Obligation Bonds," *Forbes*, January 5, 2016, https://www
.forbes.com/sites/investor/2016/01/05/beware-of-pension-obligation-bonds
/#16b1e7381bd1.

72. "States and local governments continue to turn to the bonds as the unfunded
portions of public pension systems balloon and they struggle to make annual
payments to the systems. State retirement systems had a $968 billion short-
fall between the benefits promised to workers and the funding available to
meet those obligations in 2013, according to an assessment last month by The
Pew Charitable Trusts . . . That was a $54 billion increase from the year
before . . . Across the country, governments sold $670 million in pension
bonds during the first half of [2015]." Sarah Breitenbach, "Despite Risks, State
and Local Governments Turn to Pension Obligation Bonds," *Stateline* (blog),
PEW Charitable Trusts, August 12, 2015, http://www.pewtrusts.org/en
/research-and-analysis/blogs/stateline/2015/08/12/despite-risks-state-and
-local-governments-turn-to-pension-obligation-bonds.

4. GRAY LABOR

1. "Life Expectancy at Birth, at 65 Years of Age, and at 75 Years of Age, by Race
and Sex," Health, United States (Centers for Disease Control, 2010), 134,
Table 22, https://www.cdc.gov/nchs/data/hus/2010/022.pdf.

2. See Dana Muir and John Turner, "Longevity and Retirement Age in Defined
Benefit Pension Plans," chap. 7 in *Work Options for Older Americans*, 1st ed.,
ed. Teresa Ghilarducci and John Turner (Notre Dame, IN: University of Notre
Dame Press, 2007), 212–31.

3. Charles D. Ellis, Alicia H. Munnell, and Andrew D. Eschtruth, *Falling Short:
The Coming Retirement Crisis and What to Do About It* (New York: Oxford
University Press, 2014).

4. Paul N. Van de Water and Kathy Ruffing, "Social Security Benefits Are Modest," Center on Budget and Policy Priorities, January 11, 2011, https://www
.cbpp.org/research/social-security/social-security-benefits-are-modest; Elisa
Walker, "25 Million Reasons to Give Thanks for Social Insurance," 2014
Discussion Archive, National Academy of Social Insurance, November 21,
2014, https://www.nasi.org/discuss/2014/09/bring-back-social-security-replace
ment-rates%20;%20http://crr.bc.edu/wp-content/uploads/2005/11/jtf_19
.pdf; Alicia H. Munnell and Mauricio Soto, "Sorting Out Social Security
Replacement Rates," *Just the Facts on Retirement Issues* 19, November 2005,
Center for Retirement Research at Boston College, http://crr.bc.edu/wp-content
/uploads/2005/11/jtf_19.pdf; Barbara A. Butrica, Howard M. Iams, and
Karen E. Smith, "The Changing Impact of Social Security on Retirement Income
in the United States," *Social Security Bulletin* 65, no. 3 (2003/2004), https://
www.ssa.gov/policy/docs/ssb/v65n3/v65n3p1.html.

5. Alicia H. Munnell and Anqi Chen, "Trends in Social Security Claiming," Trustees of Boston College, Center for Retirement Research, Brief IB#15-8 (May
2015), http://crr.bc.edu/briefs/trends-in-social-security-claiming/.

6. Alicia H. Munnell, "The Average Retirement Age—An Update," Trustees of
Boston College, Center for Retirement Research, Number 15-4 (March 2015),
http://crr.bc.edu/wp-content/uploads/2015/03/IB_15-4_508_rev.pdf.

7. The "labor force participation" rate, according to the Bureau of Labor Statistics,
"is the percentage of the population that is either employed or unemployed
(that is, either working or actively seeking work)." https://web.archive.org/web
/20160404113657/ https://www.bls.gov/bls/cps_fact_sheets/lfp_mock.htm.

8. "Spotlight on Statistics: Older Workers," US Department of Labor, Bureau
of Labor Statistics, July 2008, https://www.bls.gov/spotlight/2008/older
_workers/.

9. As analyses by the Bureau of Labor Statistics data show, "The relatively strong
presence of 65-and-older workers is found across age brackets: 65- to
69-year-olds, 70- to 74-year-olds, and those 75 and older. All are working at
higher rates than they did in May 2008, the only age groups about which that
can be said." Drew Desilver, "More Older Americans Are Working, and Working More, Than They Used To," Pew Research Center, June 20, 2016, http://
www.pewresearch.org/fact-tank/2016/06/20/more-older-americans-are
-working-and-working-more-than-they-used-to/.

10. Mitra Toossi, "Labor Force Projections to 2024: The Labor Force Is Growing, but Slowly," *Monthly Labor Review*, Bureau of Labor Statistics, December 2015, https://www.bls.gov/opub/mlr/2015/article/labor-force-projections
-to-2024.htm.

11. Desilver, "Older Americans Working More," http://www.pewresearch.org/fact
-tank/2016/06/20/more-older-americans-are-working-and-working-more
-than-they-used-to/. "Between 1995 and 2007, the number of older workers
on full-time work schedules nearly doubled while the number working part-
time rose just 19 percent. As a result, full-timers now [in 2007] account for a

majority among older workers: 56 percent in 2007, up from 44 percent in 1995." "Older Workers," https://www.bls.gov/spotlight/2008/older_workers/.

12. The four factors named here are the most important, but others are at work as well, including improving health and higher levels of education. For more, see Munnell, "Average Retirement Age," http://crr.bc.edu/wp-content/uploads/2015/03/IB_15-4_508_rev.pdf.

13. Teri Morisi, "Why More People Ages 55+ are Working," *US Department of Labor Blog*, November 18, 2016, https://blog.dol.gov/2016/11/18/why-more-people-ages-55-are-working/.

14. Barbara A. Butrica, Howard M. Iams, Karen E. Smith, and Eric J. Toder, "The Disappearing Defined Benefit Pension and Its Potential Impact on the Retirement Incomes of Baby Boomers," *Social Security Bulletin* 69, no. 3 (2009), https://www.ssa.gov/policy/docs/ssb/v69n3/v69n3p1.html.

15. Morisi, "People 55+ Working," https://blog.dol.gov/2016/11/18/why-more-people-ages-55-are-working/.

16. Ibid.

17. Josh Bivens, Elise Gould, Lawrence Mishel, and Heidi Shierholz, "Raising America's Pay: Why It's Our Central Economic Policy Challenge," Economic Policy Institute, June 4, 2014, http://www.epi.org/publication/raising-americas-pay/.

18. Teresa Ghilarducci, "Why Women Over 50 Can't Find Jobs," *PBS Newshour*, January 14, 2016, http://www.pbs.org/newshour/making-sense/women-over-50-face-cant-find-jobs/.

19. "Pew Research Center's Social & Demographic Trends project finds that a majority (54%) of workers ages 65 and older say the main reason they work is that they want to. Just 17% say the main reason is that they need the paycheck. An additional 27% say they're motivated by a mix of desire and need. When asked to identify specific reasons for working, older workers emphasize psychological and social factors: 'to feel useful'; 'to give myself something to do'; 'to be with other people.' Younger and middle-aged workers are much more inclined to cite classic pocketbook considerations." "Recession Turns a Graying Office Grayer," Pew Research Center, September 3, 2009, http://www.pewsocialtrends.org/2009/09/03/recession-turns-a-graying-office-grayer/.

20. See Katherine S. Newman, *The Accordion Family: Boomerang Kids, Anxious Parents, and the Private Toll of Global Competition* (Boston: Beacon Press, 2013).

21. See Sharon Hermes and Teresa Ghilarducci, "How 401(k)s and the Stock Market Crash Explain Increases in Older Workers' Labor Force Participation Rates," chap. 8 in *Work Options for Older Americans*, 1st ed., ed. Teresa Ghilarducci and John Turner (Notre Dame, IN: University of Notre Dame Press, 2007): 237–66.

22. David Neumark, Ian Burn, and Patrick Button, "Age Discrimination and Hiring of Older Workers," FRBSF Economic Letter, Federal Reserve Bank of San Francisco, February 27, 2017, http://www.frbsf.org/economic-research/publi

cations/economic-letter/2017/february/age-discrimination-and-hiring-older
-workers/.

23. This quotation appears in Nathaniel Reade, "The Surprising Truth About
    Older Workers," *AARP The Magazine,* September 2015, http://www.aarp
    .org/work/job-hunting/info-07-2013/older-workers-more-valuable.html. It is
    reporting on research done by the Sloan Center on Aging and Work.

24. Elizabeth Olson, "Shown the Door, Older Workers Find Bias Hard to Prove,"
    New York Times, August 7, 2017, https://www.nytimes.com/2017/08/07
    /business/dealbook/shown-the-door-older-workers-find-bias-hard-to-prove
    .html.

25. "Unemployed Older Workers: Many Experience Challenges Regaining
    Employment and Face Reduced Retirement Security," United States Govern-
    ment Accountability Office, Report to the Chairman, Special Committee on
    Aging, US Senate, April 2012, http://www.gao.gov/assets/600/590408.pdf.

26. Today, more than a quarter of working-age adults who are not in the work-
    force are homemakers, 97 percent of those homemakers are women, and the
    primary reason for being out of work cited is "family responsibilities." For
    details, see a 2014 poll by the Kaiser Family Foundation/*New York Times*/
    CBS News, which found that of working-age adults (aged twenty-five to fifty-
    four) who are not currently working, two-thirds (67 percent) were women;
    of those, 26 percent were homemakers, and 97 percent of homemakers were
    women. "Overall, most homemakers say they either want a job now or will
    want to go back to work someday; just 13 percent of this group says they
    don't want a job now and don't think they'll want one in the future." Accord-
    ing to the homemakers, "family responsibilities are far and away the top
    reason (84 percent)" why they weren't in the workforce. Liz Hamel, Jamie
    Firth, and Mollyan Brodie, "Kaiser Family Foundation/New York Times/CBS
    News Non-Employed Poll," Henry J. Kaiser Family Foundation, December 11,
    2014, http://www.kff.org/other/poll-finding/kaiser-family-foundationnew-york
    -timescbs-news-non-employed-poll/.

27. "$42 billion in informal economic activity took place in 1981 and . . . four
    out of every five American families purchased something from an informal
    vendor . . . Expenditures for child care in unlicensed establishments and/or in
    the homes of the families buying such care came to $5 billion." James D. Smith,
    "Measuring the Informal Economy," *Annals of the American Academy of
    Political and Social Science* 493, The Informal Economy (September 1987):
    83–99, http://www.jstor.org/stable/1046196.

28. A 2004 study by Stephen Rose and Heidi Hartmann found that even if women
    made on average 77 cents for every dollar earned by a man in a one-year
    period, over a fifteen-year period, women made 38 cents for every dollar men
    earned. Stephen Rose and Heidi Hartmann, "Still a Man's Labor Market: The
    Long-Term Earnings Gap," Institute for Women's Policy Research, February 1,
    2008, https://iwpr.org/publications/still-a-mans-labor-market-the-long-term
    -earnings-gap/.

29. Carole A. Green and Marianne A. Ferber, "The Long-Term Impact of Labor

Market Interruptions: How Crucial Is Timing?," *Review of Social Economy* 66, no. 3 (September 2008): 351–79, http://www.jstor.org/stable/29770479; Deborah J. Anderson, Melissa Binder, and Kate Krause, "The Motherhood Wage Penalty: Which Mothers Pay It and Why?," *American Economic Review* 92, no. 2 (2002): 354–58; Michelle J. Budig and Paula England, "The Wage Penalty for Motherhood," *American Sociological Review* 66, no. 2 (April 2001): 204–25.

30. A 2015 article in the Washington Post notes that "among couples who have paid the same amount into the system, those with one earner can draw tens of thousands of dollars more in lifetime benefits, compared to households with two earners." Max Ehrenfreund, "How Social Security Penalizes Working Women," *Washington Post*, October 23, 2015, https://www.washingtonpost .com/news/wonk/wp/2015/10/23/how-social-security-puts-trophy-wives -ahead-of-single-working-women/. A piece published by Urban Institute fellow Eugene Steuerle in *PBS Newshour* explains further, "Today, spousal and survivor benefits are often worth hundreds of thousands of dollars for the nonworking spouse. If both spouses work, on the other hand, the add-on is reduced by any benefit the second worker earns in his or her own right." Therefore a woman who took a break in her career or worked part time might end up with the same amount as a woman who didn't work at all, unless she made a significantly high amount of money. Eugene Steuerle, "Recent Social Security Reform Doesn't Fix Unfair Spousal Benefits," *PBS Newshour*, November 5, 2015, http://www.pbs.org/newshour/making-sense/column-recent-reform-social -security-replaces-one-unfair-measure-another/.

31. "Women Are the Majority of Workers in 7 out of 10 Low-Paying Jobs for Older Workers," October 2016 Unemployment Report for Workers Over 55, Schwartz Center for Economic Policy Analysis, The New School, November 4, 2016, http://www.economicpolicyresearch.org/index.php/wealth-insecurity -news/1682-october-2016-unemployment-report-for-workers-over-55 #owag.

32. "Highlights of Women's Earnings in 2015," Report 1064, BLS Reports, US Department of Labor, Bureau of Labor Statistics, November 2016, https:// www.bls.gov/opub/reports/womens-earnings/2015/home.htm.

33. In 2015, women made an average of 81 percent of what men made. Women under thirty-five made 88 to 90 percent of what men made. "Women's Earnings in 2015," Bureau of Labor Statistics, https://www.bls.gov/opub/reports /womens-earnings/2015/home.htm; "Issue Brief: Older Women and Economic Security," Women's Bureau, US Department of Labor, February 2015, https:// www.dol.gov/wb/resources/older_women_economic_security.pdf.

34. "Older Women and Economic Security," https://www.dol.gov/wb/resources /older_women_economic_security.pdf.

35. Paula Span, "The Gray Gender Gap: Older Women Are Likelier to Go It Alone," *New York Times*, October 7, 2016, https://www.nytimes.com/2016 /10/11/health/marital-status-elderly-health.html.

36. Carol Stack, *All Our Kin: Strategies for Survival in a Black Community*, 27th Printing ed. (New York: Basic Books, 1983).
37. "Fact Sheet: Older Women and Work," Women's Bureau, US Department of Labor, https://www.dol.gov/wb/resources/older_women_and_work.pdf.
38. Ibid.
39. Ibid.
40. The oil company he worked for was a Teamster company, but it was not part of the Central States pension fund; he still gets a check for $121 from that pension fund.
41. Scott A. Bass, ed., *Older and Active: How Americans over 55 Are Contributing to Society* (New Haven and London: Yale University Press, 1995).
42. "Fast Facts About the Nonprofit Sector," National Council of Nonprofits, https://www.councilofnonprofits.org/sites/default/files/documents/2017-Fast -Facts-About-the-Nonprofit-Sector.pdf.
43. "New Face of Work Survey," MetLife Foundation/Civic Ventures, June 2005, https:/www.psrai.com/filesave/CV%20survey%20report%206%207.pdf.

5. TWO-TIERED AGREEMENTS AND THE DILEMMAS OF GEN X

1. Carol Hymowitz, "Generation X Has It Worse Than Baby Boomers, Millennials," *Boston Globe*, June 10, 2015, https://www.bostonglobe.com/business /2015/06/10/millennials-think-they-have-bad-generation-has-worse /3vhfpB2PCGOSHD2mEX1AwM/story.html.
2. George Masnick, "Defining the Generations," *Housing Perspectives* (blog), November 28, 2012, Harvard Joint Center for Housing Studies, http:// housingperspectives.blogspot.com/2012/11/defining-generations.html.
3. This is according to a 1998 BLS study that documented union membership in the transportation sector from 1975 to 1995. Cynthia Engel, "Competition Drives the Trucking Industry," *Monthly Labor Review*, US Bureau of Labor Statistics, April 1998, https://www.bls.gov/opub/mlr/1998/04/art3full .pdf.
4. "Union Members Summary," US Department of Labor, Bureau of Labor Statistics, economic news release, January 19, 2018, https://www.bls.gov/news .release/union2.nr0.htm.
5. "Central States: Ten Years of Decline Under Hoffa," Teamsters for a Democratic Union, September 11, 2009, http://www.tdu.org/news_central-states-ten -years-decline-under-hoffa.
6. There are over fifteen tiers or "benefit classes" for Central States. Members are enrolled in benefit plans that vary according to when they started on the job, which employer they worked for, and whether they were continuously working for the Teamsters or took a break to do something else.
7. Katie Lobosco, "Pensions May Be Cut to 'Virtually Nothing,' for 407,000 People," *CNN Money*, May 20, 2016, http://money.cnn.com/2016/05/20/retire ment/central-states-pension-fund/index.html?iid=hp-stack-dom.

8. "Central States Slashes Pensions for YRCW Teamsters," Teamsters for a Democratic Union, March 25, 2011, http://www.tdu.org/news_central-states -slashes-pensions-yrcw-teamsters.

9. "Companies That Have Changed Their Defined Benefit Pension Plans," Pension Rights Center, http://www.pensionrights.org/publications/fact-sheet/com panies-have-changed-their-defined-benefit-pension-plans.

10. Ken Belson and Matt Richtel, "Verizon to Halt Pension Outlay for Managers," *New York Times*, December 6, 2005, http://www.nytimes.com/2005/12/06 /business/verizon-to-halt-pension-outlay-for-managers.html.

11. Ibid.

12. Verizon now matches 100 percent of management employees' deferrals up to the first 4 percent of pay and 50 percent of deferrals on the next 2 percent of pay. As a one-time transition, Verizon will add eighteen months of service in calculating employees' pension benefits and the amount of Verizon's retiree health care subsidy.

13. For a list of companies that have reduced or suspended their 401(k) match program, see "Companies That Have Changed or Temporarily Suspended Their 401(k) Matching Contributions," Pension Rights Center, http://www .pensionrights.org/publications/fact-sheet/companies-have-changed-or -temporarily-suspended-their-401k-matching-contribu.

14. Belson and Richtel, "Verizon to Halt Pension," http://www.nytimes.com/2005 /12/06/business/verizon-to-halt-pension-outlay-for-managers.html.

15. Steven Greenhouse, "4-Year Deals for Unions at Verizon," *New York Times,* September 20, 2012, http://www.nytimes.com/2012/09/20/business/verizon -workers-reach-4-year-tentative-pacts.html.

16. Noam Scheiber, "Verizon Strike to End as Both Sides Claim Victories on Key Points," *New York Times,* May 31, 2016, https://www.nytimes.com /2016/05/31/business/verizon-reaches-tentative-deal-with-unions-to-end -strike.html.

17. See Jacob S. Hacker, *The Great Risk Shift: The New Economic Insecurity and the Decline of the American Dream* (New York: Oxford University Press, 2008).

18. Verizon saw high profits in 2015, even with aggressive competition. Lauren Gensler, "Verizon Profit Tops Estimates As It Adds More Subscribers," *Forbes*, April 21, 2015, http://www.forbes.com/sites/laurengensler/2015/04/21/verizon -first-quarter-earnings/#2a2fed5a2ea5. Growth slowed slightly in late 2015 into early 2016, but Verizon was still relatively strong. Ryan Knutson, "Verizon Swings to a Profit, but Pace of Growth Slows," *Wall Street Journal,* January 21, 2016, http://www.wsj.com/articles/verizon-profit-beats-expectations-14533 78839.

19. Dale Russakoff, "Human Toll of a Pension Default," *Washington Post,* June 13, 2005, http://www.washingtonpost.com/wp-dyn/content/article/2005/06 /12/AR2005061201367.html.

20. Micheline Maynard, "United Air Wins Right to Default on Its Employee Pen-

sion Plans," *New York Times,* May 11, 2005, http://www.nytimes.com/2005
/05/11/business/united-air-wins-right-to-default-on-its-employee-pension
-plans.html.

21. Robert Clark, "Evolution of Public-Sector Retirement Plans: Crisis, Challenges, and Change," *The Labor Lawyer* 27, no. 2 (2012): 257–73, http://www.jstor .org/stable/23314985.

22. Mary Williams Walsh, "Detroit Rolls Out New Model: A Hybrid Pension Plan," *New York Times,* June 18, 2014, http://dealbook.nytimes.com/2014 /06/18/detroit-rolls-out-new-model-a-hybrid-pension-plan; Dustin Block, "Detroit Unveils 'Hybrid' Pension Plan; Officials Say Negotiated Plan Will Stabilize System," *Michigan Live,* June 18, 2014, http://www.mlive.com /news/detroit/index.ssf/2014/06/pension_deductions_proposed_fo.html.

23. "Frequently Asked Questions: Component I (Hybrid Plan)," General Retirement System, City of Detroit, http://www.rscd.org/grsd/Resources/FAQs-Component -I-Hybrid-Plan.

24. "Reports, Trends and Statistics," American Trucking Associations, http://www .trucking.org/News_and_Information_Reports_Industry_Data.aspx.

25. Andrew Hogan and Brian Roberts, "Occupational Employment Projections to 2024," *Monthly Labor Review,* US Bureau of Labor Statistics, December 2015, https://doi.org/10.21916/mlr.2015.49.

26. *Heavy and Tractor-trailer Truck Drivers: Occupational Outlook Handbook,* Bureau of Labor Statistics, US Department of Labor, https://www.bls.gov/ooh /transportation-and-material-moving/heavy-and-tractor-trailer-truck-drivers .htm.

27. Steve Viscelli, *The Big Rig: Trucking and the Decline of the American Dream* (Oakland, CA: University of California Press, 2016).

28. Ken Jacobs, "A Tale of Two Tiers: Dividing Workers in the Age of Neoliberalism," *New Labor Forum* 18, no. 1 (2009): 66–77, http://www.jstor.org/stable /40342795; Peter Cappelli and Peter D. Sherer, "Assessing Worker Attitudes under a Two-Tier Wage Plan," *Industrial and Labor Relations Review* 43, no. 2 (1990): 225–44, doi:10.2307/2523701; "Two-Tier Wage Discrimination and the Duty of Fair Representation," *Harvard Law Review* 98, no. 3 (1985): 631–49, doi:10.2307/1340872.

29. "Addison Group's Third Annual Workplace Survey Reveals Ambitious, Anxious Workforce," Addison Group News, October 2016, http://www.addison group.com/news/addison-groups-third-annual-workplace-survey-reveals -ambitious-anxious-work.

30. Anna Robaton, "Why So Many Americans Hate Their Jobs," *CBS News,* March 31, 2017, http://www.cbsnews.com/news/why-so-many-americans -hate-their-jobs/.

31. Laurie Goodman quoted in Shane Farro, "Gen X Is the Most Screwed Generation When It Comes to Real Estate," *Huffington Post,* March 30, 2016, http:// www.huffingtonpost.com/entry/gen-x-screwed-real-estate-housing-crisis_us _56fad298e4b0143a9b497c9c; Wei Li and Laurie Goodman, "Comparing

NOTES

Credit Profiles of American Renters and Owners," Urban Institute, March 2016, http://www.urban.org/sites/default/files/publication/78591/2000652 -Comparing-Credit-Profiles-of-American-Renters-and-Owners.pdf.

32. Paul Fain, "Withholding Social Security to Repay Student Debt," *Inside HigherEd*, December 21, 2016, https://www.insidehighered.com/quicktakes/2016 /12/21/withholding-social-security-repay-student-debt.

33. Stephen Feller, "Number of Retirees with Student Loan Debt Quadrupled in Last Decade," *United Press International*, January 18, 2017, http://www.upi .com/Top_News/US/2017/01/18/Number-of-retirees-with-student-loan-debt -quadrupled-in-last-decade/3721484698049/.

34. Louis Uchitelle, "How Two-Tier Union Contracts Became Labor's Undoing," *The Nation*, February 6, 2013, https://www.thenation.com/article/how-two -tier-union-contracts-became-labors-undoing/.

35. Ibid.

36. "The Spanish social debate on non-standard forms of employment focuses on permanent/fixed-term contracts. The rate of short temporary employment is high (95% of the total of determined fixed-term contracts are short term), and it specially affects young people. In addition to this, short fixed-term contracts lead to worse working conditions, such as less training options, higher probability of working in shifts and overtime and worse health and safety conditions. On the other hand, short part-time is an atypical form of employment rarely given in Spain, and it specially affects women, with a percentage of 2.96%, in contrast with a general rate of 1.72%." "Spain: Flexible Forms of Work: 'Very Atypical' Contractual Arrangements," EurWork: European Observatory of Working Life, March 4, 2010, https://www.eurofound .europa.eu/observatories/eurwork/comparative-information/national -contributions/spain/spain-flexible-forms-of-work-very-atypical-contractual -arrangements.

37. Katherine S. Newman, *The Accordion Family: Boomerang Kids, Anxious Parents, and the Private Toll of Global Competition* (Boston: Beacon Press, 2012).

38. "The Retirement Readiness of Generation X: The Lasting Effects of the 'Great Recession' on Gen-Xers' Retirement Outlook," Insured Retirement Institute, January 2014, https://www.myirionline.org/docs/default-source/research/the -retirement-readiness-of-generation-x-january-2014.pdf?sfvrsn=2.

39. Greg Iacurci, "Gen X Lags Boomer Generation in Retirement Savings: Study," *Investment News*, October 13, 2015, http://www.investmentnews.com/article /20151013/FREE/151019973/gen-x-lags-boomer-generation-in-retirement -savings-study.

40. "Ambitious, Anxious Workforce," http://www.addisongroup.com/news/addi son-groups-third-annual-workplace-survey-reveals-ambitious-anxious-work.

41. Rodney Brooks, "Will We Ever Be Able to Retire? Boomers and GenX-ers Are Worried," *Washington Post*, November 28, 2016, https://www.washingtonpost .com/news/get-there/wp/2016/11/28/will-we-ever-be-able-to-retire-boomers -and-gen-x-ers-are-worried/.

42. In an issue brief from March 2017, Alicia H. Munnell and coauthors tracked the shift from defined benefit to defined contribution plans from 1992 to 2010, to determine how the rise in defined contribution plans affected retirement wealth and income during that period. The authors made four key observations: "First, retirement wealth has been relatively steady or declining, depending on whether the starting year is 1992 or 1998. Second, DC wealth is more concentrated in the top quartile of education than DB wealth, and this concentration will become more evident in the aggregate wealth measure as the shift from DB to DC plans evolves. Third, the shift from DB to DC has reduced the amount of retirement income per dollar of wealth because DC participants have to pay more for annuities, and annuity rates fell as interest rates dropped. Fourth, even with later retirement ages, steady retirement income combined with rising wages has produced declining replacement rates. Thus, retirement income from employer plans has been contracting." Alicia H. Munnell, Wenliang Hou, Anthony Web, and Yinji Li, "How Has the Shift to 401(k) Plans Affected Retirement Income?," Trustees of Boston College, Center for Retirement Research, Number 17-5 (March 2017), http://crr.bc.edu/wp-content/uploads/2017/03/IB_17-5.pdf.

6. RETIRING ON NEXT TO NOTHING

1. Alan B. Krueger, "The Great Utility of the Great Gatsby Curve," Brookings Social Mobility Memo, May 19, 2015, https://www.brookings.edu/blog/social-mobility-memos/2015/05/19/the-great-utility-of-the-great-gatsby-curve.

2. As of July 2017, of the parish population overall, 56.3 percent are white, 41.6 percent are black, 2.2 percent are Hispanic, and 0.5 percent are Asian. See "QuickFacts: St. Landry Parish, Louisiana," United States Census Bureau, https://www.census.gov/quickfacts/fact/table/stlandryparishlouisiana/PST045217.

3. "Quick Facts: Opelousas City, Louisiana," https://www.census.gov/quickfacts/table/PST045215/2258045.

4. In 2015, the median property value of owner-occupied housing was $88,300, and the owner-occupied housing rate was 50.2 percent. In 2015, 71.5 percent of people over twenty-five had graduated from high school, and 10.2 percent had gone on to get bachelor's degrees. In 2015, of people under sixty-five, 9.3 percent had a disability and 23 percent were without health insurance. "Opelousas City," https://www.census.gov/quickfacts/table/PST045215/2258045.

5. The elderly comprise about 14 percent of Opelousas residents.

6. Emily Brandon, "10 Places Where Retirees Live in Poverty," *U.S. News and World Report*, May 18, 2012, https://money.usnews.com/money/retirement/slideshows/10-places-where-retirees-live-in-poverty.

7. History of Opelousas, The City of Opelousas, Louisiana, https://www.cityofopelousas.com/visitors/history-opelousas; "Why Parishes? The Story Behind Louisiana's Unique Map," *Times-Picayune*, September 8, 2017, http://www.nola.com/300/2017/09/why_does_louisiana_have_parishes_09082017.html.

8. Carl A. Brasseaux and Philip Gould, *Acadiana: Louisiana's Historic Cajun Country* (Baton Rouge: Louisiana State University Press, 2011), 67.

9. In 1863 the capital was relocated to Shreveport. "The Opelousas Area: History," St. Landry Chamber of Commerce, Town Square Publications, http://local.townsquarepublications.com/louisiana/opelousas/02/topic.html.

10. William Miller, "The Opelousas Massacre," Media Nola, A Project of Tulane University, April 11, 2014, http://www.medianola.org/discover/place/1199/The-Opelousas-Massacre.

11. Cheryl Devall, "Opelousas' Black History, Written and Lived," *Daily World*, February 26, 2015, http://www.dailyworld.com/story/news/local/2015/02/26/opelousas-black-history-written-lived/24084113/.

12. Ruth Foote, "Farm Boy to First Black Mayor," *Acadiana Advocate*, January 21, 2013, http://www.theadvocate.com/acadiana/news/article_5c5e9915-8361-5212-8605-81f67e895988.html.

13. "1985: The Oil Bust Hits the New Orleans Economy," *Times-Picayune*, December 28, 2011, http://www.nola.com/175years/index.ssf/2011/12/1985_the_oil_bust_hits_the_new.html.

14. Lisa Benoit, "About St. Landry Parish," LSU AgCenter, April 6, 2010, http://www.lsuagcenter.com/portals/our_offices/parishes/st%20landry/features/about_the_parish/about-st-landry-parish.

15. Craig Gautreaux, "2016 Was a Tough Year for Louisiana Agriculture," *Delta Farm Press*, December 21, 2016, http://www.deltafarmpress.com/cotton/2016-was-tough-year-louisiana-agriculture.

16. "Oil Bust," http://www.nola.com/175years/index.ssf/2011/12/1985_the_oil_bust_hits_the_new.html.

17. Homepage, Southwest Louisiana Zydeco Music Festival, http://www.zydeco.org/.

18. "About Us," Opelousas General Health System, https://www.opelousasgeneral.com/about_us.aspx; "Major Employers in St. Landry Parish," St. Landry Parish Economic Development, http://www.opportunitystlandry.com/data-downloads/leading-employers.

19. The hospital is one of the best places in the region for workers with modest skills. Their wages are higher and there is a 401(k) defined contribution retirement plan in place. Accordingly, serving food in the hospital is a far better job than dishing out at a fast food restaurant. Benefits, Opelousas General Health System, https://www.opelousasgeneral.com/sites/www/Uploads/files/Careers/benefit_pamphlet.pdf.

20. The hospital serves Sunset, Grand Coteau, Port Barre, Eunice, Washington, Arnaudville, Leonville, Krotz Springs, Melville, Eunice, Lawtell, Palmetto, Ville Platte, and Church Point. "History of OGHS," Opelousas General Health System, https://www.opelousasgeneral.com/about_us/history_of_oghs.aspx.

21. "Top 100 Private Companies," *Greater Baton Rouge Business Report*, July 21, 2014, https://www.businessreport.com/article/top-100-private-companies-2.

22. "Acadiana Top Employers 2015," Acadiana Economic Development, http:// teamacadiana.org/site101.php.

23. Ken Stickney, "Job Fair: Companies Seek Skilled Workers," *Daily Advertiser,* February 15, 2017, http://www.theadvertiser.com/story/money/business/2017 /02/15/book-fair-highlights-industrial-jobs/97962126/.

24. "Acadiana Top Employers 2015," http://teamacadiana.org/site101.php.

25. "Major Employers in St. Landry," http://www.opportunitystlandry.com/data -downloads/leading-employers.

26. Washington, DC, with a 17 percent elderly poverty rate, is even worse than Louisiana. Juliette Cubanski, Kendal Orgera, Anthony Damico, and Tricia Neuman, "How Many Seniors Are Living in Poverty? National and State Estimates Under the Official and Supplemental Poverty Measures in 2016," Henry J. Kaiser Family Foundation, March 2, 2018, https://www.kff.org /report-section/how-many-seniors-are-living-in-poverty-national-and-state -estimates-under-the-official-and-supplemental-poverty-measures-in-2016 -tables/.

27. "From 1966 through 2006, the official poverty rate for persons 65 or older declined from 28.5 percent to 9.4 percent. In 1966, elderly poverty exceeded that of adults aged 18–65 by 18 percentage points. By 1993, parity with the poverty rate of other adults was achieved, and since that year, the elderly poverty rate has generally been over a percentage-point lower than that registered for adults of 'working age.'" Joyce Nicholas and Michael Wiseman, "Elderly Poverty and Supplemental Security Income," *Social Security Bulletin* 69, no. 1 (2009), https://www.ssa.gov/policy/docs/ssb/v69n1/v69n1p45.html.

28. In 2012, about two-fifths (39 percent) of those age sixty-five and older received income from retirement benefits other than Social Security, such as defined benefit pensions, Individual Retirement Accounts (IRAs), 401(k) plans, and related savings. "Social Security and People of Color," National Academy of Social Insurance, https://www.nasi.org/learn/socialsecurity/people-of-color.

29. "Among seniors 65 and older, Social Security is the sole source of income for 40 percent of Hispanics, 33 percent of African Americans, and 26 percent of Asian and Pacific Islanders, compared to 18 percent of whites . . . Social Security's survivor and disability benefits are important sources of income security for many people of color. Because African Americans have lower life expectancy and higher disability rates before age 65 as compared to other races, they are more likely to receive Social Security disability and survivor benefits." "Social Security and People of Color," National Academy of Social Insurance, accessed July 18, 2018, https://www.nasi.org/learn/socialsecurity /people-of-color.

30. Officially, the national poverty rate in 2016 for seniors (over sixty-five) was only 9.3 percent, but is more when we include other factors, like the cost of health care. The Supplemental Poverty Measurement (SPM) goes beyond the federal poverty measure, which is a multiple of the cost of food, to include other expenses, including health care, transportation to work, and the like. The

SPM puts the 2016 senior poverty rate at 14.5 percent. "Poverty Facts," Poverty USA, http://www.povertyusa.org/facts.

31. Alexandra Cawthorne, "Elderly Poverty: The Challenge Before Us," Center for American Progress, July 30, 2008, https://www.americanprogress.org/issues /poverty/reports/2008/07/30/4690/elderly-poverty-the-challenge-before-us/.

32. April Yanyuan Wu, Matthew S. Rutledge, and Jacob Penglase, "Why Don't Lower-Income Individuals Have Pensions?," Trustees of Boston College, Center for Retirement Research, Number 14-8 (April 2014), http://crr.bc.edu/wp -content/uploads/2014/04/IB_14-8.pdf; "Fact Sheet: Social Security," Social Security Administration, https://www.ssa.gov/news/press/factsheets/basicfact -alt.pdf.

33. "What Is the Difference Between Medicare and Medicaid?" US Department of Health and Human Services, October 2, 2015, https://www.hhs.gov/answers /medicare-and-medicaid/what-is-the-difference-between-medicare-medicaid /index.html.

34. For more on the regional concentration of poor health, disability and a long history of inequality reinforced by regressive taxation, see Katherine S. Newman and Rourke O'Brien, *Taxing the Poor: Doing Damage to the Truly Disadvantaged* (Berkeley, CA: University of California Press, 2011).

35. Joyce Nicholas and Michael Wiseman, "Elderly Poverty and Supplemental Security Income," *Social Security Bulletin* 69, no. 1 (2009), https://www.ssa .gov/policy/docs/ssb/v69n1/v69n1p45.html.

36. Households qualify for SNAP if they have less than "$2,250 in countable resources (such as cash or money in a bank account) or $3,500 in count-able resources if at least one member of the household is age 60 or older, or is disabled." Supplemental Nutrition Assistance Program (SNAP), US Depart-ment of Agriculture Food and Nutrition Service, https://www.fns.usda.gov /snap/snap-special-rules-elderly-or-disabled.

37. Mark Ballard, "Number of Louisiana Households Receiving Food Stamps at Its Highest Ever—and Poised to Increase," *Advocate,* June 18, 2016, http:// www.theadvocate.com/baton_rouge/news/politics/legislature/article _df248098-3528-5f5d-8b80-14f07df6abd0.html.

38. "Section 202 Supportive Housing for the Elderly Program," US Department of Housing and Urban Development, https://portal.hud.gov/hudportal/HUD ?src=/program_offices/housing/mfh/progdesc/eld202.

39. "Section 202: Directory of New York City Affordable Housing Programs," NYU Furman Center, http://furmancenter.org/institute/directory/entry/section -202-supportive-housing-for-the-elderly.

40. In this, Section 202 housing is very similar to Section 8 housing, which has no age restrictions.

41. This constitutes a 10 percent reduction. Cynthia Ramnarace, "No New Homes for Poorest Older Adults," *AARP Bulletin*, November 18, 2011, http://www .aarp.org/home-garden/housing/info-11-2011/no-new-homes-for-poorest -older-adults.html.

42. Jose A. DelReal, "Trump Administration Considers $6 Billion Cut to HUD Budget," *Washington Post*, March 8, 2017, https://www.washingtonpost.com /politics/trump-administration-considers-6-billion-cut-to-hud-budget/2017 /03/08/1757e8e8-03ab-11e7-b1e9-a05d3c21f7cf_story.html.

43. See Newman and O'Brien, *Taxing the Poor.*

44. John Dupont, "Bobby Jindal Down, but Probably Not Out," *Livingston Parish News,* January 28, 2017, http://www.livingstonparishnews.com/opinion /editorials/john-dupont-bobby-jindal-down-but-probably-not-out/article _e5497c30-e28b-11e6-a5d3-e7ee83ed693a.html.

45. Stephanie Grace, "How Bobby Jindal Broke the Louisiana Economy," *Newsweek*, June 1, 2015, http://www.newsweek.com/how-bobby-jindal-broke -louisiana-economy-337999.

46. See Newman and O'Brien, *Taxing the Poor.*

47. Will Sentell, "Washington, La. Scrutinized for Being 'Speed Trap,'" *Advocate*, April 28, 2014, http://www.theadvocate.com/baton_rouge/news/politics/leg islature/article_63aacf83-eaf4-50f1-90ad-aa4324695965.html.

48. The same pattern is at play in Ferguson, Missouri, where tension over traffic stops boiled over into full-scale riots following the death of Michael Brown in 2014.

49. David Yarbrough is his real name, not a pseudonym.

50. Before Lyndon Johnson's War on Poverty, they would have been entirely without access to health insurance. Prior to the enactment of Social Security in the 1930s, they would have had no income. Indeed, people in their parents' generation were often unable to access this fundamental federal program because until the 1950s, it covered neither agricultural nor domestic workers, an exclusion demanded by southern senators who threatened to jettison Roosevelt's entire New Deal if he included these (almost entirely African American) workers. Fortunately, for this generation, who began their work lives in the 1950s and 60s, Social Security belonged to them as much as to their white age-mates.

51. The disability rolls are swelling in part because welfare regulations have tightened up, making it harder to qualify for Temporary Assistance for Needy Families (TANF, or welfare). Many people in Opelousas who might have been on public assistance in the past are on disability now. Chana Joffe-Walt, "Unfit for Work: The Startling Rise of Disability in America," *Planet Money*, National Public Radio, https://apps.npr.org/unfit-for-work/.

52. "HUD Section 202: Supportive Housing for the Elderly," Policy Guide, Community-Wealth.org, http://community-wealth.org/strategies/policy-guide/hud _section-202.html; "Section 202," US Department of Housing and Urban Development, https://portal.hud.gov/hudportal/HUD?src=/program_offices /housing/mfh/progdesc/eld202.

53. "Opelousas Colored School," Read the Plaque, http://readtheplaque.com /plaque/opelousas-colored-school.

54. There are also a lot of Baptist and Pentecostal churches in Opelousas.

55. Lester Limpele is his real name, not a pseudonym.

56. Helen K. Black, "Poverty and Prayer: Spiritual Narratives of Elderly African-American Women," *Review of Religious Research* 40, no. 4 (1999): 359–74, doi:10.2307/3512122.

57. "Opelousas, Louisiana Food Pantries," Food Pantries.org, http://www.food pantries.org/ci/la-opelousas.

58. "Single Family Housing Repair Loans & Grants," US Department of Agriculture, Rural Development, https://www.rd.usda.gov/programs-services /single-family-housing-repair-loans-grants.

59. Helen Levy, "Income, Poverty, and Material Hardship Among Older Americans," *RSF: The Russell Sage Foundation Journal of the Social Sciences* 1, no. 1 (2015): 55–77, doi:10.7758/rsf.2015.1.1.04.

60. Ira Katznelson argues that social programs like the New Deal discriminated against blacks in the 1930s and 1940s by leaving certain forms of labor that were more likely to be performed by black workers out of the Social Security system. See Ira Katznelson, *When Affirmative Action Was White: An Untold Story of Racial Inequality in Twentieth-Century America* (New York: W. W. Norton and Company, 2005).

7. KEEPING THE PROMISE

1. Pew found in 2015 that "After more than four decades of serving as the nation's economic majority, the American middle class is now matched in number by those in the economic tiers above and below it." "The American Middle Class Is Losing Ground," Pew Research Center, December 9, 2015, http://www.pewsocialtrends.org/2015/12/09/the-american-middle-class-is -losing-ground/.

2. Joe Cortright, "What America's 'Most Egalitarian Zip Code' Demonstrates About Inequality. And What It Doesn't," *Atlantic*, October 12, 2015, https:// www.theatlantic.com/business/archive/2015/10/ogden-utah/409960/.

3. Richard V. Reeves and Edward Rodrigue, "The American Middle-Class Is Still Thriving in Utah," Brookings, March 10, 2016, https://www.brookings.edu /blog/the-avenue/2016/03/10/the-american-middle-class-is-still-thriving-in -utah/; Don Lee, "In Quiet Ogden, Utah, a Surprising Glimpse of Income Equality," *Los Angeles Times*, July 19, 2015, http://www.latimes.com/nation /la-na-utah-town-income-gap-20150719-story.html.

4. See Robert N. Bellah, Richard Madsen, William M. Sullivan, Ann Swidler, and Steven M. Tipton, *Habits of the Heart: Individualism and Commitment in American Life*, 3rd ed. (Berkeley, CA: University of California Press, 2007).

5. For a discussion of federal investments in the American West, see Andrew Ross, *Bird on Fire: Lessons from the World's Least Sustainable City* (New York: Oxford University Press, 2011).

6. "What's the Mormon Community Like?" Mormon.org, https://www.mormon .org/beliefs/church-community.

7. In 2017, according to the US Census Bureau, an estimated 84 percent of Ogden residents were white. "Quick Facts: Ogden City, Utah," US Census Bureau, https://www.census.gov/quickfacts/fact/table/ogdencityutah/PST045217#viewtop.

8. At the local level, the LDS Church is organized into "wards" (congregations of 200 to 400 members) and "stakes" (administrative units made up of five to fifteen neighboring congregations). "How the Church Is Organized," LDS.org, https://www.lds.org/topics/church-organization/how-the-church-is-organized?lang=eng&old=true.

9. "Priesthood," LDS.org, https://www.lds.org/topics/priesthood?lang=eng.

10. "Relief Society," LDS.org, https://www.lds.org/callings/relief-society?lang=eng.

11. Patricia Lyn Scott, Linda Thatcher, and Susan Allred Whetstone, eds., *Women in Utah History: Paradigm or Paradox?* (Logan, UT: Utah State University Press, 2005).

12. "The Purpose of Visiting Teaching," LDS.org, https://www.lds.org/callings/relief-society/visiting-teaching-training/purpose-is-to-minister?lang=eng.

13. Bellah et al., *Habits of the Heart.*

14. For an official statement on the approach of the LDS Church to welfare, see "Providing in the Lord's Way," LDS.org, https://www.lds.org/topics/welfare/the-church-welfare-plan/providing-in-the-lords-way?lang=eng&old=true.

15. The LDS Church has organized various kinds of missionary work (conversion, welfare, humanitarian aid, etc.) around the United States and the world. The church strongly encourages two-year full-time missions for young men starting at age nineteen and optional missions for young women, and it offers seniors the opportunity to go on missions as well. "Missionary Preparation," LDS.org, https://www.lds.org/callings/missionary?lang=eng.

16. See Bellah et al., *Habits of the Heart.*

17. "Quickfacts: Ogden City, Utah," https://www.census.gov/quickfacts/fact/table/ogdencityutah/PST045216.

18. 2017 Population Estimates: Ogden-Clearfield, UT Metro Area, US Census Bureau, https://factfinder.census.gov/bkmk/table/1.0/en/PEP/2017/PEPANNRES/310M300US36260.

19. The beehive was chosen as the emblem for the seal of the State of Utah when Utah became a state in 1896. "Utah State Motto and Emblem," Utah's Online Library, Utah Department of Heritage and Arts, http://onlinelibrary.utah.gov/research/utah_symbols/motto.html.

20. Martha Sonntag Bradley, *ZCMI: America's First Department Store* (Salt Lake City, UT: ZCMI, 1991), 11.

21. Richard G. Oman, "Beehive Symbol," Harold B. Lee Library, Brigham Young University, http://eom.byu.edu/index.php/Beehive_Symbol.

22. Assimilation was not a straightforward process, nor is it complete to this day. Despite the church's new trade with non-Mormons, at the turn of the twentieth century, controversies over polygamy and statehood led most of the American public to believe that business in Utah was entirely controlled by

ecclesiastical leaders. Attacks on the Mormon economic order became more intense during the Reid Smoot hearings and climaxed with muckraking assaults from 1910 to 1913. See Thomas G. Alexander, *Mormonism in Transition: A History of the Latter-Day Saints, 1890–1930* (Champaign, IL: University of Illinois Press, 1996), 74–75; see also Brian Q. Cannon and Jessie L. Embry, eds., *Utah in the Twentieth Century* (Logan, UT: Utah State University Press, 2009).

23. Joseph Walker, "New Study Confirms Many LDS Stereotypes," *Deseret News*, December 14, 2011, http://www.deseretnews.com/article/700207176/New -study-confirms-many-LDS-stereotypes.html.

24. See chart in Matt Canham, "Mormon Populace Picks Up the Pace in Utah," *Salt Lake Tribune*, December 2, 2014, http://www.sltrib.com/news/1842825 -155/mormon-populace-picks-up-the-pace.

25. Interview with Professor Marilyn Luptak, University of Utah School of Social Work, July 12, 2016.

26. Lee Davidson, "Utah Ranks No. 1 for Share of Undocumented Immigrants in Workforce," *Salt Lake City Tribune*, November 4, 2016, http://archive.sltrib .com/article.php?id=4541055&itype=CMSID.

27. Micah Cohen, "Utah: Very Republican, but Not Quite as Conservative as It Appears," *FiveThirtyEight* (blog), *New York Times*, July 9, 2012, https:// fivethirtyeight.blogs.nytimes.com/2012/07/09/utah-very-republican-but-not -as-conservative-as-it-appears/.

28. "How LDS Charities Helps Refugees," LDS Charities, https://www.ldscharities .org/news/how-lds-charities-helps-refugees.

29. Interview with Marilyn Luptak, July 12, 2016.

30. For a discussion of federal investments in the American West, see Ross, *Bird on Fire*.

31. Unlike others quoted in this chapter, this is his real name.

32. According to the Pew Center for Research, "The top 10 middle-income metropolitan areas are more rooted in manufacturing than the nation overall." "America's Shrinking Middle Class: A Close Look at Changes Within Metropolitan Areas," Pew Research Center, May 11, 2016, http://www.pewsocialtrends .org/2016/05/11/americas-shrinking-middle-class-a-close-look-at-changes -within-metropolitan-areas/.

33. Elizabeth Gardner, "Why Does Utah Rank So High in Health Care?," *NEJM Catalyst*, May 2, 2016, http://catalyst.nejm.org/why-does-utah-rank-so-high -in-health-care/.

34. Gardner, "Utah Health Care," http://catalyst.nejm.org/why-does-utah-rank-so -high-in-health-care/.

35. "Retirement and Savings," Intermountain Healthcare Employee Benefits, https://intermountainhealthcare.org/careers/employee-benefits/retirement -benefit/.

36. "Ogden, UT," Data USA, https://datausa.io/profile/geo/ogden-ut/.

37. "Opelousas, LA," Data USA, https://datausa.io/profile/geo/opelousas-la/.

38. "The Bishops' Storehouse," LDS.org, https://providentliving.lds.org/bishops -storehouse?lang=eng.

39. "Tithing," LDS.org, https://www.lds.org/topics/tithing?lang=eng.

40. "How Are Tithing Funds Used?," LDS.org, https://www.lds.org/manual/tithing -and-fast-offerings/how-are-tithing-funds-used?lang=eng.

41. "Senior Missionary," LDS.org https://www.lds.org/topics/welfare/missionary -opportunities?lang=eng&old=true.

42. According to a 2013 study of civic life in Utah, 95.6 percent of residents frequently ate dinner with other members of the household, 92.4 percent frequently talked with their neighbors, and 58.8 percent of residents participated in groups and/or organizations. In addition, 77.9 percent of Utah residents engaged in "informal volunteering" (for example, doing favors for neighbors). "Utah: Trends and Highlights Overview," Corporation for National and Community Service, https://www.nationalservice.gov/vcla/state/Utah.

43. According to the Corporation for National and Community Service, volunteerism rates in Utah are the highest in the United States, with 43.3 percent of adults volunteering in the state, the highest ranking in the country. In 2015 in Utah, 844,023 people volunteered, putting in 75.5 volunteer hours per capita, a total of 170.36 million hours of service, with $3.8 billion in service contributed. Roughly 65 percent of volunteer activities were coordinated through religious organizations. "Utah: Overview," https://www.nationalservice .gov/vcla/state/Utah.

44. Ibid.

45. JustServe, https://www.justserve.org/.

46. Weber Human Services, https://www.weberhs.net/.

47. The Zion curtain law was struck down in July of 2017. Amy Held, "Utah's 'Zion Curtain' Falls and Loosens State's Tight Liquor Laws," NPR, July 2, 2017, http://www.npr.org/sections/thetwo-way/2017/07/02/535259524/utahs -zion-curtain-falls-and-loosens-states-tight-liquor-laws.

48. Emma Green, "When Mormons Aspired to Be a 'White and Delightsome' People," *Atlantic*, September 18, 2017, https://www.theatlantic.com/politics /archive/2017/09/mormons-race-max-perry-mueller/539994/; "Race and the Priesthood," LDS.org, https://www.lds.org/topics/race-and-the-priesthood ?lang=eng.

49. According to the ACLU of Utah: "Differences in opportunity continue to negatively affect people of color, and discrimination against racial minorities often leads to dramatically unequal outcomes in a broad spectrum of areas including education, employment, and even rates of incarceration." "Racial Justice," ACLU of Utah, http://www.acluutah.org/racial-justice.

50. Tyson Smith, "Employment by Race, Ethnicity and Gender in Wasatch Front North," *Utah Insights* 2, no. 4 (Spring 2014), https://web.archive.org/web /20170502022958/http://www.jobs.utah.gov/wi/pubs/localinsights/spring2014 /localinsightswfn.pdf.

51. "SCSEP," Easter Seals-Goodwill Northern Rocky Mountain, http://www

.easterseals.com/esgw/our-programs/employment-training/scsep.html; Senior Community Service Employment Program (SCSEP), US Department of Labor, https://www.doleta.gov/seniors/.

52. SCSEP, https://www.doleta.gov/seniors/.

53. Smith, "Employment by Race, Ethnicity and Gender," https://web.archive.org /web/20170502022958/http://www.jobs.utah.gov/wi/pubs/localinsights /spring2014/localinsightswfn.pdf.

54. "Weber County, UT," DataUSA, https://datausa.io/profile/geo/weber-county -ut/.

55. "Poverty Status in the Past 12 Months: Ogden," American FactFinder, US Census Bureau, https://factfinder.census.gov/faces/tableservices/jsf/pages/pro ductview.xhtml?src=CF.

56. A 2015 study found that Utah had the fourth worst gender pay gap in the nation. In Utah, women earn $.70 for every dollar men earn; the national figure in 2015 was, in comparison, $.79. "Utah's Gender Opportunity," Voices for Utah Children, October 20, 2015, http://www.utahchildren.org/newsroom /item/649-explaining-utah-s-gender-gap-in-wages.

CONCLUSION

1. Gary V. Engelhardt and Jonathan Gruber, "Social Security and the Evolution of Elderly Poverty," in *Public Policy and the Income Distribution*, ed. Alan J. Auerbach, David Card, and John M. Quigley (New York: Russell Sage Foundation, 2006), 259–87, http://www.jstor.org/stable/10.7758/9781610440202.10.

2. See Monique Morrissey, "Hispanic Workers Are Less Likely to Have the Opportunity to Participate in Retirement Plans," Economic Snapshot, Economic Policy Institute, October 13, 2016; see also Morrissey, "White Workers Have Nearly Five Times as Much Wealth in Retirement Accounts as Black Workers," Economic Snapshot, Economic Policy Institute, February 18, 2016.

3. "2017 Melbourne Mercer Global Pension Index," Australian Centre for Financial Studies, https://www.mercer.com.au/content/dam/mercer/attach ments/asia-pacific/australia/mmgpi-2017/au-2017-mmgpi-report.pdf.

4. Per Klitgard, "Danish Government Raises Retirement Age as Benefits System Continues to Prosper," *World Finance*, August 14, 2017, https://www.world finance.com/wealth-management/danish-government-raises-retirement-age -as-benefits-system-continues-to-prosper.

5. Ibid.; "Social Security Programs Throughout the World: Europe, 2016— Denmark," Office of Retirement and Disability Policy, Social Security Administration, https://www.ssa.gov/policy/docs/progdesc/ssptw/2016-2017/europe /denmark.html.

6. Ulf Hedetoft, "Denmark: Integrating Immigrants into a Homogeneous Welfare State," Migration Policy Institute, November 1, 2006, http://www.migration policy.org/article/denmark-integrating-immigrants-homogeneous-welfare -state.

7. Torben M. Andersen and Lars Haagen Pedersen, "Financial Restraints in a Mature Welfare State—The Case of Denmark," *Oxford Review of Economic Policy* 22, no. 3 (October 1, 2006): 313–29, doi:10.1093/oxrep/grj019; Kjetil Storesletten, "Fiscal Implications of Immigration—A Net Present Value Calculation," *Scandinavian Journal of Economics* 105, no. 3 (September 2003): 487–506, doi:10.1111/1467-9442.t01-2-00009.

8. Klitgard, "Danish Government Raises Retirement Age," https://www.world finance.com/wealth-management/danish-government-raises-retirement-age -as-benefits-system-continues-to-prosper.

9. Stephen Gadd, "Agreement Reached on Changes to Danish Pension System," June 21, 2017, CPH Post Online, http://cphpost.dk/news/agreement-reached -on-changes-to-danish-pension-system.html.

10. Klitgard, "Danish Government Raises Retirement Age," https://www.world finance.com/wealth-management/danish-government-raises-retirement-age -as-benefits-system-continues-to-prosper.

11. "Who Gets an AOW Pension?," AOW Pension, Sociale Verzekeringsbank, https://www.svb.nl/int/en/aow/wat_is_de_aow/wie_krijgt_aow/.

12. "State Pension Age Increase Boosts Immigrants AOW Rights," *Dutch News*, January 13, 2017, http://www.dutchnews.nl/news/archives/2017/01/state -pension-age-increase-boosts-immigrants-aow-rights/.

13. "AIO Supplement," Sociale Verzekeringsbank, https://www.svb.nl/int/en /aio/wanneer_bijstand/wanneer_bijstand/index.jsp.

14. Mary Williams Walsh, "No Smoke, No Mirrors: The Dutch Pension Plan," *New York Times*, October 11, 2014, https://www.nytimes.com/2014/10/12 /business/no-smoke-no-mirrors-the-dutch-pension-plan.html.

15. "Today's Dutch Pensioners 'Have Never Had It So Good,'" *Dutch News*, March 7, 2017, http://www.dutchnews.nl/news/archives/2017/03/todays -dutch-pensioners-have-never-had-it-so-good/.

16. Walsh, "Dutch Pension Plan," https://www.nytimes.com/2014/10/12/business /no-smoke-no-mirrors-the-dutch-pension-plan.html.

17. "Do the Dutch Have the Pension Problem Solved?," *PBS NewsHour*, November 10, 2013, http://www.pbs.org/newshour/bb/business-july-dec13 -dutchpensions_11-10/.

18. "Age Pension," Australian Government Department of Human Services, https://www.humanservices.gov.au/individuals/services/centrelink/age -pension.

19. Ghardilucci, etc. p. 62. Draft of their book. Fix this reference.

20. Stephanie Anderson, "Interactive: How Australia's Pension System Works," *SBS News*, June 13, 2014, http://www.sbs.com.au/news/article/2014/06/13 /interactive-how-australias-pension-system-works.

21. Professor Whiteford of the Crawford School of Public Policy at Australian National University said, "As the population ages over the next 30 or 40 years, the growth in spending in age pensions is likely to have a significant impact on future spending requirements." Anderson, "Australia's Pension System,"

http://www.sbs.com.au/news/article/2014/06/13/interactive-how-australias
-pension-system-works.

22. Emily Brandon, "10 Places Where Retirees Live in Poverty," *U.S. News and World Report*, May 18, 2012, https://money.usnews.com/money/retirement /slideshows/10-places-where-retirees-live-in-poverty.

23. Brittany Bronson, "Why Las Vegas Is a Great Place for Working-Class Women," *New York Times*, August 17, 2016, https://www.nytimes.com/2016/08/17 /opinion/how-unions-help-cocktail-servers.html.

24. Steven Greenhouse, "ORGANIZED; Local 226, 'the Culinary,' Makes Las Vegas the Land of the Living Wage," *New York Times*, June 3, 2004, http:// www.nytimes.com/2004/06/03/us/organized-local-226-the-culinary-makes -las-vegas-the-land-of-the-living-wage.html.

25. "The Culinary Worker," Culinary Union Local 226, http://www.culinaryunion 226.org/news/culinary-worker; "The Culinary Health Fund" Culinary Union Local 226, http://www.culinaryunion226.org/members/benefits/culinary-health -fund.

26. "The Culinary Union Pension," Culinary Union Local 226, http://www .culinaryunion226.org/members/benefits/culinary-union-pension.

27. Although unions have historically been strong, union membership in Nevada has been down for the past few years, particularly among public-sector workers. Given that unionized workers accounted for only 12.1 percent of wage and salary workers in 2016 (just 146,000 workers), the vast majority of residents are not in unions. "Nevada's union membership places the state in a tie for 14th nationally with Massachusetts and well above the national average of 10.7 percent." Seventy-five percent of public sector workers are part of some retirement plan, but two-thirds of Nevada's private-sector employees don't participate in any retirement plan. That means the majority of the state's pop-ulation is not likely to be in good shape for retirement.

28. Pashtana Usufzy, "Blame Growth for Much of Nevada's Poor Health Care Rankings, Studies Say," *Las Vegas Review-Journal*, May 15, 2016, https://www .reviewjournal.com/news/education/blame-growth-for-much-of-nevadas -poor-health-care-rankings-studies-say/.

29. "WCT Pension Trust 60th Anniversary: The Western Conference of Teamsters Pension Trust," http://www.wctpension.org/about-pension-trust/wct-pension -trust-60th-anniversary; "Western Conference of Teamsters Pension Trust Fund Turns 60," Teamsters Local Union 856, http://teamsters856.org/news/western -conference-of-teamsters-pension-trust-fund-turns-60/.

30. "One and Done: Nevada's Unusual, Powerful Unions," *Economist*, August 10, 2017, https://www.economist.com/united-states/2017/08/10/nevadas-unusual -powerful-unions.

31. Ina Jaffe, "Obamacare Repeal Could Threaten Provisions That Help Older Adults," *Weekend Edition*, National Public Radio, January 28, 2017, http:// www.npr.org/sections/health-shots/2017/01/28/511994587/obamacare -repeal-could-threaten-provisions-that-help-older-adults. Further improve-

ments on the ACA could include bringing annual premiums down for individuals by eliminating the 30 to 40 percent of health care spending that is essentially "waste"—in other words, expenditures that don't actually improve patient health outcomes. Our current pay-for-service system focuses on treating sickness rather than maintaining health, enables unnecessary procedures that don't help people stay healthy, duplicates services, and is rife with medical errors (225,000 people die each year due to medical errors). In addition, there could be better-quality reporting for hospitals and physicians and collaborative medical learning networks for the leadership of various hospitals and medical systems to learn best practices. Although the politics of reform are ferocious, costs would also decrease if the penalties were steeper for young healthy people who choose to opt out. Also, 20 states (including Louisiana until 2016) opted to not accept federal funding to expand Medicaid, and 3 million more people could be covered by Medicaid if these states would do so. John S. Toussaint, "Improve the Affordable Care Act, Don't Repeal It," *Harvard Business Review,* November 16, 2016, https://hbr.org/2016/11/improve-the-affordable-care-act-dont-repeal-it.

32. H.R. 676, 115th Congress (2017–18): Expanded & Improved Medicare For All Act. US Congress, February 10, 2017, https://www.congress.gov/bill/115th-congress/house-bill/676. In spite of its name, technically this would not actually be an expansion of Medicare (which allows for private supplemental insurance that is for-profit). Medicare is popular and well known among voters, but the single-payer system Conyers proposed looks to be closer to an expansion of Medicaid. Jeff Stein, "What Rep. John Conyers's Sweeping Single-Payer Health Care Bill Would Actually Do," *Vox,* August 28, 2017, https://www.vox.com/policy-and-politics/2017/8/28/16114436/john-conyers-single-payer-insurance.

33. Bob Kinzel, "Sanders Says Support Is Growing for His 'Medicare for All' Universal Health Care Plan," Vermont Public Radio, August 29, 2017, http://digital.vpr.net/post/sanders-says-support-growing-his-medicare-all-universal-health-care-plan#stream/0.

34. David Lawrence Madland, "A Wink and a Handshake: Why the Collapse of the U.S. Pension System Has Provoked Little Protest" (PhD diss., Georgetown University, 2007).

35. Richard H. Thaler and Shlomo Benartzi, "Save More Tomorrow: Using Behavioral Economics to Increase Employee Saving," *Journal of Political Economy* 112, no. S1 (February 2004): S164–87.

36. "FSP's Retirement Savings Initiative," Aspen Institute, https://www.aspeninstitute.org/programs/financial-security-program/forum-retirement-security/. For a report on the leadership forum of the Financial Security Program, see David Mitchell, "Building a More Robust and Inclusive US Retirement System amid a Changing Economy," Aspen Institute, September 27, 2017, https://www.aspeninstitute.org/publications/building-robust-inclusive-us-retirement-system-amid-changing-economy/.

37. Eric Drobelyen, "Thrift Savings Plan-Like 401(k)s Are the Key to Closing the Small Business Coverage Gap," Aspen Institute, July 17, 2017, https://www.aspeninstitute.org/blog-posts/thrift-savings-plan-like-401ks-key-closing-small-business-coverage-gap/; David Mitchell, "Secure Choice States Get Final Go-Ahead from Obama Administration," Aspen Institute, September 7, 2016, https://www.aspeninstitute.org/blog-posts/secure-choice-states-get-final-go-ahead-obama-administration/.

38. Bennett Kleinberg, "Aggregation Could Be the Solution to the Retirement Coverage Gap," Aspen Institute, July 23, 2017, https://www.aspeninstitute.org/blog-posts/aggregation-solution-retirement-coverage-gap/.

39. David Mitchell, "A Possible Solution to Meet Consumers' Short- and Long-Term Financial Needs: Sidecar Accounts," Aspen Institute, July 31, 2017, https://www.aspeninstitute.org/blog-posts/possible-solution-meet-consumers-short-long-term-financial-needs-sidecar-accounts/. They also encourage technology-facilitated redesign of the traditional 401(k) to make it easier for small businesses and start-ups to offer employees retirement accounts (through simple improvements like automatically linking payroll information or employee eligibility). Shin Inoue, "Solving the Retirement Crisis Through Better Design," Aspen Institute, July 27, 2017, https://www.aspeninstitute.org/blog-posts/solving-retirement-crisis-better-design/.

40. Patricia Cohen, "Bump in U.S. Incomes Doesn't Erase 50 Years of Pain," *New York Times*, September 16, 2017, https://www.nytimes.com/2017/09/16/business/economy/bump-in-us-incomes-doesnt-erase-50-years-of-pain.html.

41. Teresa A. Sullivan, Elizabeth Warren, and Jay Lawrence Westbrook, *The Fragile Middle Class: Americans in Debt* (New Haven; London: Yale University Press, 2000); Peter Temin, *The Vanishing Middle Class: Prejudice and Power in a Dual Economy* (Cambridge, MA; London, England: MIT Press, 2017).

42. Sherrod Brown, Senator for Ohio, "Brown Announces Plan to Protect Ohio Pensions, Keep Promises to Ohio Workers," press release, November 6, 2017, https://www.brown.senate.gov/newsroom/press/release/brown-announces-plan-to-protect-ohio-pensions-keep-promises-to-ohio-workers.

43. "Brown Announces Plan," https://www.brown.senate.gov/newsroom/press/release/brown-announces-plan-to-protect-ohio-pensions-keep-promises-to-ohio-workers.

44. "Contribution and Benefit Base," Social Security Administration, https://www.ssa.gov/oact/cola/cbb.html.

45. Paul Krugman, "Where Government Excels," *New York Times*, April 10, 2015, https://www.nytimes.com/2015/04/10/opinion/paul-krugman-where-government-excels.html.

ACKNOWLEDGMENTS

Thirty years ago, I published a book entitled *Falling from Grace: The Experience of Downward Mobility in the American Middle Class*. It was one of the first to draw attention to the waves of unemployment and occupational displacement that were reaching into previously unknown territory: the vast middle class. In the early 1980s, the nation saw double-digit unemployment figures, the worst since the Great Depression. The losses were almost unimaginable to people who thought that their education and experience would protect them against the economic insecurity that millions of poor people already knew so well. In many instances, the people who appeared in *Falling from Grace* were on the receiving end of deregulation and the occupational upheavals that followed in its wake.

In the spring of 2015, I was fortunate to be included in the annual meeting of the Aspen Institute's Program on Financial Security, a gathering of US senators, state government officials, bankers, insurance company executives, think tank economists, and academics like myself. The focus of this workshop was the nation's pension system. Ida Rademacher and her colleague Jeremy Smith, the leaders of the Aspen Institute program, brought these experts together to review the overwhelming evidence that the nation's provisions for retirees were already falling well short of what was needed and to sound the alarm that the future was going to look much worse.

At the time, I had done no research to speak of about retirement. But it became clear that the degradation of retirement security was the bookend to the unraveling I had chronicled in *Falling from Grace*. What began thirty years earlier as a wave of unemployment and a skidding descent down the class ladder for millions of middle-class Americans was now returning in the form of a tsunami of pension plan bankruptcies. Ida and Jeremy encouraged me to devote the next two years to understanding how serious the problems of inequality in retirement are, and they opened many doors to help make *Downhill from Here* possible.

Three hundred people were interviewed for this book from all over the country. Their voices were preserved by my colleague Rebecca Hayes Jacobs and transcribed by a small but devoted crew she enlisted: Claire Klinger, Sara Bloem, and Sabrina Bleich. Rebecca was nearing the end of her doctoral program at Yale University when I was introduced to her by her thesis advisor, Professor Kathryn Dudley, who was one of my very first PhD students at Columbia University many years before.

Rebecca was eager to get additional research experience, and through her prodigious talent and dedication managed to finish her dissertation and do nearly all of the primary interviews for this book at the same time. She traveled all over the country, from the Northeast, where she interviewed Verizon workers, to the Midwest, where she spoke to dozens of retired Teamsters. She moved to Opelousas, Louisiana, for three weeks in order to capture the experience of poverty-level retirement, and she settled into Ogden, Utah, to learn about how much better we could do if we followed its example. Rebecca has been a joy to work with and a major intellectual contributor to this volume, especially to chapter 7, which was her "baby" from the very beginning. She is now a postdoctoral fellow at the Museum of the City of New York, which is very fortunate to have her.

Among the very first organizations we turned to in order to find the diversity of people who appear in *Downhill from Here* was the Pension Rights Center in Washington, DC, which has played a leading role both in dramatizing the plight of working-class people whose pensions are under attack and in organizing resistance to those cuts. Karen Ferguson, the director, Karen Friedman, the executive vice president and policy director, and Joellen Leavelle, communications director, introduced me to Rita Lewis, to whom I owe a major debt of gratitude, and many other Teamsters who have campaigned tirelessly to protect the pensions they had earned in the Central States Pension Fund.

The National United Committee to Protect Pensions and Teamster locals in Cincinnati, Milwaukee, Canton, Akron, and New York facilitated interviews with their retired and active members. The Northeast Ohio, Central Ohio, and Wisconsin Southeast/Milwaukee Committees to Protect Pensions also helped by pointing the way to people whose experiences with pension loss are recorded here. David Hecker, the president of the American Federation of Teachers in Michigan, was helpful in locating Detroit teachers on the wrong end of pension reductions and health care losses.

The Association of BellTel Retirees and its public relations firm, Thomas P. Butler and Associates, helped me to tell the story of many white-collar workers caught up in the spinoff from Verizon and the demise of the Yellow Pages.

Several lawyers and nonprofit leaders helped me to understand the pension problems experienced by their clients. I appreciate the candor and the tutoring I received from Eddie Stone, who represents Bell Telephone retirees; Ryan Plecha, a lawyer for Detroit public-sector retirees; Debra Carter, Senior Community Service Employment Program national director, National Caucus and Center on Black Aging; Jerry Rubin, president and CEO, and his colleague Amy Mazur, both of the Jewish Vocational Services of Greater Boston; and Meryl Kanner, Jewish Vocational Services of New Jersey. The Easter Seals-Goodwill organization of Northern Utah, United Way of Northern Utah, and St. Landry-Evangeline United Way have my thanks for suggesting interviewees and explaining how these nonprofits work to help the elderly retirees in their midst. A number of colleagues at the American Association for Retired Persons, the nation's most vocal and effective organization to represent the voices of the nation's over-fifty population, helped me to find my way through the policy thicket and the nonprofit world.

Public officials (including Tom Christopulos, director of community and economic development in Ogden, Utah), journalists (often the best source for finding people on the ground), and fellow academics were generous with their knowledge of local history. I appreciate the contributions of journalists Nathan Bomey and Bill McGraw in Detroit, as well as David Yarbrough, dean of community service at the University of Louisiana at Lafayette, and Chancellor Daniel Little, Professor Joshua Akers, and Professor Bruce Pietrykowski at the University of Michigan Dearborn. Joshua Gotbaum, the former chair of the Pension Benefits Guaranty Corporation, now at the Brookings Institution, gave up valuable time to give me his perspective on the Teamsters' Central States Pension Fund losses and the actions of Congress during the debates over the Kline-Miller Multiemployer Pension Reform Act of 2014.

CVS Health is an important leader in hiring the gray labor force. Barbara Hoenig, a consultant to CVS in these efforts, Gregory Schmidt, and Amanda Tierney pointed the way toward finding older workers.

I have benefited from conversations with several academic colleagues whose expertise on retirement systems has been exceptionally valuable. Hence, I thank Alicia Munnell, the director of the Boston College Center for Retirement Research, Teresa Ghilarducci, director of the Retirement Equity Lab at the New School for Social Research, and Ruth Milkman, professor of sociology at the Murphy Institute for Worker Education and Labor Studies. Their work is foundational in many of the areas I touch on in this book.

The ideas in this book have been made more vivid and accessible by the devoted attention given to them by my editors at Metropolitan Books, Grigory Tovbis and Riva Hocherman, and my literary agent, Lisa Adams at the Garamond Agency. I am grateful to all three of them for partnering with me to bring *Downhill from Here* to the public.

My husband, Paul Attewell, distinguished professor of sociology at the Graduate Center of the City University of New York, has been an intellectual partner in all of my research ventures, including this one.

Our sons—Steven, thirty-five, now an adjunct assistant professor in the Murphy Center for Labor Studies at CUNY, and David, twenty-nine, a PhD student in political science at the University of North Carolina, Chapel Hill—have been tolerant of my research preoccupations since their toddler days. It is a joy for Paul and me to see both of them pursue their own intellectual passions, while leaning on them to bring ours to fruition.

This book was originally written during my time as provost of the University of Massachusetts's flagship campus at Amherst, and it was supported by research funds—for which I am very grateful—provided by its chancellor, Kumble Subbaswamy. My immediate colleagues there, including especially Diane Vayda and Deborah Gould, provided me with much-needed moral and organizational support, which is why I single them out here. I completed the book while transitioning to two new positions, as senior vice president of the University of Massachusetts system and interim chancellor of UMass Boston. Working with all of my colleagues in President Martin Meehan's office and the talented faculty, students, and staff of the Boston campus reminds me every day of the importance of public higher education.

This book is dedicated to the memory of my closest friend for nearly thirty-five years, Elaine Combs-Schilling. I was in the midst of researching *Downhill from Here* when she became gravely ill. We were assistant professors together, raised our children as neighbors, and shared the ups and downs of life in ways large and small. Never too busy to listen, never too tired to help, Elaine was a rare person in her selflessness, as dozens of her students and colleagues, not to mention her husband David and son Jonathan, would agree. She was the first scholar to bring home to me the importance of understanding the subjective realities of ordinary people, the ways in which they are impacted by and interpret the waves of social and economic change that are beyond their control and often crash down upon them without warning. Elaine passed away far too soon and she is deeply missed by everyone who knew her, especially me.

INDEX

Ackerman, Bill, 16, 44
Adams, Brad, 40
advertising sales, 49–50, 52
Affordable Care Act (ACA; Obamacare, 2010), 6, 103–5, 106, 250, 259–60
African Americans, 6–7, 9–10, 89–90, 136, 192, 251, 257–58
  Detroit and, 77–91, 105
  fines and fees and, 192
  Ogden and, 229, 241–45
  Opelousas and, 179–211, 229
  trucking and, 18–20
  voting rights and, 183
age discrimination, 67–68, 116–20, 140, 142, 249–50
agriculture, 184–86, 193, 211
Agriculture Department (USDA), 189, 206
Airline Deregulation Act (1978), 60
airline industry, 21, 48, 60–71. *See also* United Airlines
airline pilots, 46, 61–63
air traffic controllers, 23, 61
Allen, Monique, 84–85, 98, 101–4
All of Our Kin (Stack), 136

American Association of Retired Persons (AARP), 119
American Benefits Council, 8
American Federation of Labor-Congress of Industrial Organizations (AFL-CIO), 28, 33
American Federation of State, County and Municipal Employees (AFSCME), 26
America West, 71
Animal Rescue League, 144
annuities, 57–59, 74, 100–102, 156
anti-tax policies, 95
antitrust, 21, 51
Archer, Dennis, 94
Asian Americans, 188
Aspen Institute, Financial Security Program, 260–61, 265
Association of BellTel Retirees, 56, 58, 71, 73–74
AT&T, 51
Atlantic City, 258
Australia, 11, 252, 256–57, 265, 266
auto industry, 23, 79–81, 87–88, 159. *See also specific companies*
auto parts suppliers, 80, 85

Baby Bells, 49, 51
baby boomers, 11, 113–14, 130, 139, 148, 169, 176
Baker Hughes company, 187
Baltimore, 88, 108–9
banks and banking, 21, 39, 41, 94–95, 200. *See also* Wall Street
Barkley, Barry, 19
Barnett, Leon, 29, 34, 43
Barnett, Mary, 43
Baton Rouge, 180, 183, 187
Bellah, Robert, 220
Bell Atlantic, 51, 156
Bell Telephone Company "Ma Bell," 47–53, 153, 260
Berkowitz, Alison, 143–44
Bhatti, Saqib, 95–96
Big Rig, the (Viscelli), 165–66
Bloomberg, 62
blue-collar workers, 8, 16, 21, 31–44, 116, 137, 171, 175, 242–43. *See also* unions; *and specific industries and unions*
Boeing, 56, 155
Bomey, Nathan, 92
bond rating agencies, 78, 109
Boston Globe, 148
Boyle, Kevin, 89
Bristol-Myers Squibb, 59
Brown, Sherrod, 264
Brownsville-Harlingen region (Texas), 257
Bunkie, Louisiana, 193
Bureau of Labor Statistics (BLS), 129, 130, 165
Burger King, 195
Bush, George W., 250
Business Depot Ogden, 225
Butch Lewis Act (proposed), 264
Byrne, Jeffrey, 52–52

Cahan, Joe, 58, 73
California, 2, 78, 191, 261
Canada, 252
Cantrell, Fred, 238–39
Cantrell, Paige, 238–40
Carter, Annabel, 190, 196–97, 206–8
Carter, Jimmy, 21
Cataldo, Sebastian, 151–52

Catholic Church, 201, 203, 218, 223
CBS, 169
Center for Effective Government, 3
Center for State and Local Government Leadership, George Mason University, 92–93
Central Pacific Railroad, 222
Central States Pension Fund, 8, 24–45, 138–39, 149–52
Chevalier, Lydia, 190, 199, 205–7, 214, 232
Chicago, 78, 88, 109–10
Chicago Municipal Employees' Annuity and Benefit Fund (MEABF), 109
childcare, lack of, 181
childcare workers, 122–24, 126–27, 129, 131
child poverty rates, 265
Chile, 252
Christopulos, Tom, 225–26, 237–38
chronic illness, 10, 20, 189
Chrysler Motors, 80, 88, 96
cities, 2, 9. *See also* Detroit; *and other specific cities*
　bankruptcy and, 2, 76, 78–79, 81, 92–96, 105–6, 108–11, 173
　bond ratings and, 78
　crash of 2008 and, 95
　deindustrialization and, 88, 108
　municipal debt and, 95–96
　outmigration and, 88, 92–96
　poverty rates and, 108
　privatization and, 95–96
　underfunded pension funds and, 109–10
civil rights, 19, 90
civil service, 9, 77–78, 78–79, 82–83, 105
Civil War, 183, 191, 211
Clinton, Bill, 25–26, 51, 64–65
Clinton, Hillary, 4
Coleman, Roberta, 104
collective bargaining, 24, 148, 157
Colombia, 252
commodity prices, 187
Communication Workers of America (CWA), *146*
communitarian code, 220–21
Connecticut, 261

construction industry, 76, 186–87
Consumer Finance Protection Bureau (CFPB), 174
Continental Airlines, 68–70
contract employees, 106–7
Conyers, John, 260
corporations, 37, 56, 96, 155
  mergers and, 22
  taxes and, 93, 224
corruption, 85
cost of living, 115
cost-of-living increases (COLAs), 56–57, 60, 97, 156
crime rates, 108, 223
Culinary Workers Union, 257–58
CVS, 9

Dallas, 109
Davis, Tim, 150–51, 174
Day, Susan, 77, 81–85, 87, 99, 102, 104–5
Dean, Aaron, 243–44, 246–47
debt, 148, 174
defense contractors, 224
Defense Depot Ogden, 223, 225
defined benefit pensions, 4–6, 8, 56, 114–15, 149, 155–56, 158, 160–61, 226, 250–51, 258
defined contribution pensions, 5. See also annuities; 401(k)s
deindustrialization, 88, 108–9
Democrats, 21, 36, 92, 191, 264
demographic change, 11, 113–14, 144–45
Denmark, 252–54, 265
dental benefits, 181
Depression, 27, 191, 250
deregulation, 21–25, 37, 57, 60, 64, 70, 149, 153, 165–66
derisking, 58
deskilled work, 125–27
Detroit, 76, 77–111, 148, 211, 250, 263
  annuity clawback and, 100, 174
  bankruptcy and, 2, 76, 78–79, 81, 91–96, 173
  contract employees and, 106–7
  corruption and, 85
  crash of 2008 and, 94–96
  emergency managers and, 96
  future of, 105–11
  Grand Bargain and, 97–105, 107–8, 164
  health benefit cuts, 103–5
  mayoralty elections, 81, 94
  riots of 1967, 90–91
  taxes and, 84–85, 88, 91–96, 108
  two-tier agreement and, 162–64
Detroit city council, 98
Detroit City engineers' office, 82
Detroit Civil Service Commission, 80
Detroit firefighters, 76, 91–92, 94, 96–97, 103–4, 116, 163–64, 166–67, 172–73
Detroit health department, 81
Detroit Institute of Arts (DIA), 97–100
Detroit police, 90–92, 94, 96–97, 103–4
Detroit public library, 76, 87–88, 169, 172
Detroit public schools, 91
Detroit Resurrected (Bomey), 92
Detroit Transportation Department, 101
District Council 37, 26
Donegan, Jerry, 161, 167–68, 170–71
Duane Reade, 9

Eakins, Ted, 64–66
early retirement, 26, 53, 63, 67–71, 154, 196, 254
Eastern Air Lines, 71
Easterseals-Goodwill SCSEP (Senior Community Service Employment Program), 244–45, 247
Eber, Betty, 57
Economic Policy Institute, 115, 251
Edmond, James, 79–83, 85, 87, 106–7
Edwards, Edwin, 185
elder poverty, 2, 10, 182–83, 188–95, 200–211, 246, 257, 265
elections
  of 2013, 4
  of 2016, 4, 39, 104
Elsie (Detroit worker), 2
emergency managers, 96
Employee Retirement Income Security Act (ERISA, 1974), 26, 28, 58–59
employee stock ownership plans (ESOPs), 61, 64–66

engineers, 48, 60, 63–67
Ericson, Christine, 227, 233, 237
Ericson, Garry, 233, 237
Erwin, Tammy, 201, 204, 207
Europe, 175, 252–54, 265
Evangeline Downs Racetrack and
    Casino, 182, 185, 187–88
Evans, Elaine, 202–5
executive and CEO retirement plans, 3,
    71–72, 158, 240
Expanded & Improved Medicare for
    All Act (proposed), 260

families, 7, 43, 45, 136, 138–39, 149,
    159, 172–73, 176, 207, 217–18,
    230–31, 250–51
Family Dollar stores, 187
Farber, Peter, 20, 29–30
fast food industry, 194, 195
Federal Communications Commission
    (FCC), 51
federal government, 8, 10, 30–31,
    33–36, 147, 189–91, 203, 213–17,
    220, 224–29, 247 257. See also
    specific agencies and programs
FedEx, 155
Feinberg, Kenneth, 44
Felton, Clyde, 91
financial crash of 2008. See Great
    Recession of 2008–9
Florio, Patty, 66–69, 70, 71
Flynn, Doug, 16, 34, 40
food, sales tax on, 191–92
food banks, 200, 205, 228, 236
food stamps. See Supplemental
    Nutrition Assistance Program
Forbes, 25
Ford Foundation, 97
Ford Motors, 56, 79–80, 88, 106–7
Forest City, North Carolina, 257
401(k) plans, 5, 7, 9, 57, 63, 70,
    107, 115, 117, 142, 155–59,
    161, 172, 174, 181, 188,
    216–17, 224, 226, 230, 232,
    250–51, 258
  reforming, 260–61
  working poor and, 181, 188
Fox, Ray, 163, 166
French, Anthony, 164–66, 170–71

Gallup, New Mexico, 257
gambling industry, 185, 224, 258
Gary, Indiana, 88
General Electric (GE), 19, 55
General Motors (GM), 56, 59, 80
generation X, 9–10, 130, 147–77,
    264
Gerard, Milton, 196, 201
givebacks, 23–24, 55, 61, 148, 171
globalization, 57, 73–74
Goldman Sachs, 25, 31, 38, 41
Google, 52
Gotbaum, Josh, 26–27, 41
Gotbaum, Victor, 26
Government Accountability Office
    (GAO), 39, 120
gray labor force, 9, 112, 113–45,
    249–50, 263
  elder poverty and, 195–96
  Ogden and, 241–42, 244, 246–47
Great Gatsby Curve, 180
Great Migration, 79
Great Recession of 2008–9, 5–7, 10,
    26–33, 37–38, 41, 59, 94–95, 119,
    123–24, 140, 147, 156, 173, 176,
    251–52, 255, 262
GTE, 51

Habits of the Heart (Bellah), 220
Halliburton, 187
Hamilton, Shane, 22
Hannigan, John, 48–51, 55
Hannigan, Lisa, 48–55, 74–75
Harper, Janice, 240
Harrisburg, Pennsylvania, 108
Head Start, 242
health care benefits, 10, 55–56, 69, 78,
    96, 103–5, 217, 224, 250, 252,
    258–60
  two-tiered agreements and, 154–57,
    160, 149, 162–64
  working poor and, 181
health care industry, 226
Hewlett-Packard, 155
Hill Air Force Base, 216, 224, 232,
    242–44
Hoffa, Jimmy, Jr., 33
Hoffa, Jimmy, Sr., 25, 30, 33
Holland Freight, 14–15, 23–24

Holy Ghost Catholic Church (Opelousas), 200–201, 203–5, 218, 232
Home Depot, 9
home equity, 5, 176, 262
homelessness, 223
home ownership, 198–99, 205–6, 226, 256
hospitals, 96, 186–87, 191, 225–26
housecleaners, 134–36, 193, 209, 244
housing, 3, 148. *See also* mortgages
   collapse of 2008, 5–7, 37–38, 147, 173, 262
   elder poor and, 190–91, 198–99, 200–201
   racial discrimination and, 89, 242
Housing and Urban Development (HUD), 190, 200–201
Hunter, Lily, 163
Hurricane Audrey (1957), 186
Hurricane Harvey (2017), 192
hybrid pension plan, 162–64

IBM, 55, 155
Idearc (*formerly* Yellow Pages; *later* SuperMedia), 53–55, 74
Illinois, 261
immigrants, 79, 87, 242, 253–54, 258. *See also specific groups*
Immigration and Customs Enforcement (ICE), 220
India, 66–67
inequality, 3–4, 7, 116, 180, 134–39, 212, 213–47, 251, 257, 265
injuries, 10, 14, 29–30
Institute for Policy Studies, 3
institutions, loss of faith in, 35–36, 262–63
Insured Retirement Institute, 176
interest rates, 6, 147
interest-rate swaps, 94–95
Intermountain Healthcare, 226
Internal Revenue Service (IRS), 10–11, 213, 216, 224, 243, 247
International Brotherhood of Teamsters, 1–2, 8, 12, 13–45, 49, 55, 71, 86, 148–49, 211, 250, 263
   corruption and, 30
   federal oversight of, 25
   gray labor and, 116, 137–39

job quality and, 164–66, 170
   KOPPA and, 39–40
   membership declines and, 149–50
   minorities and, 19
   PBGC and, 40
   protests by, 12, 36–38, 41–42
   two-tiered agreements and, 150–52, 174
internet, 52, 74
Interstate Commerce Commission (ICC), 21
IRAs, 159, 188
   Roth, 159
   Secure Choice, 261
Italy, 176

Jacobs, Rebecca Hayes, 213
Janowski, Amy, 73
Jarvis, John, 184, 190, 196, 205, 208
JCPenney, 56
Jim Crow, 18, 79, 88, 183–84, 202–3
Jindal, Bobby, 191
job quality decline, 164–74, 235–36
Johnson, Lyndon, 90, 250
Joiner, Tim, 63, 68–70, 72–73
Jones, Gabriel, 152–54, 158–60
Jones Day law firm, 96
Joseph, John W., 184
Joubert, Zadie, 187, 195, 198, 207–8
J.P. Morgan Asset Management, 176
Justice Department, 51
JustServe program, 237

Kaminski, Albert, 166–67, 172–73
Kammerer, Larissa, 17–18, 32
Kammerer, Tim, 17, 20–21, 32
Kaptur, Marcy, 36, 39
Keep Our Pension Promises Act (KOPPA, proposed), 39
Kennedy, John F., 25
Kilpatrick, Kwame, 94–95, 100, 104
Kimberly-Clark, 56, 59
Knight Foundation, 97
Kowalski, Patricia, 87–88, 91, 100–101
Kraft, Larry, 142–43
Kresge Foundation, 97
Krugman, Paul, 266
Ku Klux Klan, 88
Kwanzaa, 204

Labor Department, 40–41, 64, 115, 136–37
labor force participation, 136–37
Lachlan, Jack, 223–24, 235–36
Lachlan, Margaret, 223–24
Lafayette, Louisiana, 180, 186–87, 202
Lambert, Jill, 231–32
Lane, Donna, 244–47
Lanter, Floyd, 13–15
Laredo, Texas, 257
Las Vegas, 257–58
Latinos, 6–7, 18, 217, 219, 223, 241–42, 188, 251, 257–58
Latter-Day Saints, Church of (LDS; Mormons), 11, 214–47, 257
  Holy Ghost Church vs., 232–33
  minorities and community beyond, 236–47
LDS JustServe, 237
LDS Relief Society, 218, 231–33
LeCompte, Ginger, 185–86, 193, 200
Ledoux, Arnold, 186, 190–91, 200
Lee, Carmen, 241–42, 246
Lee, Elvira, 242
Lerner, Irving, 117–20, 122, 124–34, 139
Lerner, Leslie, 117–18, 120–27, 129–34, 137, 139
Lewis, Butch, 12, 14–15, 22–25, 28–30, 41–42, 249, 263
Lewis, Rita, 12, 13–15, 17–18, 20, 23–25, 29–34, 38, 40–42, 44, 263
LGBT community, 240–41
Lidell, Hazel, 246–47
life expectancy, 7, 113–14, 254
Limpele, Father Lester, 204–5
Livonia, Michigan, 80
Louisiana, 10, 180, 183–85, 188–93, 198, 203, 224
low-income workers, 6–7, 180–81, 184–95, 222, 224, 242–47, 251, 257, 261–63
LTV Steel, 37
lynching, 183

Macy's, 140
Manjoo, Farhad, 64–65
manufacturing, 23, 108, 148, 225
Mardi Gras, 178, 179, 180
Markel, Theo, 94–95, 98–99

Maryland, 261
Massachusetts, 191, 225
Maurer, Ron, 234
Maurer, Sally, 234
McDonald's, 187
Medicaid, 189, 201, 229, 250, 260
Medicare, 3, 6, 36, 103–5, 145, 163–64, 188–89, 196, 217, 226, 250, 259–60
  eligibility for, 138
  expansion of, 260
  privatization of, 105
Medicare Advantage, 103
Medicare gap plans, 103, 135, 163
Melbourne Mercer Global Pension Index, 252
Mexican immigrants, 11, 220, 242. See also Latinos
Mexico, 88
Miami, 257
Michigan, 85, 92–97
Michigan National Guard, 90–91
Michigan state legislature, 92
middle class, 3, 212, 213, 263
millennials, 9–10, 148, 158, 169
Miller, James, 137–39
Miller, Joleen, 199
Miller, Mark, 210
Miller, Mitchell, 210
Miller, Valerie, 199, 207–10
Milwaukee bus drivers, 137–38
morale, 169–74
moral values, 34–38, 220, 227–37, 262–66
Moretti, Carlos, 154–55, 157–58, 160, 167, 172–73
Mormon Church. See Latter Day Saints, Church of
Morrissey, Monique, 251–52
mortgages, 6, 199
  reverse, 5
  subprime, 7, 28, 37, 41
Motor Carrier Act (1980), 21
Motorola, 59, 155
multiemployer pension plans, 24–26, 28–29, 33–40, 165
Multiemployer Pension Reform Act (MPRA, 2014), 28–29, 33–36
  KOPPA and, 39–40
municipal workers, 76, 77–111

Nathanson, Louise, 214–20, 223, 234, 247
Nathanson, Randy, 214–20, 234, 247
National Building Trades Council, 28
National Merit Scholarships, 80
Native Americans, 241
Netherlands, 11, 252, 254–55
Nevada, 258–59
Newark, 88
New Deal, 2, 250–51
New England Telephone, 51
New Jersey, 191
New Orleans, 185
New York City, 4, 78, 109–10, 118
New York State, 165, 191
New York Telephone, 51
New York Times, 108, 156, 174, 255, 258
nonprofits, 97, 139–44, 238, 244, 247
Nordic nations, 252, 266
Northern Trust, 25, 31, 38, 41
nursing, 210
nursing homes, 193–94, 196, 201
Nyhan, Thomas, 29, 33, 38, 42, 44, 149–52
NYNEX, 51, 153–54, 156
NYNEX Pension Plan, 53

Obama, Barack, 250
offshoring, 52, 148
Ogden, Utah, 10, *212*, 212–47
    Opelousas vs., 214, 216–18, 222, 224, 226, 229, 232–33, 246–47
Ohio, 36, 151
oil and gas industry, 21, 47, 186–87, 195, 224
    shocks of 1970s, 60, 71, 80–81, 147, 184
Opelousas, Louisiana, 10–11, *178*, 179–211, 226, 228, 232–33, 246, 257, 258
    Ogden vs., 214, 216–18, 222, 224, 226, 229, 232–33, 246–47
Opelousas Area Ministerial Alliance, 205
Opelousas Colored School (St. Landry Parish Training School), 202
Opelousas General Hospital, 186
Opelousas High School, 179
Opelousas Massacre, 183

Oregon, 261
Orr, Kevyn, 96–99
outsourcing, 66–67, 69, 71, 74, 157, 167–69
overtime, 155

Pagini, Vincent, 154–55, 157, 171–72
Pan Am, 61, 71
Parker, Virginia, 139–42
part-time work, 195, 244, 258
payday loans, 199–200
Pennsylvania state legislature, 108
Pension Benefit Guaranty Corporation (PBGC), 26–27, 37, 39–41, 46, 57, 63, 70, 161, 165, 264
    KOPPA and, 39–40
People Express, 60
perma-temp jobs, 175–76
Phillips, Jay, 228, 231, 233–34
Pietrykowski, Bruce, 93
pink collar jobs, 121, 129, 137
police, 15, 19, 76, 192
Polish immigrants, 79, 87–89
Portugal, 176
poverty, 89–90. *See also* child poverty rates; elder poverty; low-income workers
Powers, Werner, 54
Preston, Grant, 85–87, 110–11
privatization, 95–96
productivity, 115, 170
Promontory Summit, 222
promotions, 82–84
Providence, Rhode Island, 88
Prudential Financial, 57, 59
PTSD, 243–44
public schools, 96, 184, 191, 202, 216–17, 243
public transit, 181, 194
Puerto Rico, 108

QuickChek, 120, 125, 128

racial discrimination, 3, 79–80, 82–84, 89, 92–96, 180, 184, 201–4, 222, 241–43
Reagan, Ronald, 21, 23–24, 30, 147
recessions, 8, 251. *See also* Great Recession of 2008–9

Reconstruction, 183
reductions in force (RIFs), 67
Reich, Robert, 65
replacement rate, 114, 145, 250, 255, 265
Republicans, 21, 92, 222
Retirement Heist (Schultz), 56, 71–72
retirement funds, state vs. federal regulation of, 58–59
retirement savings, 188, 193–96, 244, 251–52, 261–62, 265
    mandatory, 256
    sidecar accounts, 261
retirement system, improving, 257–66
Rideau, Lorna, 207, 210
right-to-work states, 88, 148, 224
Rochefort, Nina, 194, 198–99
Romano, Marissa, 134–37, 139
Romney, George, 90
Roosevelt, Franklin D., 2, 250
Roosevelt Institute, 95
Rosen, Gerald, 97–98
Rossi, Joseph, 35
rust belt, 24, 35, 41, 88
Ryan, Deborah, 205

safety standards, 21
salespeople, 48–50
sales taxes, 191–92
Salon, 64
Salt Lake City, 221, 230
Salt Lake Community College, 230
Sanders, Bernie, 4, 39, 44, 260
sandwich generation, 250
Schlumberger company, 187
Schultz, Ellen, 56, 71–72
Sears, 56
Section 202 program, 190, 200–201, 204
Section 504 program, 206–7
Secure Choice plans, 261
self-employed workers, 122, 144
September 11, 2001 attacks, 62, *178*
service industry, 185, 187–88, 224, 242–43
Shaforth, Frank H., 92–93
Shannon, Kelly, 74
sharecropping, 79, 181, 211
Sherman, Trevor, 92, 105–6

ShopRite, 120, 125
Shultz, Ellen, 71–72
sick leave, 10, 162
slavery, 191
Snyder, Rick, 93, 96
social contract, betrayal of, 35–38, 55, 211, 262–64
social mobility, 180, 208–11
Social Security, 3–4, 6, 10, 36, 70, 102, 104, 117, 152, 174, 188, 200, 210, 240, 242, 250
    early retirement and, 114–15, 196
    elder poverty and, 190, 194, 196
    gray labor and, 141, 145
    reforming, 264–66
    self-employment and, 122–24, 135
    spousal benefits and, 197
    tax cap and, 145, 265–66
    women and, 122–24, 137
    working poor and, 181
Social Security Disability Insurance (SSDI), 50, 188–89, 194, 196–98
Society of the Divine Word, 204
Solomon, Steven Davidoff, 54
"Solutions Not Bailouts" (report), 28
South, 18, 79, 191–92, 211
Southwest Airlines, 60, 65
Southwest Louisiana Zydeco Festival, 185
Spain, 175, 176
Spence, Odette, 84–85
spinoffs, 53–54, 74
Spirit Airlines, 60
spousal benefits, 69–70
Stack, Carol, 136
Staples, Kevin, 18
steel industry, 23
St. Landry-Evangeline United Way, 185
St. Landry Parish, 182–88, 191–92
St. Landry Parish Community Action Agency, 199
St. Landry's Catholic Church, 203
stock market, 3, 7, 8, 25–27, 37. *See also* Great Recession of 2008–9; Wall Street
    crash of 2008–9, 27, 33, 59, 94–95
    401(k)s and, 174

Stone, Eddie, 54, 58–59
student loans, 148, 174
suburbs, 88, 90–92
Sugrue, Tom, 89, 90–91
superannuation "super" fund, 256–57
Superior energy, 187
SuperMedia Inc., 55
Supplemental Nutrition Assistance Program (SNAP; food stamps), 10, 135, 189–90, 196, 200, 229, 246
Supplemental Security Income (SSI), 189, 190, 197, 208

Taco Bell, 187
Tale of Two Retirements, A (report), 3
taxes, 6, 191–92, 237
  Denmark and, 253
  Detroit and, 88, 92–96
  KOPPA and, 39
Teamster Locals. See also International Brotherhood of Teamsters
  Local 25, 50
  Local 707 (New York), 44
  Local 1000 (Cincinnati), 15, 19, 22
tech bubble burst of 2001, 27
telecommunications, 21, 47–57, 73–74, 232
Telecommunications Act (1996), 51
temporary workers, 175–76
Texas, 192
3M, 155
Thrift Saving Plan (TSP), 261
Tilton, Dan, 91, 104, 106
Treasury Department, 8, 25–26, 29–31, 33, 36, 40–42, 44, 71, 152, 264
trucking industry, 1–2, 13–45, 71, 149–52, 164–66, 249
  Central States pension fund and, 24–28
  deregulation of, 8, 21–24
  minorities and, 18–20
Trump, Donald, 6, 104, 191, 259
two-tier agreements, 61, 146, 147–77, 264
  truckers and, 148–52
  white-collar workers and, 152–62

Uchitelle, Louis, 174, 175
unemployment, 23, 37, 119–20, 147, 184
Union Army, 183
Union Pacific Railroad, 222, 243–44
unions, 5, 36, 215. See also specific unions
  decline of, 30, 32–33, 88, 148–52, 149, 166
  deregulation and, 21–23
  Detroit Grand Bargain and, 98
  generational divide and, 15, 148–52, 174–75
  racial discrimination and, 19
  Verizon and, 53, 158
United Airlines, 2, 8, 46, 48, 60–71, 73, 148, 160–62, 167–68, 170–71, 211
  bankruptcy and, 60–71, 73, 161, 168
  Continental merger and, 68–70
  ESOP and, 61–62, 64–66
  401(k)s and, 161–62
  job quality and, 66, 167–68, 170–71
  outsourcing and, 66–67, 69
  recovery of, 73, 263–64
  two-tiered agreements and, 61, 160–62
United Automobile Workers (UAW), 159, 258
United Mine Workers, 25
United Parcel Service (UPS), 86, 149, 151
United Press International, 174
United Way, 200
UNITE HERE union, 258
US Air Force, 10, 213, 215, 223, 224
US Congress, 2, 4, 6, 21, 28, 34–36, 38, 41–42, 44, 191, 263
US House of Representatives, 36
US Marine Corps, 19
US Navy, 50
US Senate, 13, 264
US Supreme Court, 21–22, 58
Utah, 214, 222, 246–47, 257
utilities, 47, 199, 245

Verizon Communications, 2, 8, 51–60,
    70–71, 73–74, 153–62, 167,
    171–73, 211, 232, 263
  annuities and, 57–59
  deregulation and, 70
  401(k)s and, 158
  outsourcing and, 71
  profitability of, 71, 73–74, 159–60
  retiree suit vs., 58–59
  spinoffs and, 53–56, 66, 263
  strike of 2016 and, 146, 153
  two-tiered agreements and, 153–62
  union vs. nonunion workers and,
    158–59, 175
  white-collar workers and, 55, 148,
    155–58, 167, 171–73
  work conditions and, 167, 171–73
Vermont, 191
veterans, 202, 223, 243–44
Vietnam War, 14, 243
Viscelli, Steve, 165–66
volunteer work, 214, 218–20, 229,
    232–38
voting rights, 183

wages, 3, 21–23, 61, 115, 147–48, 175,
    185, 259. See also low-income
    workers
  gender inequality and, 123, 129–30
Walgreens, 9
Wall Street, 159, 251. See also banks
    and banking; Great Recession of
    2008–9; stock market
  bailouts and, 37, 39–41
  crash of 2008 and, 27–28, 94–95
  deregulation and, 21
  pension funds and, 31–32, 37–38,
    40–41, 71, 94–95, 110
Walmart, 9, 133, 188, 207
"Walmart economy," 22

Walsh, Mary Williams, 108, 255
Warmth of Other Suns, The
    (Wilkerson), 79
War on Poverty, 250
Warren, Elizabeth, 36–40, 44
Washington, DC, 88, 109
  Teamster protests in, 12, 13, 36
Washington, Louisiana, 192
Washington Post, 89
Washington State, 191
wealth distribution, 3, 10–11, 251–52
Weber County, Utah, 223
Weber Human Services, 238
White, Carter, 169, 172–74
white-collar managers, 8, 47–75,
    154–62, 171–74
Wilkerson, Isabel, 79
Williams, Larry, 17, 20, 22, 40
Wilson, Todd, 227–28
Winters, Jocelyn, 193–94
Wisconsin, 40, 150, 174
women, 82–84, 121–23, 197, 258
  gray labor and, 134–37, 140
  LDS and, 222, 244–46
  pay inequality and, 129–30
working conditions, 165–70
workman's compensation, 196
World War I, 89
World War II, 47, 79

Yarbrough, David, 192
Yates, Colin, 229–31
Yates, Karla, 229–31
Yellow Pages (later Idearc), 49–55, 57,
    60, 66, 73, 74, 155, 263
Young, Coleman, 81
younger workers, 9–10, 146, 149–77,
    250. See also generation X;
    millennials
YRC Worldwide, 150

ABOUT THE AUTHOR

KATHERINE S. NEWMAN is the author of fourteen books on topics ranging from urban poverty to middle-class economic insecurity to school violence. Her *No Shame in My Game: The Working Poor in the Inner City* received the Robert F. Kennedy Book Award and the Sidney Hillman Foundation Book Award. Newman, who has held senior faculty and administrative positions at Columbia, Johns Hopkins, Harvard, Princeton, and UMass Amherst, is currently the interim chancellor of the University of Massachusetts Boston and the Torrey Little Professor of Sociology.